242   2009

Thank you!

Gary I. Pool

XỨC MÂY
(NEVER HAPPEN)

Ramblings of my everyday life
while serving in an EOD unit in South Viet Nam

By GARY POOL

Published by Gary Pool
Tabor, Iowa

XứC MÂY

(NEVER HAPPEN)

Ramblings of my everyday life
while serving in an EOD unit in South Viet Nam

I would like to extend a special thank you to my wife Jan and daughters Andi, Loretta, Lorna and Pam for their opinion, support and encouragement and to Pam for the photo touch up work and cover design.

Published by Gary Pool
Printed by InstantPublisher.com

ISBN: **978-0-615-31698-7**

DEDICATION

I am told that every book must be dedicated to someone or something. In this case these writings are the result of my association with EOD men everywhere, but in particular it is the 3rd Ord EOD and the men who served in Viet Nam that made these stories possible. It was these men in the bad as well as the good times that forged an everlasting bond of brotherhood.

It is my hope that anyone who reads these simple tales will gain some degree of understanding of the connection that is shared by this tiny group of men.

I would like to thank all of the 3rd Ord EOD men for their patience and understanding that gave direction to my life in these post Viet Nam years.

THE MEANING OF THE
EXPLOSIVE ORDNANCE DISPOSAL UNIT BADGE

The Wreath
Symbolic of the achievements and laurels gained in minimizing accident potentials, through the ingenuity and devotion to duty of its members. It is in memory of those EOD officer and military personnel who gave their lives while performing EOD duties.

The Bomb
Copied from the design of the World War II Bomb Disposal Badge, the bomb represents the historic and major objective of the EOD attack, the unexploded bomb. The three fins represent the major areas of nuclear, conventional, and chemical/biological interests.

Lightning Bolts
Symbolize the potential destructive power of the bomb and the courage and professionalism of EOD personnel in their endeavors to reduce hazards as well as render explosive ordnance harmless.

The Shield
Represents the EOD mission, to prevent a detonation and protect the surrounding area and property to the utmost.

XỨC MÂY

(NEVER HAPPEN)

INTRODUCTION

As I checked out of a small chain store the other day the young female cashier looked at my cap and said, "You're a Viet Nam veteran, so is my uncle but he won't talk about it." A comment I have heard repeatedly.

I was wearing a veteran's cap on my return from one more trip to the V.A. hospital. The cap is my credentials, a sign right there on my forehead that states I am a Viet Nam veteran.

"Yes, I know the kind." I replied to the young cashier who now appeared a bit uncomfortable at having raised the subject. "It's sort of an unwritten code of silence and humility." Then trying to ease the girl's nervousness I added. "But I talk about the war all the time, possibly too much." She smiled and we continued the conversation until another customer approached her register to be checked out.

I have known a number of veterans over the years, WWI, WWII, Korea, and Viet Nam who subscribe to that code of silence. My father was a WWII combat veteran who seldom spoke of the war but then my father seldom spoke of anything. I always assumed it was just his nature to refrain from telling stories or humorous antidotes. But then I began to realize that most of the other veterans I met lived by the same restrictions and I wondered if they signed an agreement on being discharged not to tell tales out of school. This oath of secrecy was very disturbing to me and I pondered on it a great deal as a youth.

I troubled every old man I met for information concerning their military service most especially any remembrances of WWII, but most replies dealt with Pearl Harbor Day or rationing, usually its pros and cons. On the rare occasion that I did get a different response it centered around sea sickness on the transport ships or how hot the Pacific Islands were or how cold the Battle of the Bulge was. Still I persisted in my interrogations and eventually became something of an expert on Pearl Harbor and rationing.

I realize that many of these men were subjected to unacceptable levels of violence in the war, scenes that the average person would find impossible to describe. They were short of the vocabulary necessary to describe incidents that shocked the veteran's senses and moral values. But even if a person could find a way to relate a particularly memorable event they did not wish to relive such unnerving times. Besides it was considered impolite and/or immodest to speak openly in first person of any subject that might reflect in a positive way on the teller.

Personally I considered this false modesty, for each individual knows full well what activities they participated in while in the military. I also think that the reluctance on the part of veterans to confirm or deny the truth of military service provides an open field for writers with overactive imaginations. Far too many books and movies make gross exaggerations about war to heighten the interest of the story they tell.

I enjoy a good story as much as the next person but I also think being factual about such a serious subject should outweigh any attempt to enhance the tale. Not every event can be interesting and exciting; some exploits that begin with a bang will end in a fizzle and should be related that way. The human brain could not withstand 365 days of life-threatening activity or boredom without some type of breakdown. Story tellers should stress the truth of every day military life.

What I would like to see is a military writers program that would encourage in-depth records of

2

everyday life in the service. By this I mean personnel from the enlisted ranks, the privates and corporals who served in support roles to the most active combat soldier. Part of this being humble is upbringing and normal human logic leads us to believe that whatever role we played in the military we were inconsequential to the big picture. This misguided attitude could not be further from the truth. The military has a reason for every job from postman to sniper, or cook to pilot. The military is one big team and each individual must do his or her part in order to accomplish the mission at hand. All of this activity must have resulted in interesting stories of what transpired in fulfilling these everyday tasks under government control.

I would encourage all men and women who served in any military capacity to record their experiences for posterity. But more importantly for their families who invariably tell me they wished their loved one would share whatever they experienced in the honorable service of their country.

Many people have asked how I can remember all of these stories after so many intervening years. To be truthful, I have a difficult time remembering things like dates and unit numbers but I have a pretty good recall of events and situations. I started to write these tales for my family so I have included a couple of lines about my youth as well as my early days in the military. I wanted them to know the path I traveled that lead to my in-country tour.

The title XựC MÂY or 'never happen' was an appropriate title for this rambling collection of tales because there are days when I question if any of this ever truly transpired. Of course on other days a sound or a smell will trigger some vivid image to sneak out of my brain's lock-box and it will reassure my conscious world that it was not all a dream. All of this and much more really did happen to me and the men I served with.

Be assured there are many more such tales but some of them would cause embarrassment to me or the good men and women in uniform. You must remember that South Viet Nam was a huge combat zone and that the citizens of that zone were living in the early 1900's. The common everyday items that were available in the United States were unheard of in country. It behooved a person to be creative, ingenious, and persuasive; qualities that I do not possess. I had to rely on others or steal to survive. I, not knowing the statutes of limitation on such inter-service activities, chose to delete tales that might sound incriminating.

I, Gary Jay Pool have recorded this long rambling narrative for the sole purpose of massaging my old ego in an effort to recapture my youth. If any of my children or friends should desire to wade through these tales of Viet Nam, I say welcome and wish you luck in trying to interpret their meaning or reason for the retelling.

I was born July 18, 1946 in the small railroad town of Pacific Junction, Iowa. Supposedly this event occurred on the right side of the tracks. I always questioned this declaration of status as the community was cut into 1/4 by the Burlington and Union Pacific railroads. Who ordained our section of town as the right side of the tracks, I never knew but they must have been wise indeed. However I have very little recall of my birthplace because my father had an itchy foot and everyone knows the only treatment for such an ailment is moving every year or two. Mother, on the contrary considered a trip to the grocery store a big event and wished for good or bad to be planted in one place for life.

Our family quest for a better life finally ended on a dead end dirt road three miles north of Bartlett, Iowa. The banks of the mighty Missouri River lay about a mile west of the small four room house except in times of inclement weather; then the river bank was somewhere east of the house. At such times the occupants of the house was treated to a panoramic view of the Missouri River on all four sides. My parents always referred to this place as the "river house" and with good reason because it had been filled with flood water on several occasions.

The house had no central heating or air conditioning; these luxuries of life were fulfilled by a large wood stove for heat and one small green metal fan for cooling. In the fall and winter of 1959 we were fortunate enough to gain access to several hardwood trees that the whole family endeavored to cut up for firewood. We proudly cut, split and stacked the prized wood certain in the knowledge that we would be able to heat the river house for many months to come. In the spring of 1960 the mighty Missouri River escaped its banks and flowed unrestricted through the river house and all of our outbuildings. That rampaging muddy water also liberated every stick of our precious pile of firewood. Pieces of the cut and split wood could be seen peeking from mud banks and fence rows for several miles downstream. My mother who had split much of the wood was never known to touch another axe handle as long as she lived. And she was the one for a change who insisted on moving to any house that didn't heat with wood.

I want to explain that I was born and raised in poverty with most of my formative years were spent at the wrong end of a dead end dirt road. When not in school I spent my days both winter and summer hunting, with a rifle in my hands and a dog at my side. Although we had nothing except the ability to wish for everything we didn't have, I will admit these were some of the best days of my life.

My mother was a very strict religious woman with a gift of gab and a saying for every situation. My father, a man of few words, was also strict but about completely different subjects than mother. Father was a troubled World War II veteran who had seen and experienced more than a normal human should be exposed to. Both were a product of the great depression.

I was out with a patrol in Viet Nam's rice paddy covered delta one day when it occurred to me out of the blue that my father had spent his life trying to raise me to survive being a soldier in a war that he somehow knew was coming. I couldn't thank him that day for all his efforts but I did so many times after my return home.

My parents were good people who I loved and respected to the day they died, or more accurately until the day that I die. But I know they had some serious doubts about their only son.

Report cards from the tiny school I attended (the town's population was only 99 people) always reflected below average marks and the notes sent home by the teachers always contained the words, disruptive, day dreamer, no scholastic skills, no leadership skills and doesn't even follow well. In other words I was a non-educable social misfit. My only response to these remarks is that it's difficult to argue with the truth. I was fortunate enough to fall into the timeframe in education when an undesirable student was passed along because the faculty refused to deal with such a problem student year after year.

I found college much more to my liking because no one cared what you did as long as you paid your tuition on time. Of course this was during the beginning of the Viet Nam war and the draft had every male citizen over 18 wanting a deferment. The greedy folks in higher education pounced on the opportunity to vastly enlarge existing schools or to build completely new ones. They would accept nearly any male with money regardless of scholastic ability. Unfortunately I hadn't any money.

The dilemma quickly unfolded to remain an uneducated college student or join the military. Secondly, peer pressure decreed that only a fool would enter the military, which most folks agreed was my prime qualification.

I was an uncompromising patriot that hated all the hiding cowardice and arrogant draft dodgers that filled the evening news. The obvious finally became evident and I enlisted in the U.S. Army.

Why enlist in the Army? That is a question I have been asked many times and the truth of the matter is this: I had carried a rifle nearly every day since the age of 7; I could shoot and track, use camouflage and stealth, and was not raised in the lap of luxury. Additionally, I did not read or write well, could not do math or comprehend social studies or science. In other words I could have been an accomplished woodsman of the 17th or 18th century but could not grasp the skills required for success in the 20 century. I was repeatedly told I would never live to see 21, but that was just a reflection of the community's wishful thinking. So it was with heavy heart that I abandoned my lackluster quest for higher education and enlisted in the Army.

The Army had generously offered to train me in some useful skill and I chose small arms repair. However, they neglected to tell me the school had been closed for over a year when I enlisted. Somehow small arms repair was replaced with Ammunition Storage School to be attended after basic training. I drew Ft. Bliss, Texas up on Logan Heights for my basic training base. I would like to say basic at Bliss was the highlight of my enlistment, but it really wasn't. I admit to liking the El Paso area except I never got over the feeling that this place was the bottom of some long-ago dried up ocean. It seemed the sand got into everything including the food. I remember vividly eating watery jello that crunched if you chewed it.

I was fortunate to be given some leave time after basic training and before reporting to Redstone Arsenal for Ammunition Storage School. Those few days of freedom allowed for a great deal of reflection on what I wanted from the Army. It was then I decided that if I must be in the Army, I wanted to be part of the war. I could never be satisfied expending three years of my life without experiencing the war that was the cause of my military commitment. I departed for Alabama with the intention of learning all I could about ammunition storage. My goal proved much too easy to attain, in fact it lacked the challenge that I soon discovered in EOD School.

I graduated from Ammunition Storage School at Redstone Arsenal, Huntsville, Alabama only to discover that all personnel with a U.S. designation of draftee were given orders for Viet Nam; on the other hand all R. A. or personnel who had enlisted received orders for the U.S. or Germany. I believe this policy was implemented in order to receive a full year of service from the draftee's two year term while in Viet Nam. The R.A.'s who were enlisted to serve three years could be reassigned at a later date for service in Viet Nam. Obviously the draftees were bitterly displeased with the situation while the R.A.'s were elated at the reprieve. That is all the R.A.s except me.

Upon receipt of my orders for Germany, I made a beeline to our training company headquarters to register a complaint. At that time our First Sgt. and C.O. were two of the nicest men I met in uniform. They were shocked to hear that I did not want to go to Germany, but instead wished orders for Viet Nam. They made several calls on my behalf to have my orders changed but each call received as firm "no".

It was only then that the kindly First Sgt. suggested applying for EOD School. I always wanted to be in Bomb Disposal but hadn't the slightest idea of how to join the elite group. The First Sgt. said he had friends in EOD and would call and inquire about the possibility of my volunteering for their school. It was late afternoon when the First Sgt. hung up the phone. "They want you down there right now." He exclaimed.

"What?" I demanded.

9

"They are going to convene a board for you." The First Sgt. explained. "You'll have to run to get there on time." He continued ushering me out the headquarters door while giving me directions on how to find the EOD building. And run I did, for I hadn't any other type of transportation and it was some distance to the EOD building.

When I arrived at the EOD building I found an impromptu board consisting of one officer and two NCO's. I cannot recall any of the men's names but they fired questions at me for about 15 minutes then told me I was dismissed. The board didn't render any verdict at its conclusion causing me to believe I had been rejected. I walked slowly back to our company where the First Sgt. waited eagerly for the results of the interview. I explained what had taken place and that no decision had been announced. Well, the First Sgt. just couldn't accept being kept in limbo so he called his friend in EOD. The First Sgt's smile was, if possible, larger than my own when he hung up the phone and announced that I had indeed been accepted.

FORT MC CLELLAN MOO SORORITY DANCE

Ft. McClellan at Aniston, Alabama was one of the homes of Army chemical warfare during the Viet Nam war and where potential EOD personnel started their training. The fort was built in a lush tree covered hilly area and showed its age even in the mid 60's. Military installations are cut from the same piece of cloth like Volkswagens; that is they never change in style so it is impossible to tell at a glance how old they are.

I had been to Ft. McClellan previous to beginning EOD training while taking the chemical phase of ammunition storage schooling. The entire class of ammunition school males was excited to find on arrival at Ft. McClellan that not only was it the home of chemical warfare but also a Women's Army Corp. basic training facility. Of course the WAC training area was located on a completely different part of the camp but we occasionally saw these young women march by or heard them in the distance counting cadence in their high pitched female voices. Still we were kept at greater than arms length from any female until one night we were invited to a dance at the Enlisted Men's Club. Not knowing what to expect, several of us privates put on our best civilian clothes. Now remember we were paid less than a hundred dollars a month so you can imagine how elegantly we were attired when we walked into the EM Club. The only way I can describe the affair is to refer to the scene from the movie Revenge of the Nerds and the party held at the frat house when they invited the girls from the Moo Sorority.

We arrived on foot, dressed in less than our Sunday best; the WACS wore Aunt Samantha's latest design of green frocks that somehow managed to conceal everything faltering about the female form. They wore the latest in foot wear; at least my grandmother would have thought so. The girls were bruised and battered with sunburned faces and hair like windblown straw. In all fairness I am sure we presented much the same unattractive image to the young ladies. All of this was compounded by the fact that the WAC's were exhausted from the rigors of basic training and seemed more interested in falling asleep than fraternizing with their male counterparts.

The evening was spent in two groups divided by sex and an empty dance floor. As the music played, the WAC's snoozed and the men drank. But as all things eventually change the young ladies finally began to wake from their naps, stretch and smile indicating they were now ready to party. It was at this opportune moment that a hefty looking WAC Sgt. walked into the E.M. Club and announced it was nearly time for lights out and that all of the female trainees must return to their barracks "post haste".

We politely thanked the girls for a wonderful evening and slowly walked back to our barracks discussing which of the young ladies we might have spoken to if they had been alert enough to register the greeting. No names were exchanged, no pick-up lines were hopefully rendered, no homesick or hard luck stories were sobbed out in hopes of softening a fair maiden's heart.

Thus ended my first experience with the wild members of the Women's Army Corp.

I wish to make a disclaimer for I fear some of my off handed references to the Woman's Army Corp might be misconstrued by the reader.

The truth of the matter is I have a very high regard for service women. I consider females in the military to be very patriotic, possibly more so than their male counterparts.

The majority of women who join the military realize that the lifestyle can be spartan, if not harsh. The pay is low compared to their civilian contemporaries, while the rewards are few. They serve in silence, seldom attaining fame or high position for the years of volunteer service. How often do you hear of a female running for political office based on the strength of their military record? In fact it is rare to meet a female ex-soldier who just happens to mention their service career, let alone brag about receiving medals or awards. No, that right seems to be reserved for the males of our species. The female soldiers are offered very little for enlisting and for the most part receive even less. But still they enlist and without the threat of being drafted.

I proudly salute the women of the military (post and present) and offer a sincere hearty thank you for your selfless service.

CANDLE LAND

On my return to Ft. McClellan to begin the chemical phase of EOD I discovered a whole new Army with an older and more professional minded group of men. However I had my doubts about the organization itself. During this more advanced chemical school we were given the opportunity to experience giving ourselves shots with the atropine auto-injectors and the unique experience of having mustard gas dabbed on three places on our left forearm in what is known as a "confidence test". I began to wonder what type of "confidence test" might be in store in the conventional and nuclear phases.

In any case we were given much more freedom to explore the base than on my first visit. We often used the big buses that made regular runs to the PX and the other base facilities. On one particular day a large air force Sgt. and I were seated in the rear of one of these buses when several W.A.C. trainees boarded and sat down near the front of the bus. As we approached each stop the driver would call out the reason for the stop, such as Infirmary, PX, Provost Marshall and so on.

At the first bus stop in the W.A.C. training area the driver announced first stop in "Candle Land". Now, I had heard this reference several times during this schooling such as in class or when given directions to a specific place. The driver continued to use the term "Candle Land" as we passed thru the WAC area and at each stop some of the young women would leave the bus.

As the bus approached another stop the driver called out "Last stop in Candle Land". I could no longer contain my curiosity and turned to my friend and asked. "What is all this Candle Land business?" He pointed to the WAC's who were seated just in front of us and shook his head without saying a word.

"I don't understand what these girls have to do with Candle Land". I blurted out. A couple of the young women still standing in the bus isle waiting to exit turned around and gave me a strange look that was a cross between disgust and pity. The Air Force Sgt. waited until the WAC's had stepped off the bus and we began to move again before he spoke. "I don't know what they teach you boys in Army basic training but they definitely are lacking in some of your education." He drawled out.

"These ladies are in the Women's Army Corp., WAC's right?" He asked in disbelief.

"Right." I agreed.

"Well this is called Candle Land because it's where you come to dip your wick in the wax". The big Sgt. declared with a touch of scorn in his voice.

I was glad when our chemical training a Ft. McClelland ended because it marked the end of my being teased about "Candle Land".

EOD SCHOOLING

I got my first real taste of the long standing rivalry between the military branches at Anniston, Alabama. As for the inter-service rivalry it must be stated that strong loyalty and a sense of competition will always exist in the military as long as there are separate branches of the service.

At the time of these stories all branches of the U.S. military attended the Naval Ordnance EOD School at Indian Head, Maryland. This was a very small intimate school where all branches and all ranks except the Navy attended classes together. Navy EOD had separate classes. It was not unusual for friendships to form among members of differing service branches. We lived together, eat together, attended class together, and studied together. I neglect to mention drinking alcohol all together because it is such a massive subject. We had a bar in the basement of our enlisted men's barracks, and the first three businesses as you exit the main gate were bars owned by EOD personnel. The first one ran what would have to be termed as unlimited credit in the form of punch cards for EOD men and students who wished to eat or drink there.

The school policy prevented a student from being excused from class to use the latrine; however anyone, including the instructor, could and would stop class to vomit on a morning after. Hang-over's among students and faculty were standard procedure and no one was laughed at or looked down on for such ailments as long as you could continue to perform your duties.

I believe that the time I spent at Indian Head was by far the most educational period of my life. I had a couple of years more or less of college, Army basic training and had graduated from the Ammunition Storage School at Huntsville, Alabama before being accepted into EOD. All that had passed before was typical education, where the instructors provide the information and you pass or fail on your own volition. No one really cared if you learned the material and you had to commit a heinous crime in order to be expelled from the school.

Indian Head however was the exact opposite of the American education system. The instructors were experienced real-life bomb disposal personnel who for the most part were dedicated to the student becoming the best EOD man possible. They always maintained their extra effort was derived from the fear that they might have to work with you in the field sometime and didn't wish to risk their lives teamed with an idiot. But in truth their drive to produce the best people possible stemmed from their pride in bomb disposal itself and the desire to perpetuate a breed of daring self-reliant men like themselves.

Admittedly the school at Indian Head was not easy but many of the instructors and all of the students graciously tutored me at night and in weekend study groups. I might have graduated without these men's assistance but I would never have learned all that I needed to know. I do know that without the guidance and understanding of the men in the EOD that my short stint in the military might have ended on a different note. I wish to thank all of you men once again for your friendship and your many acts of kindness that helped make me into a better person. It's been a good life and you all played a big part in the path that I have followed.

An explanation is in order here for anyone reading this, an old man's reminiscences, so they might fully understand. As I have stated the Naval Ordnance School did not have the strictest discipline or military bearing, but they have one rule that set this school apart from any other I have ever heard of, especially in an all volunteer organization. This rule stated that "any qualified EOD personnel could protest any man of any branch or rank who wished to become an EOD man". In other words any man with an EOD badge and MOS could state that he, for whatever reason, did not like and would refuse to work in the field with a particular student and that student would be thrown out of school. These reasons could vary from trivial to serious, most however were for good reason. Once a student was protested, a board was quickly convened, usually within minutes or at least a couple of hours. The student could if he were so foolish, face the board and fight the charge but most were open and shut cases.

I was present when two such boards convened and was witness to one man being removed from school. This confrontation occurred between a white Army E-5 and a black Army Major. The E-5 had a long list of military infractions that was coupled with a combative personality. The black Major had always seemed to be a fair man when dealing with the students and the school cadre. One day the major approached the E-5 and warned him that he had received complaints from some of the instructors that the E-5 had been wearing non-military shoes and displaying an illegal medal.

The E-5 replied that the necklace in question was a surfer's cross and was a legal piece of jewelry. The Major stated the necklace was an iron cross that Germany had given to its soldiers during WWII. He continued to explain that several W.W.II veterans were serving in the school cadre and were offended at seeing this medal being worn by a soldier in uniform. Well, the debate continued until the Major asked the E-5 if he did not like him. The E-5 who was from the south and lived to refight the civil war replied very bluntly that he did, in fact, not like the Major.

At that point the Major politely informed the E-5 it was now 16:30 hrs and to have his bags packed by 18:00 because orders for his dismissal would be ready by that time. The E-5 demanded a board be convened and the Major promised there would be with plenty of time to spare. The Major also admonished the E-5 to not only have his bags packed but don't count on eating dinner in the mess hall.

Now this was an obvious gross error in judgment by the E-5. Seldom do E-5's win arguments with any officer let alone a major but all he had to do was agree to stop wearing the necklace and smile while telling the black Major how much he respected his rank and his work.

This rule was written in stone and a wise student kept it firmly in mind. Still there are times when a person must live by their own code even if it means never attaining a personal goal. I believe the E-5 in the above tale was unable step beyond certain personal standards and it cost him dearly. On the other hand there are people like myself who do not think before they speak, suddenly words, usually hot words just pour out of their mouths without checking with the brain first.

When I attended Indian Head the first time I was a one stripe private first class, not a very powerful position in the scheme of military rankings. The non-Navy classes were made up of men from E-2 to E-6 enlisted men and officers up to the grade of Captain. The Army, Air Force, Marines and Coast Guard as well as a few foreign military students attend classes together.

19

Now as noble or progressive as this may sound it could be a bit more intimidating than sharing space with your own peers. The age and military experience of these groups differed greatly not to mention the variations in pay, marital status and education. My pay as a P.F.C. was roughly one hundred dollars a month before expenses while the older NCO and officers earned an actual living wage. The Naval Ordnance School made many financial demands on its students that were difficult for me to meet. But the EOD personnel are a generous group who made every effort to help those of us who needed transportation or additional non-issued equipment.

There was however a very important lesson to be learned from the mixed rank classes and the cadre made a concerted effort to bring the point home. This odd experiment of equality in the ranks was carried to such an extreme that everyone in the class was called upon to take his turn as team leader on practical problems. The instructor would take the class out on the demo range which was nothing more than a barren sand spit in the Potomac River. Here a clip board with a written problem was presented to the instructors newly appointed team leader. Again this could be any member of the class regardless of rank, a real point of irritation to some of the officers. Being officers they felt they were trained to take charge and to lead men and that it was degrading to be under the authority of some underling.

They never considered that even the lowest ranking man would someday find himself in charge of a critical situation. But more importantly it was essential to instill trust within the EOD team. The EOD student must be able to recognize tens of thousands of conventional explosive items. In addition to immediate identification of these items the student had to remember

20

a dozen or so pertinent facts about each item as well as any peculiar traits that might prove hazardous. Few minds can retain all of this information let alone be able to recall it accurately under stressful situations. It is for these reasons that team leaders must learn to rely on every bit of brain power at an incident sight rank notwithstanding.

Although it may go against the grain of every ramrod stiff military types, many of our render safe plans were reached by a democratic vote of all the team members, or at the very least through a discussion where no better plan was suggested. It often paid to keep an open mind, a calm demeanor and a sense of humor when formulating the proper procedure to disarm an explosive situation. Now with that lengthy description of the inner workings of the EOD School at Indian Head made I must tell you of my run-in with one of the instructors.

RUN-IN WITH INSTRUCTOR

Our class had been bussed out to the demolition range on a cold wet winter afternoon. The wind off the Potomac River was unusually sharp causing us much discomfort. This miserable state was due in part to the fact that we non-Navy personnel were unable to draw winter issue gear because we hadn't a supply sergeant present to handle such matters. But suffice it to say we were all poorly equipped and suffering as we huddled up in a small shack waiting for the instructor, an Air Force Sgt to begin the practical exercise.

The instructor began by handing me (the lowest ranking man in class) the clip board that held the scenario for the problem we were to overcome. I began by reading aloud the short description of the reported call. The problem consisted of a U.S. 500 lb bomb armed with an impact nose fuse and a chemical delay tail fuse. The bomb had impacted and was buried directly under a generals head quarters that contained all of his worldly goods and military papers. In other words this dud bomb could not simply be detonated in place. The chemical tail fuse was one that detonates after a certain amount of time at a given temperature; however increased heat would lessen the time available for our render safe procedures. Being cold and miserable, plus hard headed and arrogant I took charge and started making plans without consulting the team members when the instructor spoke up.

This interruption is known as 'throwing shit in the game' (TSG). It was an often used device limited only by the instructor's imagination and was predictable because of the grumbling of one of my classmates, an officer who highly disapproved giving authority to anyone that was not commissioned. I admitted that my eagerness to take charge and to complete the mission in the shortest time possible added to the instructors meddling.

The instructor began his TSG by adding to the problem at hand by stating that there was a fire burning in some rubble near the 500 pounders chemical tail fuse. This meant a reduction in the amount of time allotted to safe the ordnance. The class began to make alternate plans to handle the fire when the instructor stated that a company of enemy soldiers were a short distance away and moving in our direction. Of course this new information made us regroup in an effort to come up with an alternate plan, which we did but the instructor countered with another dire situation that prevented implementing our new plan. This back and forth went on several times until I knew for certain that no matter what we decided the instructor would throw another insurmountable obstacle in our path.

The problem had now become a nightmare that could not be completed. The combination of cold, the instructors overzealous testing and the lack of support from some of my classmates combined to trigger my temper. I threw the clipboard on the ground while yelling a string of profanities at everyone present.

I was fortunate to have a couple of good friends in the class who stepped forward and subdued me before I committed any real court martial offenses. One, a very large Air Force sergeant I will call Sgt. Jim grabbed me from behind and pulled me away from the center of the fracas. The clip board was recovered and one of the other men took over as team leader. The problem was begun again, this time with much less outside interference. I recovered my temper and assisted wherever possible to successfully complete the day's problem. I waited for the hammer to fall but nothing more was said about the incident but I knew that the end of my career in EOD was at hand.

After class I returned to the barracks head bowed, feeling like a fool. I had let my temper ruin the one thing I had found about the military that I really cared for. This bomb disposal was my field, something I had dreamed of doing since a kid after watching an episode on TV of two second world war Navy men removing an explosive round from a live sailor's body. I had held that golden opportunity in the palm of my hand but my uncontrollable temper just like a gust of hot wind had blown it away.

The typical day of classes at Indian Head ended with supper after which most everyone returned to the school building for a couple hours of study. Sensing the worst, I walked from the mess hall to the empty barracks and began to pack my duffel bag in anticipation of the transfer orders that were sure to come any minute. The big brick barracks building was unusually quiet due to the large number of students who were at evening studies. I was nearly finished packing when I heard heavy footsteps on the wooden stairs leading to the second floor army wing.

"Let's go up town and get a drink." A voice bellowed from the hallway and I turned to see my friend the big Air Force Sgt Jim who had stopped my angry outburst on the demo range come strolling in.

"I gotta pack." I replied but he insisted that we have one more drink together.

Now Sgt. Jim was a huge powerful man with a glib tongue, a southern drawl, and very persuasive reasoning so I agreed to go downstairs and have a goodbye drink. But Sgt. Jim wouldn't hear of such a thing, he insisted that we go up town where there was food and drink as well as slot machines. I reluctantly agreed but stated I didn't want to go into the bar that was partially owned by the instructor that I had exploded at earlier in the day.

Sgt. Jim argued that he was sure the instructor would not be tending bar that night, so we ended up going into that particular establishment. Sure enough the instructor welcomed us like old friends from behind the bar as we entered the front door. There was no turning around now so we took a seat at the bar and Sgt. Jim ordered beer and chili for the both of us. I for once in my life thought it wise to keep my mouth shut not wishing to further damage my lowly position in the military. The two Air Force sergeants had a pleasant conversation across the bar as we consumed the chili and I secretly cussed my friend for putting me in such an uncomfortable position.

As we finished our meal and the instructor/bar tender's business slowed down Sgt. Jim suddenly blurted out that I had something to say. I choked out something like "I do?" Sgt. Jim elbowed me firmly in the ribs and growled that I should speak my peace. I then attempted to stumble and stuttered through an apology for my actions on the demo range.

The instructor smiled and replied that he knew I had a temper and wanted to know just how far he could push me. He was glad to see that I had continued to assist with the problem; he added that my grades were very good and I had a good record in class.

At that point Sgt Jim jumped in saying. "Then you ain't going to throw him out of school?"

"No." The instructor replied setting all three of us up with a drink on the house. There was no lectures or warnings other than he hoped I would remember the lesson he had tried to get across. I lost my temper many times over the years but I did learn that day to pick my moments to get mad. I was never so relieved in my life as I was that night when the old Sgt. decided not to throw me out of EOD School and I do really believe that Sgt. Jim's insisting on going to that very bar and facing the situation made all the difference in the outcome. I know now that both of those wise old sergeants did me a huge favor that day, one that served me well throughout the years.

Thank you gentlemen.

OH VERY WELL DAY

While waiting for orders to attend EOD School, I remained at Redstone Arsenal in Huntsville, Alabama. During this time I pulled C.Q. duty in the same company I had been assigned to for Ammunition Storage training. It was here that I heard numerous stories about the difficult EOD training that I would receive at Indian Head. There were tales of intentional exposures to chemical and radiological material. It was often reported that the physical training was harsh, to say the least and of course a terrifying example was always forthcoming. But the stories that worried me the most were second hand accounts of the maniacal inspections.

I listened to all of these dire warnings about the schooling and the inevitable predictions that I would not last a week, let alone graduate. These are typical examples of the barracks ghost stories that are told and retold around the light in the latrine at night just after lights out.

I was often advised to drop out before ever getting to Indian Head. A smart person discounts all but a few of these accounts but one always wonders if there might not be a fragment of truth in what is said.

At this time there were two other privates waiting for EOD school openings and we were often assigned to assist Master Sgt. Starret who ran an EOD test and training range at Redstone Arsenal. We were fortunate to spend a lot of time with this talented man who provided an ongoing education if one paid attention. It was through our association with Sgt. Starret that we realized that the horror stories had been greatly embellished and that we should remain in the program.

Later, after finishing EOD training, I often wondered if the wild tales were not the handiwork of some of our very own EOD instructors, some of them certainly had the talent and imagination for the task.

The military inspections at the EOD School at Indian Head, Maryland were somewhat different than any I had experienced in my short time in the service. These inspections were held on Friday mornings and usually alternated between a barracks inspection and a formation outside the school building. The ceremony at the school required Class A or dress uniforms and was known as "Oh Very Well Day".

The master of ceremony at Oh Very Well Day was the base commanding officer, a Navy man named Commander Ploof. He was tall and thin with a long narrow face and a black mustache that reminded me of the cartoon character Snidely Whiplash. But the man's claim to fame in EOD was "Oh Very Well Day".

You see, each branch of the service would fall into formation before being called to report in. At this time the unit leaders would respond by calling out how many men were present and how many were absent. A typical report would be "Army: all present and accounted for", "Marines: all present and accounted for", "Air Force: 31 present, two in sick bay".

Now this all sounds typical military except that no matter what the unit leaders reported, Commander Ploof would reply "Oh very well". If the Army were to report 28 present, 13 absent, Ploof would respond in his low monotone but official voice, "Oh very well".

It seemed no matter how bad the head count was reported the only form of recognition was an unemotional "oh very well". That is how the formal inspection became known as "Oh Very Well Day" among EOD men around the world.

This may sound very casual to you so let me tell you about one of the in barracks inspections I stood while in school at Indian Head.

The Army wing of our quarters was an open bay divided up into cubicles using wall lockers and large movable panels. On this particular Friday morning inspection was not to be of the open wall locker variety but it had been an off-and-on thing with no one knowing for sure if it would even take place. Finally the word came to stand by our bunks.

I stood silently beside my bunk confident in passing the inspection for my uniform and boots were in good shape and my bed was made up tight and straight. We had stayed out late the night before knowing that this was to be a closed locker inspection. I had crammed everything I owned into my locker and slammed the door shut before anything could tumble out.

However my air of confidence quickly evaporated as I listened to the inspecting team enter our wing and begin to order locker doors to be opened. Although I couldn't see the officer in charge I easily recognized his voice. It was an Army Captain who I did not get along with very well. I listened intently to the Captains speech and determined that he was still intoxicated at 8 o'clock in the morning.

The inspection team drew nearer and at each cubicle the Captain ordered the locker doors opened and at nearly every one he found fault with something. Suddenly the Captain and a Sgt carrying a clipboard to write down each soldier's infractions burst into my cubicle. My suspicions of the Captains inebriation were immediately confirmed by the smell of his breath and the fact that he could not stand still without weaving to and fro.

29

We immediately locked eyes and he tried his best to stare me down but the Captain found it a difficult task thru half-closed eyelids and the swaying back and forth made focusing on me nearly impossible. I was given a quick once-over before the Captain snarled out an order for me to open my locker.

I kept my eyes locked on the Captain's eyes while I reached over and flipped the latch on my locker allowing it to burst open under the pressure of all the junk dammed up within. An avalanche of boots, clothes, dirty socks, underwear and old food cascaded out of the locker; part of it landing on top of the Captain's feet.

The intoxicated officer took a deep breath and without looking at the pile of junk or uttering a word staggered out of my cubicle. The Sgt with the clipboard stepped over the accumulation of goods on the floor, flashed me a quick smile and disappeared behind the Captain.

The instant the inspecting team was out of my sight I silently stuffed the mound of clothing and personal items back into my locker and with great care closed and locked the door. I feared that the Captain's alcohol fogged brain might clear long enough for him to realize what had happened and I wanted to make his finding me as difficult as possible.

When the inspection ended many of the men complained that the captain had punished them for the tiniest infraction of the rules. Several men asked how I had managed to pass the inspection knowing that I was never a straight trooper. I insisted that I had expected just such an open locker inspection so I had been prepared for the Captain.

The truth of the matter is I have no idea what happened that day other than to think the Captain could not believe his own eyes or that he felt so bad that

30

reporting me would have caused him a lot of work. Whatever the reason, I walked away from the inspection with my weekend free of extra duty or black marks on my record.

The EOD School at Indian Head held many surprises for us students, weekly inspections was just one small part of this unusual facilities mystique.

SGT JOHN'S RUN-IN WITH THE COOK

I witnessed or took part in several memorable occurrences while attending school at Indian Head, but the two that follow are high points from our training trip to Quantico Marine Base in Virginia. All of the classes before ours had spent the last days of training at Egland Air Force Base, Florida. It was winter and we were all looking forward to the trip to sunny Florida but at the last minute it was announced that our classes would be the first to travel the few miles across the Potomac River for our finals.

Naturally the huge Marine contingent at Quantico did not want us there and were not prepared for our stay so we were housed in a non-heated metal quonset hut that lacked bedding and had poor showers and latrines. Needless to say our welcome was less than enthusiastic. Our class had one lone Marine and he was a character right out of an adventure story. I'll call this Marine Sgt. John and his home town was New York City. The man stood about 6' tall, had black hair and perfect white teeth while sporting the build of a professional boxer. He also had the attitude of a fighter plus a temper to match my own. Actually there were two Marine Sgt's in school at this time that would fit this description, difference being the Sgt John in my class had been at the siege of Khe Sanh and was late starting EOD School because he chose to remain until the base was relieved. He arrived at Anniston, Alabama's Ft. McClellan with only a dress brown uniform and a chip on his shoulder the size of world. We immediately had a disagreement that ended quickly with Sgt. John throwing an angry punch at me. I moved slightly and his hurried off-balance hay-maker resulted in little damage so we walked away only later to become good friends. Sgt John told me later that he admired the fact that I had stood my ground that day but I had to confess that it was not an act of bravery but rather my slow wittedness and poor timing that kept me frozen in place. It is truly amazing how fast some men can deliver a blow and just as amazing at how slow some of us are at avoiding those blows.

Sgt. John was a very intelligent man holding one of the highest grade point averages at graduation from the EOD School but he also had an independent streak that the Corp did not appreciate. I was a Private First Class that means one step above the bottom and Sgt. John was an E-5 buck sergeant which according to the Marine Corp are two incompatible ranks. Our being friends and the difference in rank caused Sgt. John no end of trouble because the Marine liaison officer at Indian Head had been Sgt. John's commanding officer in Viet Nam. The man held every Marine to a higher standard than the other students but Sgt. John was expected to do even better than the average Marine.

It will come as no surprise when I say that most of the students and instructor's drank every night, after putting in a couple hours of study time. Friday night especially found everyone who could hold a drink in their hand in that very position, usually without the benefit of study time.   Sgt. John and I were no different than the rest and we would end up in one of the many local drinking establishments.   Monday morning ritual saw Sgt. John being called from class to report to his Marine liaison officer for a dressing down. It seems the Major didn't condone fraternization among the ranks, especially since Sgt. John had been seen drinking with an Army private. Now for the record, our little group of friends were no hell raisers, there were no fights, or rowdy behavior, just friends having a drink.

I told Sgt. John several times that I was not worth the trouble he had to endure for a night on the town. But he would not knuckle under, saying the Corp had no right to tell him who he could spend his off duty time with. So we decided to go to other towns on Friday night or go into Washington D.C. but somehow the Major's spies always found out about the trips. We had several non-Marine close friends in our group who we began to suspect but we could never prove that anyone was a double agent. Sgt. John received reprimands for times that he and I would independently stumble into the same place, exchange hellos and go our separate ways.

The Major hated me and loved Sgt. John to the point he became obsessive but no matter the punishment Sgt. John remained a loyal friend until I graduated from conventional ordnance. Sgt. John was a man unto himself; I say that in the most complementary way. He was proud to be a Marine and yet he did not succumb to the brainwashing or bonding activities like the Marine Corp birthday celebration. Sgt. John was much too strong willed and independent to blindly follow the crowd.

One Friday morning Sgt. John and I were dressed in class A uniforms on our way to "Oh Very Well Day" inspection with just enough time to run by the mess hall for breakfast. We were fortunate that no other troops were in line as we approached the civilian cooks to order our breakfast. This was a Navy galley after all and they not only had civilian cooks but real china plates and cups and clear water glasses. The cooks stood behind their huge flat steel grills that were covered with bacon and eggs and sausage and hash browns, all in various stages of preparation. A short glass barrier topped with a metal shelf divided us from this wide array of food but still allowed each person to select the specific item they desired.

Sgt. John politely gave his order to the civilian cook, and then as was customary held his clean dish covered tray over the shelf to await the food. What happened next I'm not sure but for some reason the cook using a spatula slapped an egg order onto Sgt. John's white china plate with such force that it spattered grease all over the sleeve of Sgt. Johns newly cleaned dress uniform. Now I had witnessed Sgt. John's temper before and it was truly a thing to be reckoned with. He made no pretense of hiding his anger as his body became ram rod stiff and his face turned bright red. I didn't know what to expect exactly other than an explosion of some sort would erupt that would result in a fight.

In the second it took to think of what might happen Sgt. John leaned forward turning his tray upside down dumping its breakable contents in the middle of the large cooking grill. The heavy white china plate shattered into a thousand pieces when it collided with the steel grill top. Of course the cup, saucer and glass followed suit showering the cook and the grill full of cooking food with shards of glass.

Suddenly there was a lot of yelling and cussing, with Sgt. John wanting to fight the cook while all the cooks were wanting to fight Sgt. John. I knew there wouldn't be any breakfast that morning so I caught Sgt. John off guard and quickly ushered him out the door. I managed to hustle us both down the back street of the little post to the main building where the "Oh Very Well Day" formation was held.

I was surprised to find a welcoming committee waiting our arrival at the main building. It did not seem like enough time had elapsed for word to have spread from the chaos of the mess hall to an outdoor inspection only a couple blocks away. I was amazed at the ruckus the brass was making over this incident but they were mad and Sgt. John was mad. A lot of threats were made that ranged from loss of rank to expulsion from school. Sgt. John was far too irate to present a defense and I felt as if I were being railroaded for something I had no control over. So I calmly explained that the cook had slopped hot grease on Sgt. John hands which caused him to accidently dump his tray on the grill.

The interrogators accused Sgt. John of spilling the tray on purpose but I denied the charge saying that anyone would react the same way if burned by hot grease. One big old Sgt insisted I was lying; that of course trigger my temper and the argument was on. I told the Sgt. that I did not lie although I just had and for some reason he accepted my statement. I believe the whole matter ended in a stalemate, both sides deciding that the other was too hard headed to argue with. We were then directed to join our respective units and from this day forward to walk softly in the mess hall. It is truly amazing how much trouble a person can get into just trying to get a square meal. Now at the hazard of being branded a kitchen commando or a chow hound I must tell one more mess hall story.

ANOTHER MESS HALL STORY

The star of this mess hall misadventure was Sgt. John again and I can assure you that this Marine was not a chow hound. The man never carried and extra ounce of fat or showed an interest in food or drink.

As I said before, our class was the first to spend their last days in school at Quantico, Virginia instead of Florida. We were unceremoniously bussed the short distance from the tiny naval school at Indian Head to the bustling over-crowded Virginia Marine Base. It was obvious from the first that very little thought or planning had gone into the major change in the schools itinerary.

The Marine EOD were prepared for our training but word of our stay had not trickled down to the NCO's who were in charge of quarters and meal's. Although there were some rough places at first our little class managed to settle in.

Quantico was a Marine training base that was filled to the brim with young men full of vim and vigor who knew little of life outside of the Corp's indoctrination. Their reaction to our presence was made clear from the minute we stepped off the bus. We were few in number with two air force officers, one army lieutenant, a handful of Army and Air Force enlisted men and one lone Marine. For some reason the whole class was a bunch of babes in the woods as we entered the designated mess hall for the first time. I suddenly knew how General Custer's men must have felt at the Little Big Horn for we too were surrounded by about a hundred men who hated us with a passion. It is very eerie to have that many people fall silent while every eye was turned in our direction. Instantly a young Marine blocked our way saying we could not enter the building. He then turned and called out a distress signal for the mess Sgt. A huge man came on the run to the scene of the ruckus, demanding to know what was taking place.

I have a serious question to ask at this point and that is why are all Marine mess Sgt's big enough to play tackle for any professional foot ball team? It seems to me that such big rugged men should be serving in the field during a war and not counting the silver ware. The only reason I can see of assigning such tuff characters to mess halls is the possibility that they might have to also serve as bouncers when the men get out of hand.

In any case, the mess Sgt. declared that none of us were welcome and that we should find somewhere else to eat. A few heated minutes of conversation established that this class was assigned to eat in this mess hall. It was with a great deal of reluctance that the mess Sgt. gave in to our argument but only if we lived by his rules.

The first rule sent the officers to a segregated area for officers only, second the N.O.C.'s had to set at certain tables and the third rule stated that I and another E-3 could not eat in this building. He then in no uncertain terms directed us underlings to find another mess hall. Of course Sgt. John would hear none of it for we were all in the same class and we intended to remain so to the end. And so another fight was on; Sgt. John and the mess Sgt were getting in each other's face while yelling as only Marines can with their respective argument. Finally in frustration the mess Sgt relented allowing all of the class to eat in this building but anyone below the rank of E-5 had to carry out their own trays. Sgt. John once again became enraged but I argued it was better that we should all eat together and carrying out my tray was no big deal.

38

With the mess Sgt half-hearted blessing our group of enlisted men made its way to the serving line and it seemed that the confrontation was over. We filled our trays and found a couple of empty tables where we quietly settled in. Everyone remained passive by walking around anyone who might purposely bump you to start a fight and we especially avoided locking eyes with any of the hundreds of pair of eye's that were boring holes in us.

Sgt. John was still steaming from our reception at the front door but we all reassured him that no offence had been taken. At that very instant a young Marine approached our table gave each one of us a hard glare then took the salt shaker from our table. Seconds later another Marine repeated the first man's actions then picked up the pepper shaker from the table and departed. None of us said a word but I could see Sgt. John's face welling up to a brilliant red, a positive indication that an explosion was about to occur. When the third young Marine stepped up to the table gave everyone the evil eye then reached for the ketchup, Sgt. John boiled over. He grabbed the third Marine by the forearm and in one quick motion lifted the surprised man off the floor and threw him across a nearby table. The third Marine landed with such force that food and tableware went flying in all directions.

Now everyone in the mess hall sat in a silent state of shock, heads all turned in our direction but that was not a harsh enough statement for Sgt. John. While still on his feet Sgt. John jumped up on his chair and bellowed that the next, _____ - _____, (you can fill in the words) who touched this table dies!

This overt challenge is just like a 98# bookkeeper in a three piece suit walking into a biker bar and declaring that he can whip any man in the house. It just isn't done. But Sgt. John did, he then sat down and

39

quietly finished his meal. I confess that I remained all eye's and ear's because I expected at least one if not several of these physically fit well indoctrinated young Marines to pick up the gauntlet and the fight would be on. But to my surprise and indeed great pleasure not a man moved. We finished our meal and departed in an orderly fashion without so much as a harsh look.

I must report that the class dined in a perfectly tranquil mess hall for the remainder of our visit. I even ventured to the small nearby PX alone on several occasions that resulted in nothing more threatening than a few muffled whispers as I passed. I asked Sgt. John about his little display of anger and how the results might have been entirely different but he considered it just another day in the Marine Corp. That maybe so but I have never forgotten Sgt. John actions that day and have enjoyed retelling his story on many occasions.

QUANTICO BASE GRASS FIRE

Once that our quarters, (an empty quonset hut that lacked everything including bed linens) and our food needs were resolved it was time to go to work. Quantico Base is a huge installation that covers a great deal of Virginia real estate. One of our first stops was an abandoned test range; our assignment to find and destroy dud fire ordnance.

This will be of interest only to other EOD men when I relate that we discovered a Stokes mortar shell. The Stokes mortar was a relic of the First World War and was known to be very hazardous to move once fired. The instructor at school had told us not to worry about ever working on one because they were very rare. Well here we were - our first day in the field and the first explosive item we find was a rare Stokes mortar. I don't know how others felt but to my way of thinking this was great fun.

Our next training session was a real treat in that we were to be on hand while some new explosive ordnance was tested. We were bused to a large open grassy area where some man-shaped targets had been erected on one side and some wooden bleachers on the other. The bleachers were soon filled with government officials and Marine Corp officers. Both groups were dressed in their best Sunday suits and uniforms. Our class was attired in dirty fatigues and was kept off to the side and out of view of the dignitaries.

The first weapon tested was a 40 mm machine gun that was intended to be mounted in the side door of the famous Huey helicopter. This weapon was designed to fire the longer range air craft 40 mm round that would provide much greater range than the shoulder fired

41

round. A Marine Huey helicopter landed on a small knoll not far from the bleachers to give the V.I.P.'s a chance to view the new machine gun in its normal habitat before being test fired.

After a quick inspection the Huey took off and lined up with the targets and began the test firing. The first rounds missed the targets, striking low of their mark. We had been instructed to count the numbers of rounds fired and the number of detonations in hopes they would be the same and if not, to try to determine where any duds had impacted.

On the second pass and the gunner did manage to put some of his rounds on target before the front sight fell off of the weapon. The loss of the weapons front sight put an end to the test before very many rounds had been fired. The huey landed and we were directed to inspect the targets for hits and to identify any dud rounds if possible. With that done we were ordered back to our little hiding place to await a second demonstration.

This particular Huey had 2.75 inch rocket pods mounted externally on its sides. The longevity of a weapon is one of the true indicators of its success and the 2.75 inch rocket has been in the U.S. arsenal for decades and is still issued to this day, so this is in no way meant to detract from that weapon's fame. However the individual who thought up the second innovation to be tested must have lacked any common sense or mechanical understanding.

The experiment called for the explosive warhead of the 2.75 inch rocket to be removed and replaced with a piece of rocket motor body containing a smoke grenade. The hoped for results was to produce a cheap tracer or spotting round for the 2.75. The obvious fallacy that most of the class members spotted right away was the original explosive warhead weighed something like eleven pounds while the smoke grenade would be no more than a couple of pounds. Another possible defect; the piece of motor body holding the grenade had an open nose that would allow strange wind deflections. Also a slot had been cut in the side of the motor body skin to allow the lever on the smoke grenade to swing out and ignite the grenade. This also meant that the rockets would have to be loaded tail first into the pod tube until the smoke grenade lever was held in place by the tube before the safety pin could be removed and the rocket inserted completely into the tube.

This loading operation sounds much more complicated than it actually was and the class watched intently as the ground crew loaded the rockets for the test firing. The Huey pilot started up the engine and rose eagerly into the sky. He took up his firing position, aimed at a target and let one fly. The rocket was gone in a tiny puff of smoke and no one including the pilot could determine where it went.

We all knew that the tracer rocket had not come close to the ground target. Once again the pilot took up his position and fired a second rocket that didn't even give off a puff of smoke but merely disappeared over the horizon. The pilot radioed to the spectator's on the ground that he was unable to keep visual contact with the rocket after firing. Of course that was the point of the whole exercise, to enable the pilot to spot where the rockets were going. It was then decided to stop the test and the Huey was directed to land in front of the bleachers.

As the pilot set down it was announced that some unknown item had impacted a public highway some distance from our test range. It was assumed and later confirmed that the unknown ordnance on the highway was indeed the wayward 2.75 rocket. The poor results brought an end to the test allowing the ground crew to begin the down loading of the remaining 2.75 inch rockets.

The Huey pilot had shut down the motor and dismounted from the craft when one of the ground crew who was carefully removing the loaded rockets from the pod had the misfortune of dropping the smoke grenade. He had failed to replace the safety pin so the grenade functioned as intended and began to emit white smoke. The crew attempted to pick up the smoking grenade but failed due to the high temperature of the device's metal case. The smoke cloud grew rapidly as did the heat produced by the burning grenade until it ignited the dry grass of the test range. The tall flames spread rapidly under the air craft's body causing a great concern for the Huey and crew.

The pilot raced thru the fire and jumped aboard the Huey in a wild attempt to quickly restart the big jet engine. However the Huey's slowly rotating top blade just fanned the grass fire to higher pitch. The smoke became so thick that it was difficult to see the pilot inside the cockpit fighting furiously to start the balky motor. It was at this point that everyone present realized the seriousness of the situation.

The crew who were frantically fighting the grass fire was quickly joined by the Marine Corp officers from the reviewing stands. It was exciting to see all those important officers on a dead run removing their brown dress uniform coats to use as make- shift blankets to beat the fire. Several members of our class, wearing dirty fatigues started in a dead run towards the endangered Huey but were stopped in their tracks by the Marine instructor. That instructor was Gunner Vick, a man we all came to respect during our short stay at Quantico. Sadly I understand Gunner Vick was killed in Viet Nam by a 122 mm rocket during an attack somewhere up north.

I remember being stopped on my way to assist with the grass fire by Gunner Vicks calling us back. "We are not firemen." Gunner Vick declared in a powerful voice. "This is the brasses show; let them take care of it." He added.

"But won't you get in trouble?" I asked worried that the Marine would be reprimanded for not acting. But my concern was wasted on a man who was confident and completely sure of himself.

"I guess you're right." I agreed walking back to the class. "I don't see any of the V.I.P's in the expensive suits running out there to fight the fire." I laughed.

The pilot finally got the Huey's motor started and he lifted off the ground in a whirl of smoke and black soot generated by his rapidly rotating blades. The officers who tackled the fire were covered with debris and their dress coats were blackened and dirty from being beaten on the ground. All in all this had been a very entertaining event what with the disastrous rocket firing and the impromptu Marine fire brigade. I for one hoped we would be invited to more of these weapons demonstrations but I think some of those singed V.I.P.s held a grudge.

I was glad to leave the Spartan quonset hut of Quantico for the meager barracks of Indian Head as we finished conventional ordnance school. Those members of the class who were E-5 rank or above advanced to Nuclear Ordnance School while those of us below that level were assigned to EOD units around the world.

CLINTON COUNTY AIR FORCE BASE

       I drew the 71st EOD at Clinton County Air Force Base in Wilmington, Ohio. The 71st was a very small undermanned Army EOD unit stationed on a very small reserve air force base three miles outside of a very small midwest town. Our building was an old fire station situated just off the runway that served four F 100 fighters, a fleet of refueling planes plus a school for antique C-119 cargo planes. This school was a lame attempt to convert the C-119 aircraft into mini gun-toting gunships.

       The lack of success apparently centered on the Air Forces' inability to keep the aged aircraft from falling out of the sky. Our building was a typical Government Issue building, hotter than hell in summer and twice as cold as the outside in winter. It was however a ring side seat for all the air traffic or possible crashes that might occur on the runway. Our telephone was on the crash line so we received a call every time a landing plane was in trouble. I never knew why they called us because we could not leave the building unattended to either avoid a crashing plane or to help if one did crash.

       I always thought the base was laid out a bit strange because all of the fuel trucks filled with JP-4 were parked right beside our building. It always seemed to me that if one of those big refueling planes was to crash and burst into flames, our old fire station could be trapped between the inferno and the loaded fuel trucks.

       On the occasion of emergency the crash phone would ring one long continuous ring day or night until someone answered. Once answered, a cold passionless voice would declare that an air craft with an in-flight emergency would attempt to land with thirty thousand pounds of fuel and seven souls aboard. I never got accustom to that sinister sounding voice on the telephone nor the reference to souls rather than lives. I often wondered if the caller was trained and practiced to sound that disinterested and if the military considered all of us as just so many souls already counted as dead before we met our fates.

In any case living near an Air Force runway could be noisy and disruptive and at the same time very interesting. The old fire station I'm sure was never intended for continual habitation but rather it was to be used by rotating fire crews. The single enlisted men however were forced to stay in the building at all times except when given permission to leave for chow or to make a mail run.

Being short of staff and in EOD we had to keep the person on duty in the building aware of our location twenty four hours a day. As a for instance, if I left the building in the evening I had to tell the duty-man that I was going the three miles into town to the movie show. Now remember that this was 1968 and there were no cell phones, or pagers, just land line phones. So once I arrived at the movie theater I would call the unit and report that I was in the show building. Once the show was over I would have to call and say that I intended to stop to eat; then at the restaurant I would call in again and report my location. As you can see time off was not really time off. We were always told that at such times EOD men were not allowed the luxuries of being considered absent without leave, if your presences were not known 24 hours a day you were considered a deserter. The charge of desertion especially during a time of war can carry a very heavy penalty.

During the time I was stationed at the 71st I never got to know a single citizen in the small friendly town of Wilmington, Ohio or for that matter on the tiny Air Force base. The single men spent 24 hours a day in this tiny drab building while the married men were allowed to go home at night and weekends. I will admit to getting an occasional day pass to go to Dayton but they were few and far between.

I want to state that I do not blame our commanding officer, John A. Barbush for any of these problems, he was an honest man who did the best he could with what little the Army provided. This was at a time of social unrest when the 71st area included the southern half of Ohio, part of West Virginia, and part of Kentucky. This was also during the 1968 presidential campaign and the Army EOD units were required to supply personnel to support the Secret Service. The 71st seldom had a full ten-man roster and since a call required at least a two-man team response, being short handed was very common. In fact there were times that I would take an incident call on the phone knowing that we had only two men to respond, leaving one man on the phones. At such times we all prayed a second call did not come in for there would be no one to send except the man on the telephone.

That remark about Army EOD assisting the Secret Service to protect the presidential candidates in the 1968 election is hush, hush. If anyone asks I didn't say that the federal government bought us new suits and we traveled around in civilian clothing pretending to be Secret Service agents. We were sworn to secrecy because there was a law preventing the military from such activity. Still it was a great experience meeting or at least watching the rich and famous cavort around the country. Actually the only candidate I met that impressed me was

General Curtis LeMay who was running for vice president on George Wallace's ticket. My highlight was getting to meet Bob Hope. The governor of Ohio, Bob Hope and Spiro Agnew, who became Richard Nixon's Vice President for a while, played a golf game at a very elite golf course in Columbus, Ohio. Mr. Hope, who was performing at the Ohio State Fair, invited Agnew to join him in the show that night so we were required to work both the golf match and the fair. I shared the elevator with Mr. Hope at the Hilton Hotel that afternoon and we chatted through the ride. He appeared to be a very nice down-to-earth man. I also met Bob Hope back stage when he put on his Christmas show at Long Binh, Viet Nam. I believe that Mr. Hope enjoyed that long hot afternoon on stage nearly as much as the twenty five thousand GI's who were watching from in front of the stage. What a great show it was too!

Clinton County Air Force Base was located on the east side of the small town of Wilmington, Ohio and there was an Army missile site on the west side of the town. Now the interesting thing about this arrangement was the fact that we had absolutely no association with them. All of our paper work, including pay, promotion, training and medical records was at Ft. Knox, Kentucky, a three hour drive from Wilmington. There were no fax's or computer emails in those days so all correspondence was by mail or we drove down there.

Our demolition range was at Washington Courthouse, Ohio also a couple hours' drive from Wilmington. This range was a Union Army Camp during the Civil War and in the 1960's was operated by the local National Guard Unit. They had placed a five pound per detonation limit on the range which made destroying anything larger that a dud hand grenade questionable. Taking everything into consideration, locating an Army

EOD unit at Clinton County Air Force base was not one of the military's smarter moves. It was almost as if the Department of Defense threw a dart at the map of Ohio and said that no matter where it stuck they would make it work.

During this period of time the Marine, Navy and Air Force were restricted to performing EOD operations only on their own bases or on their ordnance off base. In contrast the Army EOD provided services to all police, fire departments or government agency's who requested assistance. This allowed us to travel around a specific area in answer to official calls as well as training fire and police departments in basic explosive identification and handling.

During my time with the 71st we responded to many calls for such items as war trophies, old dynamite, a couple of police raids, some Civil War items and a couple of bombings. One of these resulted in a hot conversation between the Army and Air Force EOD.

This particular incident occurred on one of the many weekends that I was pulling duty in the 71st old fire station. I was watching TV in the afternoon when one of the other enlisted men called telling me that he was hurrying back to base. It seems there was a story on the local radio station that a bomb had been found in Dayton and that the 71st was on its way to the rescue.

I had not heard the broadcast nor had I received a call from any of the authorities for assistance. The other man returned and we listened intently as the on-scene action news reporter stated repeatedly that the 71st EOD team would be on site any moment, which would have been a good trick because our squad was nearly an hour's drive away and had not left the building yet.

We spoke to the C.O. by phone and informed him we had enough people to roll but he refused to allow us

50

to leave without an official request from a government agency. As we spoke the news reporter described the action around the scene of the bomb, as the police struggled to wrestle a 55 gallon drum of water to the roof of the building where the supposed explosive item was located. The reporter speculated as to what had happened to the Army Bomb Disposal Unit as he gave a detailed description of the Dayton police picking up the bomb and dropping it into the barrel of water.

For the uninitiated, it is considered bad form to pick up any explosive device without first checking for anti-lift or anti-disturbance devices but even then such an item should never be thrown in water. The reasoning against such action, no matter how often it is portrait in the movies, is that the water could short out an electrically fired device and cause it to detonate. Fortunately for all concerned, applying water to this particular improvised explosive devices electrical system failed to cause a detonation.

The radio reporter made the whole episode very interesting for all the listeners, including our EOD team as we waited for the urgent telephone call. That call never came but we did receive one from the First Sgt of the Air Force EOD unit at Wright Patterson Air Force Base in Dayton, Ohio. He claimed that he had spoken to me and demanded my head on a platter for not responding.

Needless to say I got a good raking over the coals by everyone from the lowest private to the C.O. I stuck to the fact that I had never received a call that day from any police or fire department, and certainly not from the First Sgt. of the Wright Patterson EOD.

A little bit of research disclosed that the telephone calls had gone to the Army missile site on the other side of Wilmington. It seems that someone on C. Q. duty was taking the calls for help from Dayton police and replied that the EOD was on its way. I was finally vindicated by this little revelation but I don't recall a single apology for the accusation made against me.

The next Monday I and a Sgt were instructed to drive to Dayton and pick up the remains of the device from the Air Force EOD team at Wright Patterson. The police had hauled the barrel of water containing the explosive device to Wright Patterson's main gate where their team finally took possession of the dynamite. I was advised not to go because of the bad feeling between me and the Air Force Sgt but truthfully I would not have missed the trip for anything.

We arrived at the main gate of Wright Patterson Air Base and were quickly directed to the EOD unit. At the air force EOD building we were shown the soggy red paper globs which was all that remained of the sticks of dynamite after being stored in water for a couple of days. The unit's top Sgt, a Master Sgt as I recall, began to denounce the Army EOD and me in particular for the bomb incident.

The man became very irate so I asked him why his team who was much closer did not respond to the call. I already knew the answer but I just had to ask. The first Sgt growled that they did not ever go on off-post calls because it simply was not their job.

At that point the first Sgt began to curse whoever was on duty at the 71st the day of the bomb call. I told him I was on duty that day and that neither he nor the authorities ever called our unit. In fact, I even explained that much of the responsibility lay on his shoulders because he had telephoned the Army Missile Base and not our unit. All military telephones are answered with the name of the unit, as in this case "71st EOD Specialist Pool speaking." If the Sgt had been paying attention on his many calls to our unit he would have realized that was not how the phone had been answered.

The Air Force Sgt and I exchanged a few heated words that ended when my teammate thought it was best if we leave. I of course was lectured about talking back to the Sgt but I was not about to be cussed for his mistakes. I had done nothing wrong and I wanted him to know it. It's a well established fact that I have the rare ability to say the wrong thing at the right time. This happened to be just such a time because the first Sgt relayed his disappointment to my C.O. It seems that no matter how hard a person tries to do the right thing it all comes out wrong.

TRAINING THE FIRE MARSHALS

During my time in the old fire house that served as garage, barracks, offices, and day room for the 71st EOD we took on the task of training fire department personnel as well as the Ohio state fire investigators.

In truth this was not a bad job in that most of the time we traveled to the fire department's station house to put on our presentation. On a few occasion we spent the night in the station house and were feed their home cooked meals. Somewhere along the line it was decided that the classes could be improved by having some samples of clandestine devices. This idea was expanded to allowing members of the class to attempt a render safe on these homemade training aids.

I questioned the wisdom of making mock explosive devices knowing that in the end students would want to attempt to disarm the devices. This would have been fun in practice but no one can become a bomb disposal expert from attending four or five hours of class. But "rank rules" and we set to work building fake explosive devices. This bomb building was right down my alley so I gathered up every empty cigar box in the little town of Wilmington, Ohio. We proceeded to produce a number of different bombs, each one illustrating a different form of ignition system. There were cigar box bombs that had anti-lift devices, anti-disturbance devices and anti-tip igniters. These training-aid bombs used flashlight batteries for power and remote flashbulbs that fired off if the student failed to disarm the device. It soon became apparent that the citizens of Wilmington did not consume enough cigars in order to keep the supply up to our demand and the brass thought we were consuming too many batteries and flash bulbs. I was told to find a more permanent source of power and a replacement for the flash bulbs.

I went into town and searched the second hand and junk stores for any cheap items that might be converted to an explosive device. I selected such things as a hair curling iron, a hand iron, and a waffle iron. We quickly dismantled the appliances and filled them with white clay to represent C-4 then added batteries so that the simple act of unplugging the unit from the wall socket would not defuse the items. Still it seemed the class needed some type of devices that the students could more easily practice on, so we were back to using cardboard boxes. After our experiences with converting small appliances it became clear that things like shoe boxes, or even shipping containers would give the students a proper feel for clandestine explosive devices.

Now thru all of these classes we had used large photography flash bulbs to simulate detonations when the student made a mistake in disarming a device, however the Army decided that this was too expensive and we were told to find a cheaper alternative.

Many ideas were passed around and several things tested before we got a hold of a jeep horn that was rated at 24 volt D.C. Let me tell you that the little 24 volt horn produced a big, big sound when connected to 110 volt. Most people would describe the sound of the horn as startling. It was clear we had found the replacement for the flash bulb shortage. In using the vehicle horn we had found the answer to a reusable explosive simulator problem or so we thought. The unit was now prepared for our next class, a group of state fire investigators who came to the 71st for training.

We cleaned the old fire house from top to bottom making a special effort to remove the stains and dirt from the concrete floor of our truck bay. The powers-that-be decreed that the truck bay would be a fine place to set up our newly manufactured training aids for the fire investigators to apply their new knowledge of bomb disposal.

I will admit to having a feeling of pride as we set up tables in the truck bay area. The new bombs were placed on the tables in such a manner that each one could easily be connected to the horn as well as the old reliable 120 volt electrical outlet. With all the preparations completed, the state fire investigators were lead into our dayroom where they received about four hours of class on explosives and bomb disposal and then adjourned to the truck bay.

The game rules were explained to the students that they could not cut the power cord or the jeep horn as part of the render safe procedure. It was made clear that any procedure must be done within the device itself. Then we turned our middle-aged class loose to do their best at disarming the devices.

These men were all old friends which possibly produced a too familiar atmosphere, one that I never would have allowed in later years. But we were trying to be good hosts to a group of men who had worked hard to attain some status in the state of Ohio. Additionally, they had been attentive students.

I'm sure that I am not giving away any trade secrets when I describe one of the bombs that I had made for the class. I started with a standard card board box roughly 12" square that I wrapped with heavy tin foil. Next the box was wrapped with heavy brown paper followed by another layer of tin foil, then an outside covering of brown paper to make the whole thing appear to be a package ready for shipment. An electrical wire had been connected to each of the layers of foil covering.

The idea being that any metal object, a bullet or metal knife should penetrate both layers of the tin foil the bomb would detonate. The metal knife blade passing thru the foil acts as a switch making a complete electrical circuit that would cause the electric blasting cap to detonate.

We had instructed in class that a metal knife should never be used to open a suspected package. In fact knowing that one of the training bombs was rigged to prevent entry with a metal implement we stressed the danger of such a practice.

We began to hook up our devices and the students eagerly stepped forward to match their wits with our in-house mad bomber. Unfortunately taking the devices one at a time proved too slow so the process was sped up by hooking up multiple units. I suddenly felt that the practical part of the school was rapidly getting out of control, still we continued on.

At this time one of the older men dressed in a nice sport coat and slacks stepped forward wanting to try his luck on the brown paper wrapped box. Before we knew what had happened, the man pulled out a pen knife and plunged its steel blade into the brown box.

The little horn screamed out its distress as the 120 volts coursed through the horn, the tin foil and the man's knife. The man grabbed his chest just before flopping over backwards on the grease stained garage floor.
"He is recovering from a recent heart attack." One of the other students yelled out in shock as he crouched to aid his stricken friend.

"Oh that's great." One of the other men exclaimed. "He just had 120 volts of electricity ran through his heart." There was a sudden moment of panic that was quickly overcome by the professionalism of the highly trained fire men who quickly began to assist the heart patient.

Fortunately the shocked man quickly recovered and did not hold a grudge. He stated that we had warned the students repeatedly about using metal instruments and he knew that 120 ac was present in the exercise. The incident did produce some deep thought and long discussions of how to present such an incident in the future.

I learned several valuable lessons that day, the main one centered on the fact that booby traps can prove fatal even in the absence of high explosives. This was just another case where good fortune smiled on a pack of fools and I admit to being the biggest fool of all. Anyone with the slightest bit of common sense would have seen the inherent dangers in the use of 120 volts of electricity to power devices designed to be dismantled by such poorly trained individuals.

EXPLOSIVE DOLLS

Another story from Ohio centers around a mythical plastic doll that troops in Viet Nam were reportedly shipping home as souvenirs. I'm not sure if this started as a practical joke or was instigated by some half wit news man who neglected, as usual, to research a story. In either case the news media spread the word around the nation that dolls were coming into this country from Viet Nam that were manufactured from or filled with plastic explosives.

The dolls in question were about twelve inches tall with black hair, Asian features, and dressed in traditional Vietnamese clothing. Most dolls wore long colorful satin dresses but some were attired in the pajama pants, split skirt dresses and funnel-shaped straw hats. The doll bodies were fabricated from very thin skin toned plastic. I can only guess, but I believe that someone confused the cheap plastic used in the doll body with plastic explosives.

The 71st received its fair share of calls from worried citizens who had been gifted with a suspected doll. As far as I know there was never an instance of a doll exploding or for that matter one that contained any explosives. However it was in my mind a legitimate reason to escape from the old fire house prison, so I jumped at any chance to play with these dolls.

If any explosive dolls were ever found, I hope the team that found them would let me know.

VOLUNTEERING FOR VIET NAM

I learned a great deal about life in and out of the military while stationed with the 71st but I had joined the Army to see the war. Living beside a long concrete sidewalk in the middle of an Ohio corn field was not what I wanted. I began to volunteer for assignment in Viet Nam but although EOD men were in demand transfer orders never came through. After completing paperwork several times, I finally discovered that my 1049 requests were not being forwarded to our head quarters at Ft. Knox. This of course enhanced a long smoldering feud between me and those who were interceding with my plans.

This was during the 1968 presidential campaign and the violent anti-war unrest that was dealing the authorities fits. The Army EOD, although short of stateside personnel due to the Viet Nam war were the only bomb disposal people available to respond to domestic calls. Only large city police departments had very small poorly trained and equipped bomb disposal departments and the Secret Service didn't have units at all. This created a high demand for well trained EOD men causing the Secret Service as well as police departments to begin courting many of us younger members of EOD teams. They offered a six month early out and advanced rank and starting pay. Now the argument I received continually centered on the fact that I had less than a year on my enlistment so I could avoid duty in Viet Nam. It was also pointed out that if I were that unhappy being held prisoner at Clinton County I could take advantage of one of these government programs. Yes, I could have stayed at the 71st and counted down the days to discharge or taken an early out but it seems to me cowardly to have taken advantage of so much Army training then not put it to good use. Beside, being a person who never believed what I read in the newspaper or saw on TV, I had to see the war first hand. I did accomplish this goal but I was more of an observer than a participant. By this I mean that I was able to visit many of the famous towns and cities as well as land marks that were in the news every day.

I was fortunate enough to explore the city of Saigon many times, ride swift boats on the Mekong, and visit Da Nang and its beaches. We flew a lot and traveled by helicopter which provided a magnificent view to the rural villages, jungles and farms of South Viet Nam. As much as I enjoyed Viet Nam I had an equal dislike for duty in Ohio. Now this was a personal thing because this little out-of-the-way squad had some great people serving there. I know that most of these men did their best to make life pleasant at the 71st but I just did not fit the life style. An example of the kindness of the EOD families and these people in particular can be best illustrated in my Thanksgiving Day of 1968.

THANKSGIVING DINNER

When the Thanksgiving holiday rolled around the two single enlisted men who shared our building, lived very close to Wilmington asked for the weekend off and of course the married men wished to have a long weekend at home with their families, so I volunteered to pull duty for the four day weekend. This meant that I would be locked in the building from Wednesday night until Monday morning. I went to town and bought enough food to last the four days thinking I could eat and watch TV while holding down the fort.

The Army had just issued the 71st a new color TV for our day room/kitchen/lounge/meeting room/ and sometimes office for it was used for all of these purposes and more. The members of the unit were very pleased with the new TV for very few people owned color sets in 1968 but it's nice wooden console cabinet did look a little out of place in our run down fire station.

Thursday morning of the big day I began to fix my Thanksgiving dinner. I thought a turkey too much trouble and a bit of over-kill for just one person so I selected a nice big ham that could be spread out over several days of feasting. I prepared several side dishes and had purchased a nice German Chocolate cake from the bakery in town. By noon everything was ready including the holiday football games on the new color TV.

A Thanksgiving dinner spent totally alone may seem antisocial but after being confined to our small building day and night with the same men can also prove very trying. The four days alone would be a real tonic for a loner like me. With my dinner ready I sat down in front of the new color TV to watch the holiday football games and eat. Shortly after I finished eating my dinner, one of the married enlisted men and his wife dropped by. They were a young Latina couple from New York City who were concerned that I would miss Thanksgiving dinner. To alleviate this concern they brought me part of their traditional Porta Rican meal. It was nothing like I had ever eaten before but it was just as delectable as it was different. I sat at the chrome kitchen table and consumed a second meal while they sat on the couch in front of the color TV with their backs to me.

This young couple had just gathered up their dishes and departed when another Sgt and his wife, who were suffering the same guilty pangs, arrived. This couple was from the south originally and the food they brought reflected the geographic influence. The food was great but it was difficult to eagerly partake a third meal in about as many hours. Once again the couple occupied the couch in front of the new color TV while I looked at their backs.   The good natured southern couple policed up their dishes and departed leaving me with a larger stomach than usual but I could finally get in front of the new TV to watch the football games.

At least that was my intent until another Sgt with wife and children in tow arrived with more food from their Thanksgiving Day feast. This lady was from Mexico as was the meal she had prepared. I attempted to explain that I had eaten three dinners already and had a great deal of leftovers from them. They sat together on the couch watching the new color TV while I tried to eat yet another highly unusual meal. The Sgt. and his wife sat with their backs to me on the day room couch while their two children stood beside me as I ate. The Sgt's children were still hungry for momma's home cooking so while the parents were watching the TV, I fed the two kids nearly everything on my plate.   Near evening the Sgt and family gather up their belongings and headed for home. Shortly thereafter I received a phone call from the C.O. and his young wife who wanted to stop by with food from their dinner but I politely declined the offer the same way I did the call from the First Sgt. I know this was the biggest Thanksgiving dinner I ever consumed and certainly the most varied.

I didn't see anyone for the next three days and I began to wonder if the Thursday visits were just an excuse to watch football on the new color TV, but deep down I knew that these were good people and every one a special lady who was genuinely concerned that I would be deprived of a home cooked meal. I would like to thank every one of these people for giving me a truly unique Thanksgiving Day even if I did miss the color TV broadcast of the holiday football games.

GOING AWAY PARTY

As I think back now, duty at Clinton County would have been far more appealing to the old man I have become. It certainly was a disappointing back water place to a young single soldier who wanted to see the war. A certain amount of personality difference drove my desire to transfer out of the 71st, with Viet Nam being the logical destination. In the end Sgt Dick and I received orders for Viet Nam at the same time. In fact our going away party was held on the same night but since we were short handed and someone had to be on duty, I stayed at the building to answer the phone. As the evening progressed the party goers called several times to keep me up dated on the celebration and the state of their intoxication.

The next morning I was handed the engraved metal cup that had been presented to me in my absence the night before. I was told I should have been there but I knew that staying at the building was a much wiser choice, now that I was so near to escaping the old flight line fire station. The members of the 71st were some fine people and I wish I could have enjoyed my time there more but departing the 71st was much less heart wrenching than the end of my tour in Viet Nam.

In contrast, a going away party in Viet Nam, at least in the 3rd Ord was basically just another excuse to drink for each man just sort of oozed in and out of the unit. The departing man faded away without fanfare or an organized celebration. The good-byes among comrades and friends were more sincere because the departing felt guilty about leaving their teammates with a hazardous job unfinished, while those being left behind were jealous as well as glad for the lucky soldier returning to the world.

Returning to the states was a distinct moment in time that we all hoped to live long enough to achieve. It was a goal that men prayed for, a day that was counted down to with short-timer calendars and posters. And yet that day of clearing the post was a defining moment in life that we all knew would never pass again. It was a summit you had fought to reach and at the same time a low, nearly depressing unavoidable life altering event. Each man signed out of the unit to slip away alone hoping to find a new life without the aid of the closest friendship he would ever form. It was also understood no matter how many promises were made to keep in touch, that the chances of ever meeting again were slim at best. Still we exchanged addresses and shook hands reluctant to be separated from the bonding brotherhood forged by heat of danger and tempered in the waters of compassion for one another.

We may have served at the pleasure of the President but not the popular vote of the people and yet we did serve. It was service out of loyalty and love of country even though many thought the cause unjust; we suffered and perished in an alien land for a strange people.

TRANSFERRING OUT OF THE 71ST

When the end finally came and orders were issued transferring me from the 71st to some unknown unit in Viet Nam I celebrated in private. Actually the feeling was mutual because I wanted out of the 71st and the 71st wanted me out of the unit. Now it was time to clear post, which to nonmilitary people is a ritual that all personnel must go thru before departing from an installation. You must be released by the bank, library, Post Exchange, doctors, and any other place you might have had dealings with during your stay on base. Due to our restrictive lives I had little or no contact with these facilities.

At this time the Army required that ownership of motorcycles would be allowed only after obtaining permission from your C.O. and the base commander. I wangled around until both men gave me the O.K. to own and ride a motor cycle on Clinton County Air Force Base. The base, being very small, I believe I owned the only bike that was kept on base making me something of a marked man.

I had made most of my rounds clearing post when I had to report to one office that was run by a beautiful young blonde haired civilian woman. I had only seen this woman from afar but everyone on base knew of her and commented on her great looks. She politely signed my paperwork then asked what I had planned for my motor cycle. (Now remember this was January 1969, mid way through a very cold winter.)

I replied that I intended to ride my B.S.A. the 800 miles back home. The beautiful blonde offered to ship my bike by air to Offutt Air Force Base which is located about 30 miles from my parent's home. "No," I insisted I would ride all the way home, "no problem". I must admit that my over active male ego would not allow me to look weak in front of this attractive lady that I had never met before and would never meet again.

I thought of that pretty blonde about once a mile for the entire 800 mile ride home. The motor cycle itself hadn't a windshield or any other form of wind protection as I struggled westward with the air temperature in the mid teens every day. I could only ride for about 10 to 15 minutes before my hands became frozen inside my insulated gloves. It was a painful ordeal that brought a lot of questioning stares and pointed fingers as I rolled west thru the ice and snow on Interstate 80. But I finally made it home not much worse for wear but I learned not to be so foolish in the future. At least I had 30 days to thaw out before heading for the tropical paradise of South Viet Nam.

HOW I FOUND MY HOME IN COUNTRY

My in country experience started by reporting to Ft. Lewis, Washington where we waited several days to be assigned a flight out. We departed from Ft. Lewis in the middle of the night landing some six hours later in Anchorage with a beautiful winter sun rise.

This stop was very brief and we were soon back in the air aboard a four engine commercial jet whose body had been lengthened to haul more troops per flight. It could be a matter of perception but it seemed the seats were also closer together and the food was nonexistent for the 13 hour flight to Japan. From Japan to Cam Rahn Bay, South Viet Nam seemed a short hop after the long hours spent crossing the Pacific Ocean. The flight had originated in the dark of night in Washington State but from Anchorage we had flown in bright sun shine, finally arriving half way around the world in the middle of the afternoon. Talk about jet lag!

The flight home originated near midnight at Bien Hoa Air Base and landed in Okinawa at sunrise; the sunset was about four hours later. We stopped in Hawaii in the dark and landed in Oakland, California at sunrise. The flight over was in all daylight while the return trip had to be endured thru the long dark night. This made for an uncomfortable ride for me as I had become used to registering land marks while flying around in country but there was nothing to see high over the middle of the Pacific in the middle of the night.

I had been offered the opportunity to go by ship to Viet Nam which was reported to take 21 days off of my time in country but I declined. I was in too much of a hurry to get in country to waste my time on a pleasure cruise. However I will admit that I often had second thoughts about my rapid decision to go by air.

On arriving at Cam Rahn Bay we were nearly overcome by the searing heat of the day; something that we were not accustomed to coming from winter in the states. We were formed up and marched down the street to a tent with long rows of tin troughs where we were told to brush our teeth. I never knew the reason for this exercise other than the cadre could not deal with our bad morning breath after the long flight.

We were then instructed in the use of sun screen and insect repellant not to mention the hazards of the many varieties of dangerous critters indigenous to Southeast Asia. Our group was given the typical army bums rush being moved from point A to point B for some fabricated pretense just to keep everyone busy. There were never any real answers as to what or where we went. Suddenly we were told to grab our gear and prepare to be loaded on a plane to be sent south. The ride was a C 130 cargo plane and the southern destination proved to be Bien Hoa Air Base.

We GI's were loaded on the C 130 thru the rear tail gate and told to take a seat on the hard metal deck that served as the main floor. Just before take-off a group of South Vietnamese civilians were brought aboard and were directed to the canvass web seats that lined the plane's exterior walls. It was interesting to note that these civilian's carry-on baggage consisted of pigs, chickens, and a couple of small goats.

The big C-130 backed out of its protective revetment then lumbered up and down the runway a couple of times before finally gaining enough velocity to break the law of gravity. I thought it odd that the plane's crew chief waited until the very last moment to close the rear loading ramp. But it wasn't long before the tropical heat and the close confinement of the planes interior combined to release odors from the on-board livestock that only a sewage plant worker could love. I knew then that the crew chief had left the tail gate down in a futile effort to maintain a well ventilated aircraft for as long as possible.

The big old cargo plane lumbered and jumped and bucked across the clear Asian sky for what seemed hours to my butt's way of thinking. We were originally told this would be a short flight but then it was reported that storms lay in our path so we had to change course. After a time I became envious and then resentful towards the local civilians whose animals were resting semi peacefully in the much more comfortable web seats.

The flight continued on and on before it occurred to me that either we were flying in circles or South Viet Nam was a larger country than I thought. Of course, it could have been we were on a very slow air plane, which made me glad that C-130 were not used to transport troops from the states to Nam.

We finally set down on the runway at Bien Hoa Air Force Base and no one had to tell us twice to exit the plane; of course that happened only after the civilians and livestock had leisurely deplaned. This was my first experience with the Asian life style which proved to be much slower and more casual than anything in the states. The adjustment came easily to some GI's while others never fully accepted the relaxed, timeless attitude of the natives.

At Bien Hoa the C-130 was met by military buses that rushed us to the 90th replacement depot at Long Binh. This establishment proved to be another exercise in controlled confusion. It was here that I was warned that I might not be assigned to an EOD unit. It was here that I warned them if I was not assigned to an EOD unit there would be hell to pay. Perhaps this is not the proper military attitude but then I never claimed to have the proper military attitude. The Army had cried and begged for EOD men to come to Viet Nam and I had volunteered repeatedly and fought like hell to get in country so I had no intention of being stuck in some ammo company. I felt certain if I were wrongly placed, simply making contact with any EOD unit would immediately rectify the problem.

At the replacement depot life seemed to stand still. I thoroughly disliked such companies, they were so unsettled. I couldn't wait to be assigned nearly anywhere in order to escape the ever moving sea of green fatigues of the new replacements. We were forced to endure days of limbo waiting to learn their fate.

One might think that a post is a post but there can be a great deal of difference from base to base and job to job in places like South Viet Nam. The luck of the draw might land one man in a tent compound that was nothing but a tiny mud hole in the middle of nowhere, while another man with the same M.O.S. might very well find his place in a nice barracks, with a good mess hall and a big post exchange next door.

The common GI's idle mind is a play ground for a fertile imagination, which in a replacement company keeps the air filled with ridiculous rumors and false scuttlebutt. No matter what orders a man might receive there are those who are willing to recount the horror and danger of that base. These tales usually originate with those who have never been in country before let alone have any firsthand experience with the subject at hand. Many men take these erroneous reports as the gospel truth and become so upset that they dream up schemes to avoid the duty. The permanent parties of these replacement companies who probably have never been to these bases often make matters worse for the young impressionable GI's by reinforcing the distressing myths. The replacement companies were also famous for fights and the theft of anything not nailed down. Needless to say I could hardly wait for orders to whatever fate Uncle Sam had prepared for me.

SMALL WORLD

Late the first night in the 90th replacement a large number of men were, for the lack of anything better to do, lounging on the ground around the headquarters building. This always reminds me of the prison open recreation area scene from some old black and white movies. A sea of men, all in the same uniform were lying around with nothing to do but talk and gamble and fight. It seemed hardly an hour passed without the sounds of a heated argument or full-fledged fight didn't interrupt the tranquil night's rest. The bored adventurous types who were not involved in the confrontation would race to the sound of the fight which had often ended by the time they arrived.

I was seated on a grassy bank listening to one GI after another relate sorrowfully what they had left behind. It was always the prettiest girl in the state, the fastest car in the county or the highest paid job in town. Of course this terrible deprivation that had settled on the land was always the fault of Lyndon Johnson or Richard Nixon. Some of the better educated troops blamed their loss on John F. Kennedy or the great military industrial complex that was so famous with the anti-war faction in those days. I for one always doubted the latter theory on the grounds that such a group of powerful people would surely be intelligent enough to conspire together to produce a much more efficient and profitable war.

A small fight had just ended when the GI setting next to me whispered. "That fella over there is staring at us." "I noticed him looking over here a while ago." He groaned. I studied the mass of green jungle fatigue clad men about 30 yards away on the opposite bank but didn't spot anyone I knew. I was about to give up when I spotted a strange soldier wearing army issue black frame eye glasses looking straight at me. "Don't know him." I declared to the man who had first seen our observer. "Well he either knows you or he is gay." The man replied. "Oh, look out he's coming over here." He quickly added while in the act of rising to leave.

In just a couple of seconds the stranger crossed the void between us and approached me saying "Hello" to which I politely responded just the way my old grey-haired mother had taught me to do. The stranger sat down and explained that he recognized me but could not remember my name or where we had met. Now began the old military twenty question game of exchanging information that people play when they are in such a situation. The problem with this game when played in the military is that everyone looks pretty much like everyone else and nothing like they did in civilian life. We wasted a good twenty minutes going back over our short military careers in an effort to establish a common link. At the end of this time I still didn't know who this guy was but we had discovered that we were both native Iowan's but had lived in small towns quite some distance apart. It was the stranger who asked if I knew a girl named Mary from another small town where I had been registered in a community college. Notice I did not say attended for the college got my money but I never got an education. There were some administration people who had branded me a rebel, trouble maker and an instigator. Of course none of this was true.

College rules required all freshmen to live in the newly-built dormitory in order to help pay for its construction. The problem being that this dorm was full of rebel's, trouble makers and instigators that had been expelled from other more reputable schools who were now enrolling in any college that would provide them a draft deferment. During the height of the war enrollment in many small schools doubled or tripled so fast that several new colleges were opened just to handle the demand. It was this group of misfits that led this poor innocent quiet farm boy astray. The difference between the poor farm boy and the student rabble was one of money. They had money and I didn't. When these party boy's got in a fix their parents would buy off the authorities while my parents just wished me good luck.

In any case I replied that I had known the pretty young lady named Mary, in fact you might say we dated. That is her father was a local doctor and of course I being a rebellious poor farm boy did not meet the standards her family expected of her suitor. Mary was a pretty woman with a very pleasing disposition and despite associating with me, I am glad to say she went on to have a meaningful career and became highly respected in the community that she settled in. A life I am sure she could never have attained in my company. I hate to admit it but time has proven the old doctors judgment to be pretty sound (as were a couple of other wise old father's with pretty young daughters that were of my acquaintance.)

Maid Mary became the key that unlocked the question of where the stranger in new jungle fatigues had met me. He had actually attended the community college that I called home for a couple of years while avoiding the draft. I must explain to those who might read this and were not alive during the Viet Nam era that avoiding the draft was the national past time for any male over the age of eighteen. The schools and the media preached such actions and you were branded either a dunce or a fool if you didn't do your best to avoid service. In my own self defense I want it recorded that I quit college and enlisted in the Army on my own accord. I of course was ridiculed and branded an idiot by everyone in the area, including the ex-military men.

At this point the stranger explained that he remember me dating Mary because his best friend had a crush on the girl too. He confessed that he had been the best man at their wedding and then went on to state that I was a fool for breaking up with Mary. Being labeled a fool has followed me all my life to the point that I feared that people were confusing my last name of Pool with fool. Some folks have maintained the two words were interchangeable in my case.

I informed the stranger that breaking up with Mary was not of my choosing. I made repeated attempts to change the subject by mentioning some of the college instructors or campus characters but the stranger insisted on returning to the subject of Mary. I began to think he was the one who had a crush on the young lady. After a few minutes of this ongoing aggravation, I excused myself and wandered off into the balmy South East Asian night. I never saw the stranger again and had no desire to reestablish our association. In fact I have been in his home town on several occasions but I never felt the need to inquire about him.

ASSIGNED TO THE 3RD ORD

The intense February sun beat down unmercifully on me as I sat in uncertainty on a bench just outside one of the 90th replacement company's buildings. I had just entered Viet Nam 36 hours before at glorious Cam Rahn Bay. I now was biding my time waiting for orders to be typed that would send me to Pleiku far to the north of Cam Rahn Bay. "Typical military" I thought to myself, sending me down south so that I could go back up north. But I had little time to ponder the wisdom of the green machine for there was a whole new world unfolding around me that first real day in country. I noticed right away that my shiny dark OD jungle fatigues set me apart from the more experienced troops whose faded dull uniform and worn jungle boots were worn like a badge of distinction. This green horn image was noticeably not only by the GI's but also by the Vietnamese who laughed at us after making disparaging remarks to one another in their native language.

Suddenly in the distance a string of powerful explosions ripped thru the hot humid late afternoon air drawing everyone's attention. "EOD team." One of the GI's clad in very faded fatigues said nonchalantly to no one in particular. "Have your orders ready in just a minute." The clerk inside the building behind me called out thru a battered screen door. He had, like everyone else rushed outside to see where the explosion originated.

"Good." I replied weakly, wishing I had been with the EOD team that had just set off the attention attracting shots. The troops in the area quickly returned to performing their everyday tasks as the excitement of the explosion waned and was soon forgotten. Forgotten by everyone but myself, for I have always been drawn to explosives in any form. This fascination with anything that goes boom has been in my blood since I was just a child. I have always been intrigued by anything from fire crackers to nuclear weapons and this afternoon was no different.

A combination of envy, curiosity and boredom drew me from my seat in the sun to a nearby narrow blacktop street where I hoped for a better view of the demolition area. As I moved to the edge of the road a fast moving Army jeep sailed by, locked up its brakes and slid to a stop. It was then that I recognized the jeeps red fenders and emergency lights denoting it as an EOD vehicle. The unseen driver suddenly began backing up only to slide to a second stop directly in front of where I stood. The driver was a man I'll call Dick, his passenger was named Dave, both of whom I had known back in the world (as the U.S. was referred to). Although I wore no EOD insignia, Dick recognized me as he sped by.

"What are you doing?" He called out. I explained I was waiting for orders to go north. My reply lit a fire under Sgt. Dick. He pulled his jeep off the road and raced inside the building as if the devil were after him. It was amazing to watch Sgt. Dick as he descended like a duck on a June bug on the replacement company's young clerk. Dick was a large man who seldom took no for an answer and no matter how much the clerk refused; he insisted that my orders be changed. The men of this building were totally unprepared for the sudden attack that consisted of a combination of rapid speech, odd reasoning, threats, cajoling, and he was not about to take no for an answer.

The next thing I knew my duffel bag and I were in the back of the 3rd Ord jeep headed for Long Binh Post. On the ride I learned my new first Sgt was one of the toughest NCO's in the military. A hurried drive thru the countryside brought us to the famous Long Binh Post. We drove past the entrance to the Army's massive ammunition dump and turned into a guarded gate at the edge of a grove of rubber trees. The 3rd Ord EOD building sat about a block from the main road surrounded by these tall evenly spaced ancient rubber trees.

Now, I was raised in dilapidated tenet houses usually on dead end dirt roads so I was far from accustomed to a luxurious life style, but my first view of the 3rd Ord's EOD office / barracks was a true shock. I had seen many a broken down farm with better hog houses than this structure. Actually it was very reminiscent of a beach comer's shack or the shelter one might build of junk salvage from the sea when marooned on a deserted island. In fact, that is very nearly the case for the roof was corrugated tin, the walls were plywood and screen wire. O.D. colored sand bags were stacked 3 feet high against the building's exterior walls in a futile effort to protect those within. I suspect that whoever held the contract to supply sand bags to Viet Nam made more money than any other contractor. Ninety five percent of U.S. buildings in country had just such green sandbags adorning the exterior, not counting all the bunkers and shelters that were completely covered with sandbags. The wet tropical climate took a heavy toll on these bags whether made of canvas or woven plastic. It was not unusual in the midst of torrential monsoon rains for one of more of these sand bag walls to collapse with a roar. In the 3rd Ord Battalion area this roar was often followed a few seconds later by the detonation of a hand grenade. It seems the drug dealers and users of which there were many found the sand bag walls ideal places to hide their illicit stashes. The hand grenades were placed, pin pulled, lever held secure by the sand bags as an unseen security system. (but getting off subject) A small porch and open doorway marked the entrance to the office where the unit's top NCO sat peering out at his returning jeep.

"Come on." Dick declared in a positive voice while parking the jeep. "Top Sgt is at his desk so this is a good chance for you to meet him." I grabbed my duffel bag and followed Dick and Dave thru the door to the desk occupied by a very stern faced Master Sgt. "Good evening Master Jack." Dick called out in his most charming voice. "Here's your new EOD man", "Worked with him in the states".

"But we haven't got a man coming." Came Master Jack's firm objection.

"We got one now." Dick smiled stepping out another office door. "I'm late for chow." He announced, quickly disappearing from sight, leaving Dave and I to explain how I come to be assigned to the unit that didn't need or want me.

As consequences of my unexpected arrival, I spent the next two weeks policing up cigarette butts and polishing spittoons until the Powers that Be decided I was fit for EOD incidents.

DESTINED TO BE IN THE 3RD ORD

During this process of transferring stations I was given the opportunity to go to Viet Nam by ship. It was explained to me that this boat ride would be a 21 day reprieve from duty in country. I declined fearing I would spend 21 days as a deck hand or moving freight in some hot cargo hold. I now regret not accepting the offer to cross the Pacific Ocean by ship; still I fear I would not have been assigned to the 3rd Ord if my timing had not been prefect. It may sound foolish but I always felt destined to be in the 3rd Ord and really never wanted to transfer to any other unit in country.

I don't believe man is important enough to be a piece to some grand mystical plan that predestines the fate of each of us. On the other hand I feel that win, lose or draw I must play out the hand that was dealt to me. In this case the 3rd Ord was the cards dealt to me and I thank God for it. I was fortunate to meet some of the best men I will ever know during my time at the 3rd and I also know that without these good understanding men I might have failed as a soldier and EOD man.

In summation I must state that my all too short experience with the EOD program was a great experience. I have always been intrigued in the mechanical workings of ordnance and that combined with a keen interest in explosives proved enough incentive to keep me out of serious trouble.

I willing admit now that the only punishment I feared in the Army was that I might lose my EOD badge for one of my many indiscretions. I never seemed to quite fit the military mold but fortunately those around me were conscious of that fact. I always said to do EOD

82

work a person had to be smart enough to do the job but not smart enough to know better. Nearly every EOD man I met fit those specifications perfectly. Many people have asked me why anyone with any sense would volunteer to disarm explosive ordnance. The only way that I can answer that is to state how many times the members of the 3rd Ord fought for the right to go on a bomb call. Big John, Tex, Junior and I were especially annoying to our clerk who often gave out the assignments. Dick was very efficient at dispatching the proper team to a particular situation. We may have done our best to persuade the man to send us on calls but he always won any ensuing argument.

3RD ORD EOD CLERK

The EOD clerk was often the back bone of the unit, a fact that I was slow in learning. Our clerk (and this time I will name him) was Dick Hause, and he was absolutely a member of the 3rd Ord EOD team. He slept in our building instead of ambling in from some distant barracks. Dick manned the radio and the telephone 24 hours a day in an attempt to keep us out of harm's way. It was a rare occasion when he did not know the location of every man in the unit. He knew who was TDY, who was on R and R, who was sick, who had appointments and somehow managed to keep us on time for all of these things and more.

Dick was far from a Radar O'Rielly but for such a young man he did have an innate ability to predict the future. He often foresaw upcoming transfers, disagreements, replacements, promotions, and assignments long before they took place. The man willingly took it upon himself to gently break bad news, praise a good job, or ease disappointment, none of which were part of a clerk's job description. It took awhile but I too learned how important a good clerk was to easing the torment of daily life of an EOD unit in Viet Nam.

I had the privilege of taking our clerk Dick on at least one bomb call. It happened on a day when our unit was unusually short-handed and we had received an urgent call for assistance from some influential people. Because of the "two man team" rule Dick volunteered to go along but worried he didn't know what to do. I asked him why he thought that I knew. Calls in Viet Nam were not like appliance repair where you diagnose a problem, install a new part and go on your merry way; every call was a different unique experience.

I put a cap bearing an EOD badge on Dick and before leaving for the incident sight gave him instruction to act nonchalant or if possible look bored. The person who calls in the incident is the one who will look nervous, while the EOD man must appear cool and casual at all cost. I had known Dick long enough to know he did not scare easily or lose his head in touchy situations so I was quite sure he could pull off this charade without any difficulty.

We arrived at the incident sight to find a very young and very nervous officer fretting over an M-26 hand grenade with the safety pin still in place. The officer was certain that the hand grenade would detonate at any second and destroy the greater part of Long Binh post. We politely reported to the Lieutenant who was relieved to see us, but at the same time not quite sure if he should trust us with such a hazardous weapon. I assured the man that we could handle the situation without calling in any back-up personnel but just to make his day I went into my bomb disposal expert act. Dick caught on to the ploy immediately and assisted as I closely examined the M-26 while discussing in very earnest tones all the hazards involved in the movement and handling of such an item. I praised the Lieutenant for his alert reporting of a potentially deadly situation, picked up the grenade and returned to the building. Dick had become very knowledgeable about the EOD business and the ordnance that we commonly encountered in Viet Nam. I had no doubt in my mind that he would perform professionally on an incident call and in this case even more so than I because I pulled the naive lieutenant's leg a bit.

I'm afraid I was often guilty of putting on an act for those who were overly concerned about a particular explosive situation. I meant no harm and I felt certain

85

that these men returned home and vividly recounted time and again how insane those bomb disposal people were in Viet Nam.

The easy availability of quality 35 mm camera's turned many a veteran into avid camera bugs. Everyone carried a Yashica or Minolta around their neck in the hope of catching that one shot that would embody the Viet Nam story but most clicks of the shutter captured a friend clowning around or a farm family in a rice paddy. We struggled to capture dots in the sky that were passing air craft and the water buffalo became so accustom to being photographed they would stop in mid-step to strike a powerful pose. The Vietnamese children on the streets begged to have their picture taken but not realizing you didn't have a Polaroid camera they would get mad when you didn't give them the picture. Many of the older natives resented having their photo taken claiming that you were stealing their soul. Personally I believe they feared their images could fall into the hands of the V.C. who might take exception at their assisting our side. I do know some of our house girls would liberate any photograph of themselves that they happened across. I never took offense at this minor theft, reasoning that I had taken their picture without permission and it was only fair they retrieve it without my permission.

Our clerk, Dick became very handy with his Yashica but we were all very impressed when he borrowed the units issue Liecha camera to photograph the Bob Hope show. This camera was a rather difficult piece of German equipment that was intended for the team to use to photograph unusual ordnance or booby traps. Since everyone had a personal camera that was far easier to use the Liecha saw little use, however the accompanying Government Issue color slide film seldom got out of date.

The 3rd Ord was called upon to help provide security for Bob Hope and his performers at Long Binh's amphitheater, which in reality was a large semi circular bowl carved out of a barren hill side. This of course was the great entertainer's annual Christmas show that reportedly some twenty five thousand GI's endured an afternoon of sweltering heat to see the legendary show. We being part of the security were allowed back stage before the show and had reserved seats right up in front of the stage during the performance. Luckily for us Dick was dressed in an EOD arm band and badge and once again became one of the team. He managed to take the best close ups of Bob Hope, the Gold Digger dancers, Connie Stevens, Neil Armstrong and the rest of the cast. I don't know how many copies of those slides that Dick had made but everyone who saw them requested a set. I still have my set that bring back fond memories of that hot afternoon so many years ago when a few good people traveled half way around the world to bring a little Christmas joy to a bunch of homesick GI's.

It seems to me, a person with very limited recall, that Dick was confined to our building day and night because he was always present to answer the phone and radio. His unenviable job was to serve as a buffer between the teams in the field, the decision makers and the rest of the world. Sometimes late at night when business would pick up Dick would be in the office trying to coordinate personnel with the messages coming in and the instructions going out. The demands and confusion must have been very trying at times to say the least.

One particular night that I remember well involved what appeared to be a heavy V.C. attack on Long Binh's north perimeter. Several of us interested in the situation entered the office by way of the sleeping quarters only to find the radio and phone unmanned. I exited the office by way of the outside door that opened on to a small porch. I looked all around but could not spot Dick anywhere so I called his name.

"Up here." He answered softly. I was able to follow his voice to the top of our new begged, borrowed, bartered, and stolen shower room water tanks. The tanks were mounted on high stands providing gravity feed to our shower heads.

"What are you doing up there?" I called up to Dick who was laying flat across the large metal tank.

"Come on up." "There is a great view of the fire fight going on up there." He answered.

Dick was absolutely right; the elevated tanks were a great vantage point for witnessing the tracer firing helicopter mounted mini guns. The combination of traces and illumination rounds dumping flares in the night sky produced a real photographic spectacle. Dick had a knack for capturing on film the usual and unusual in an interesting light. He also had the ability to capture the importance of the everyday happenings and verbally expressing them in a clear concise sentence. But I believe that one quality that EOD men and the many people who passed through the 3rd Ord will remember most about Dick was his unwavering smile. The man wore an infectious friendly grin even in his sleep. Always the first to offer help, that kindly facial expression carried over into every act of Dick's daily life.

All these years I've wondered how different life at the 3rd Ord would have been if our clerk had been one of those common run of the mill army issue typist. I know that without Dick's quick thinking and insightful advice my tour in country could have ended in a completely different manner.   Thanks Dick.

DON'T SHOOT – YOU MIGHT PISS HIM OFF!

Once properly authenticated as an EOD specialist and allowed to go on off-post calls I was told to accompany a man who I will call Junior. Our instructions were to drive to a large fire base just off the highway named Bear Cat. We hurriedly loaded the jeep with explosives, weapons, ammo and canteens full of water then raced off base with Junior at the wheel for he knew the way to Bear Cat. The highway was a well maintained black topped road that wound south out of Long Binh post. We sped past little thatched farm houses that in the darkness of night looked abandoned. There were the ever-present peasants working bent over nearly knee deep in rice patty mire or what passes for mud in Viet Nam.

This being my first real trip off base, I felt like a kid in a candy store, my senses taking in every sight, sound and smell of my new world when Junior asked if I saw the rubber tree grove ahead.

"Sure," I replied to his obvious question.

"Well, we have to make a 90 degree left hand turn just on the other side of those rubber trees." Junior informed me as if giving me a tour on how to get to Bear Cat.

"Now look in that rubber tree grove and see if you can spot an Armor Personnel Carrier." He instructed me.

"No, there isn't an APC that I can see," came my casual answer. "Why do you ask?" I wondered. "Well," Junior drawls out with a smile. "If there's an APC there, we won't get shot at as we slow down to make the turn." "If there ain't one there, we will be shot at." He explained calmly as we sped toward the rubber tree grove.

This bit of information quickly jogged my brain from an innocent wide eyed tourist mode to that of a soldier and I began to ready my M16 to return fire.

"What the hell are you doing?" Junior demanded.

"I thought you said we would be fired on when we pass those rubber trees." I nervously shouted back.

"Don't shoot back, he ain't never hit anyone before and if you shoot back you might piss him off and next time someone will get hurt."

"You're kidding me?" I asked not taking my eye off the rubber tree grove just ahead. "No, I ain't kidding." Junior roared. His words were mingled with the sound of a rifle firing in our direction along with the whine of bullets ricocheting off the blacktop in front of our jeep. We managed to make the sharp left hand turn without tipping over or being shot just as Junior predicted.

In the next year, I made many trips past that particular rubber tree grove and each time I looked for that ARVN APC. If the APC was absent, I prepared myself for the possibility of Charlie shooting at us. I have always wondered if the rubber tree grove sniper suffered from poor vision or a tender heart but whatever the case, I never heard of anyone being shot at the Bear Cat turn off.

SURPRISE IN A SAIGON BATHROOM

I had only been in country about a month when Sgt Dick called on me to accompany him to Saigon. I'm not sure of the reason or excuse for this particular outing but a stop at the 170th EOD was at the head of Dick's list of things to do. This unit occupied a large French Villa with all the stately appointments one would expect in such an opulent residence, quite the reverse of our housing on Long Binh post, the décor and furnishings were late GI issue and mostly borrowed or stolen. However, I believe it was the bar at the 170th that attracted Sgt. Dick to make a visit more than an interest in French architecture or history.

We were given a cordial welcome and of course a first drink on the house. I never drank alcohol while in Viet Nam but watched as Sgt Dick consumed several First drinks while swapping stories and renewing old friendships. I drank a can of coca-cola while listening intently to every word of wisdom these more experienced EOD men had to offer a new man in country. Of course, there was no need to announce to these men my green horn status for they had spotted my shiny new fatigues and pale untanned skin as I entered the bar.

Sgt Dick began to speak of leaving and suggested we use the latrine before departing. I agreed and was given instructions on how to find the large building in the back yard that served such needs. Sgt Dick was deep into another story and indicated that I should make the trip out back first. I wandered about the first floor of the ornate old villa until suddenly blundering thru a door that opened into a large back courtyard. There, just as described sat a large, well constructed permanent structure that could only be the latrine. I had never seen such a well appointed outhouse in my life. It was certainly well beyond any such facility I had seen in or out of Viet Nam.

My instructions were very specific as to which door to enter and what to look for within. Sure enough the floor was hard surfaced; I had already become accustomed to dirt or gravel in latrines. The far wall held a horizontal half inch pipe that ran water down the wall to a wide trough. This long open trough was about 2 feet wide and 4 inches deeper than the surrounding floor, and contained several brass plates that resembled shoe soles mounted on pedestals to equal the height of the floor. It was obvious even to me that the idea was for the occupant to stand on these shoe prints in order to keep our feet dry while urinating.

I quickly stepped on the brass pads and began to tend to business when an outside door opened and a petite young Vietnamese girl entered. She hurriedly occupied the brass foot prints next to me and without so much as a by-your-leave she dropped her black silk pants and squatted down. There were no dividers between us. My mind was in a whirl but not for the reason you might think. I immediately recalled all that Vietnamese training especially the area of escape and evasion. I figured it would be my luck to be captured so I paid particularly close attention to this phase of the training. We were taught that the Vietnamese were very casual about communal bathing and all things involving natural functions. To be embarrassed or reluctant about such activities would be a dead give-away to authorities searching for escapee GI's. I did my best to remain nonchalant about the half naked young woman squatting beside me; while she glanced my way, covered her mouth and giggled repeatedly. This incessant mirth on the girl's part made concentration difficult on my part so I buttoned up my fly and stepped back onto the dry floor again.

I made a quick and quiet return to the bar where Sgt Dick and his friends were still telling stories. I reminded Sgt Dick that we were going to leave and that he had better use the latrine after having consumed so many beers. Sgt Dick confessed that he didn't need to use the latrine, but thought it only fair that I relate my recent experience on my trip out back. The entire bar broke into laughter and it was only then that I realized the whole thing was a set up. They had sent the Vietnamese girl into the latrine behind me with specific instructions as to how to behave. This was just another initiation for the pale skinned new guy in shiny green fatigues.

WHITE PHOSPHOROUS FOR THE UNINITIATED

White phosphorus is a chemical that burns quite fiercely and can set cloth, fuel, ammunition and other combustibles on fire when exposed to the atmosphere which means it must be suffocated out. If a person is so unfortunate as to get WP on exposed skin, it will burn into the flesh until extinguished by lack of oxygen – not a pretty thought I will admit.

When used in most ordnance WP (white phosphorus) needs a fuse as an initiation device that minimally employs a rather sensitive explosive. This sensitive explosive is very susceptible to fire and heat; exposure to either can cause a normally safe piece of ordnance to detonate. Now this may sound complicated but this initial highly volatile explosive is used to detonate a less sensitive explosive which in turn detonates a burster tube. The bursting charge is required to rupture the heavy steel container and to disseminate the WP into the atmosphere where the oxygen causes it to ignite. If a WP round has a leak that allows air to enter a bright white smoke will appear, this is the dreaded leaker. If the leak is not stopped, heat will cook off the explosive charge and the burster tube will throw shrapnel and burning WP all over anyone unlucky enough to be in harm's way.

WP is a common tool of war, often employed to ignite napalm or as an artillery spotting charge. It has also been favored to be the ultimate skin irritant, so much so that the Viet Cong avoided all contact with such ordnance. WP may be likened to a genie in a bottle, for once its container is opened there is a puff of white smoke followed by riotous excitement. The big difference

94

between the two is that the genie will grant you three wishes, while WP makes you wish you were somewhere else, anywhere else!

Ordnance filled with WP has become the bane of all EOD personnel and the shout "leaker" produces a myriad of immediate responses. Most people take flight like a flushed covey of quail. They run blindly away from the source of the warning, thru dangers that would normally produce cold sweats, in hope of finding a mystical protective sanctuary. This mad rush for safety is undertaken solely on someone else's word "leaker", regardless of the fact that you have not personally seen this terrifying hazard.

A few people, those who must analyze every situation, will freeze in place hoping to weigh the facts before reacting. A somewhat smaller group, a nearly nonexistent group, proceed directly to the dreaded leaking WP round in hopes of snuffing out its white hot heat before it can get worse or explode.

One fine Viet Nam summer day my partner Tex and I responded to a call at the PDO (Property Disposal Yard). This PDO yard area is where all sorts of military issued items were taken to be destroyed. Who made the decision to burn new HD motorcycles still in the crates or much needed canteens we will never know, but the PDO performed such tasks. The calls to the PDO yard were usually minor in nature, unfired small arms ammo or possibly a new hand grenade. This trip however was different for we were directed to a 105 mm artillery projectile partially buried in the ground. It became obvious the round had been there for some time and was filled with WP which upon being exposed had begun to leak white smoke from a crack in the body where the sensitive fuse screwed in.

We were quickly informed the leaking round could not be detonated where it lay because of other volatile material stored nearby. Also it was considered bad practice to blow WP into the ground fearing it might be exposed at a later date causing unknown problems. The more Tex & I did to remove the leaking round, the more it leaked and the more white smoke it produced. We mixed and applied more and more mud to the smoking crack but it became clear that we were losing the battle with this leak.

We quickly formulated a plan, maybe not a good plan, but a plan. In this master plan one of us would drive the jeep as close as possible while the other one would pick up the leaking 105 mm round and with the proper timing arrive simultaneously at a predetermined spot.

Tex, though young, was well known as a calm cool character with considerable ability driving or repairing any motor vehicle. It was obvious who would drive and who would carry the leaking 105 through the stacks of ill fated equipment. I watched intently as Tex raced down the blacktop road before sliding around a corner near where I stood. I pulled the leaking WP round from the ground and raced thru piles of condemned back packs and new two-way radios. Our timing was perfect; I stepped onto the edge of the blacktop just as Tex slid to a halt.

"Put it in back and let's get going." Tex calmly declared, knowing that time was of the essence. But I couldn't safely place the hopelessly leaking WP round on the sand bags that were kept in the back of the jeep for just such a purpose because the jeeps rear tire had come to rest on top of my left foot. "I can't!" I replied. "You stopped with the tire on my foot!" A strange expression spread across Tex's youthful face as he released pressure

96

on the foot brake. This allowed the jeep to roll backward freeing my foot, but at that instant Tex let out on the clutch which caused the jeep to peel out right over the top of my foot. I never knew if my howls of profanity or look of pain on my face ever registered with Tex for his next words were true to his calm demeanor. "Put it in back and let's get going."

We raced to our demo range where we managed to destroy the heavily smoking WP round. The pain in my foot quickly subsided probably due to the M151 jeeps light weight. Still I whined and moaned for days about my injured foot just to have something to hold over Tex's head.

WHITE PHOSPHOROUS AND THE MARINE

White Phosphorus has a peculiar ability to instill instant respect that can be recognized in an EOD man's voice as he begins to speak on the subject. The tales of encounters with WP are legendary in the EOD field, some humorous, others quite serious but all are related with respect for a formidable and unpredictable adversary.

In one incident while clearing the remains of an exploded ammo dump, I became involved in a foot race with an anxious young marine and a WP round. I believe cleaning up blown ammo depots must be one of the most hazardous duties an EOD man can encounter. This particular clean-up seemed extremely dangerous for it contained everything from 750 lb low drag bombs to small arms ammo and everything in between.

The landscape of a blown ammo depot is made up of piles of charred wood, tangled metal that hides every conceivable peace of ordnance in every conceivable condition. Some items are unarmed; some are armed just waiting to be touched to initiate detonation. There are items that have been subjected to intense heat, or blast pressure or violent impact. There are hundreds of varieties of ordnance that number in the hundreds of thousands waiting to do their designed function and that is to explode.

The men who are to clear this overwhelming smorgasbord of explosives line up shoulder to shoulder in the sweltering heat or monsoon rains and begin to move cautiously through this field of destruction. They must evaluate every piece of material in front of them to determine what if any hazard it presents. If the item is deemed safe, it is picked up and handed to the man next

98

to him who passes it along to the next much like a bucket brigade of old.

You must have complete trust in the men in this line even though you have never met them before. It is taken for granted no one will move an unsafe item or attempt to pass it down the line. Any piece of ordnance thought to be questionable is called out so that everyone will be aware of the hazard of handling the item. Some of the more dangerous units are hand carried by the original finder to a place of safety. In this instance a young marine located a 3.5 inch bazooka shell filled with WP. The round looked safe until he started to pick it up which caused it to leak, but keeping his head, he did not call out leaker which would have caused a stampede but rather the marine nestled the 3.5 in his bare arms and stepped back out of line.

The physically fit youth moved quickly out of the area to a line of red 55 gallon drums with their tops cut out. These drums were set out on an already cleared make-shift road and filled with water just for the purpose of dunking leaking WP rounds. By the time our young hero had performed a fine broken field running through 50 yards of trash, the 3.5 was smoking somewhat heavier than before.

The first fire barrel he encountered was filled to over-flowing so the marine moved on to the second barrel that was placed about 10 yards away. The second barrel, as well as the third and fourth were also full and by now the 3.5 was trailing a healthy column of smoke as the young marine raced from barrel to barrel pausing only long enough to quickly assess its contents. The whole cleaning line began to encourage the young man to move faster or to get rid of the leaker. I don't believe he ever thought of his own personal safety or of throwing the leaker away, he was so intent on putting out the smoke.

I could see that the long line of fire barrels ahead of the marine were also full so in desperation I stepped out of line and began to chase the pair. It was apparent from the marine's actions and sounds that the profusely leaking WP was now burning his arms and chest but still he ran on. I ran at full speed along the line of fire barrels but could not close ground while the suffering young man no longer slowed his pace to examine each fire barrel. He was now running in pain and adrenaline with no idea of where he was going. Some of the fire barrels I passed had room for the leaking 3.5 and I called repeatedly to the marine to stop and come back so that I might help but he ran blindly on to the end of the line of barrels. It was at the last barrel that he hesitated, lost as to what to do next that I finally caught up to the suffering marine and pried the leaking 3.5 from his grasp. After extinguishing the leaker, I began to throw water on the man's burns in an attempt to soothe his discomfort. We were quickly surrounded by other men from the clean-up line who saw to it the marine found medical attention.

This is just one example of how Mr. Willy Peter can influence a normally calm rational persons thinking. The young marine did his best to protect those of us working the line and to follow the recommended procedure for handling leaking WP. Those actions placed him in more danger but he never gave up. I remember wishing that day that I had been in better physical shape; it might have shortened the race.

LEAKER – MARINES PANIC TOO

I had another W.P. experience on my second T.D.Y. to help in cleaning up the exploded ammo dump at Da Nang. However in this particular incident a leaking W.P. round was only the instigator of the trouble. The depot which had detonated some month's before my return trip still had many area's not cleared of hazardous explosives. The depot was laid out in a grid pattern that made good reference points as to what was safe and what remained dangerous.

The E.O.D. men would line up shoulder to shoulder along the end road on one of the oblong grids. We would then walk the length of the grid picking up all the explosive material and passing it to the next man. This worked much like an old fashioned bucket brigade with each safe item passing from man to man eventually coming to rest in the side road. If a hazardous explosive item were found the discoverer would pick up the item and call out the type before stepping out of line and hand-carrying it to a safe area. These grids were absolutely covered with a tangle of burned and twisted steel, charred wood and unexploded ordnance. It behooved the men in line to be ever watchful of what lay before him because the wrong movement or stepping on one of these damaged explosive items could prove fatal.

On this particular sunny Asian day I was in the middle of the line that had slowly worked about half way through the grid. Suddenly someone to my right called out the familiar warning "leaker". As usual the entire line broke and ran in a panic to the left, away from the clearing line. Everyone except me that is. I stepped into the uncleared area and turned to the right and headed toward the leaking W.P. round.

I had just touched my left foot on the ground when the biggest Marine I have ever seen ran directly into me face to face. The huge man was up to full speed when we collided and impacting with my 230 pounds didn't slow him down one bit. The big Marine sped on by as I was thrown up into the air and backwards. I landed in a shell crater about four feet deep that was half filled with water and sharp twisted piece of metal. I lay on my back in the bottom of this smelly water-filled carter gazing up at the beautiful blue South East Asian sky. Although stunned by the blow I kept trying to replay in my mind what had happened. It was obvious from the pain that being run over by a green two legged truck and unceremoniously dumped into a shrapnel-lined hole would take time to heal.

The other E.O.D. men had fled to the safety of the boundary road, and regrouped before sending two men in to tackle the leaking W.P. round. In fact, the pair that volunteered to handle the leaker walked by my resting place without so much as a 'by your leave'. A couple of minutes later the big Marine appeared at the edge of my shell-hole and extended his massive hand down to me.

"What the hell were you doing?" he asked in an astonished voice while effortlessly pulling me from the crater. He was genuinely sorry and was worried that I might be injured but a quick inspection of my body revealed nothing more than a lot of cuts and scrapes. However I'm sure an x-ray would have shown massive internal bruising and a brain that was spinning like a carnival ride. Now if you have ever had any dealings with the military you would know my response to the big Marine when he inquired if I were hurt.

I smiled and replied "it's nothing. I have been hurt worse tripping over my own two feet and falling down." Still he remained concerned, but I knew he really wanted an answer as to why I had turned in the wrong direction.

I took a deep breath before attempting to explain to the big Marine and the several others who pressed me for the answer as to why I turned towards the leaking W.P. round. The fact of the matter is Junior and I discussed the subject on several occasions and decided that it was counterproductive to run away from a leaking W.P. round then be forced to walk back up on the item again. To us it seemed that the sooner you got to the leak and shut the air off to it, the less chance of the round cooking off. The big Marine looked at me sort of funny then to my surprise agreed that it truly didn't make sense to run away only to return.

I have no way of knowing if other E.O.D. personnel put our plan into practice because there is something instinctive about running away when someone calls out "leaker". It is similar to the cry grenade or snake; people just panic. I have seen more injuries from the crazy head long flight after such warning calls than I have from the W.P. or snake or grenade for that matter. This time I was nearly injured by the panic because I was going the wrong way. I guess sometimes it is better to run with the herd than to stop in its path.

SPARE TIRE AT DONG TAM

Late in '69 as the American troops were pulling out of IV corp., or the delta area my EOD unit was assigned to cover much of this vast area. This change meant that security would be provided by a few "gung ho" Aussie's and a lot of questionable ARVN troops. In order to cover the area and be more centralized we took over the EOD unit at Dong Tam, making it a temporary station. Dong Tam was a beautiful base designed with great care as a brown water navy base that had been mostly built on muck and mire dredged from the bottom of the Mekong River. In the dry season water stood in huge puddles all about, while in the monsoon season it was difficult to tell the high ground from the river channel. Still it was a lovely place to spend a few days of sun and fun.

Our unit typically sent down two-man teams on temporary duty as the old unit seemed to slowly rotate out of country. I felt from the first that much of the old team had spent too much time in this little Garden of Eden, and in fact we were warned not to take a couple of its members on off-post calls. And one individual in particular was not allowed to go on any calls, on or off post. Let's call him Willard. Willard seemed to be a fine young soldier with a pleasant personality who was always eager to be of help. Still there was something different about the youth that one could not quite put your finger on.

Sgt. Ford and I were finishing up a quiet week of rest and relaxation in sun drenched Dong Tam when we ruined a tire on our jeep trailer. Try as we might we could not come up with another tire and we hated to start for Long Binh with a heavy load and no spare.

The night before we were scheduled to leave I was still trying to find a spare tire when Willard said he knew a fella on base who could provide us with a good tire. The only catch to this little plan was that Willard would have to drive the jeep alone to find this man. I reminded him that we were under orders not to allow him to drive any vehicle but he promised not to leave post nor get into any trouble. After being overtaken by a lazy streak and giving due consideration of the fact that the post itself was very small and that the gate guards would not permit Willard off post, I decided to take a chance and let Willard take our jeep and trailer to retrieve the needed tire.

The sun was setting in the west, wherever that was at Dong Tam, before Willard was ready to leave on his expedition in search of a spare tire. In fact the evening was turning into one of those soft lovely moments that one can only experience along the banks of the romantic Mekong River. It seems Charlie also appreciated the magical beauty of the South East Asian twilight for Willard had no more than cleared the unit's driveway in our jeep before the V.C. began to rein 120 mm mortars down on the little base.

Just for your information, the Communist 120 mm mortars are a big ugly piece of ordnance that makes a lot of unsettling noise and more than its share of damage when detonated. Now, I and some of the more foolish members in our little field shun bunkers and shelters during such events; however a couple of 120's in close proximity to our position quickly instills a new found wisdom. I suddenly found the dank confines of our bunker less repulsive than when I had inspected it several days before. I worried about the safety of Willard and the jeep but reasoned that he knew Dong Tam much better than I did and that he would surely find shelter until Charlie was tired of providing the evening's entertainment.

It's funny how even a few rounds of enemy fire while confined to a large coffin-like box seems to last forever so I have no way to gauge just how long Willard was gone but it felt like hours. Suddenly I realized the mortars had stopped falling so I edged out of the bunker hoping to see our jeep and trailer parked safely in its birth. Unfortunately the parking place was empty and there was not a sign of Willard or anyone else moving about the base. I climbed on top of the bunker hoping to see Willard returning safely, but the area was now in total darkness. My mind filled with images of the young soldier laying dead somewhere, the victim of chance and a V.C. mortar round.

I angrily paced back and forth across the top of the bunker, impatiently waiting for the M.P.'s to come by and notify me of poor Willard's untimely fate. But time passed and no one came with condolences which actually made waiting that much more difficult. I ached for another vehicle to drive in search of the wayward soldier but I could not beg, borrow or steal a ride on this dark night. Finally in disgust and aggravation I climbed back down from the top of the bunker and as I rounded the corner of our building I could hear a jeep approaching far down the road. Our building sat very near the base perimeter and running lights were the norm at night but this vehicle was moving fast without any illumination.

The jeep turned into our driveway sliding to a stop just a couple of feet from a sandbag wall. Willard jumped from the driver's seat and ran behind the building like a child who feared getting a spanking. A quick inspection of the jeep and trailer quickly revealed the reason for Willard's desire to distance himself from the vehicle. Both jeep and trailer were filled to over-flowing with spare

106

tires plus a few personalized tire covers that had become a big fad in Viet Nam.

After a game of hide and seek in the dark I managed to locate young Willard hiding under his bunk. I furiously demanded that he come out from hiding and explain where all of these tires came from. It was very simple Willard began; we needed a tire so he had driven around base looking for an easy mark to steal but had no luck until arriving at the officer's club. It was clear that everyone including the guard on the parking lot had taken cover during the mortar attack so it was a simple matter to move from jeep to jeep and remove their spare tires. I could see Willard's disappointment that the mortar attack ended before he could relieve more officers of their spare tires and personalized covers.

I spent the next hour sneaking around Dong Tam base unloading jeep tires and covers in places where they would not be easily found. Come morning we snuck off base as early as possible amid conversations about the missing tires and the intensity of the previous night's mortar attack. I will admit that we had our spare tire proudly mounted on its bracket when the gate guard remarked how lucky we were not to have had our spare stolen during the night. Lucky indeed!

AFRO-AMERICAN STUDY GROUP

The 3rd Ord. Battalion area on Long Binh Post was fairly centrally located allowing easy access for soldiers wishing to visit for whatever reason. It was, except for the occasional fragging or drug-dealer war, a quiet compound. The majority of the 3rd Ord residents spent long hot days moving ammunition in the main depot whose entrance gate was just across the road from our main gate. These ammo humpers were for the most part quiet neighbors who wanted nothing more than a cold beer and a place to lie down after a day of working in the hot Asian sun.

However, humans have a never-ending desire to change, no matter the subject at hand they are driven to alter in some way everything within reach. The 3rd Ord Battalion area was a large compound, maybe three or four blocks wide and five or six long. There were two main gates and the whole rubber tree grove was protected by questionable fencing. A small chapel was located on the main street about half way between the two gates. The little church lent a peaceful air of contradiction to a compound dedicated to supporting the war. I will admit that I do not remember ever being inside the 3rd Ord Chapel unless it was in the line of duty. The Chaplin we had early on would, on occasion, stop by our building and visit with the men and compliment them on their various collections of Playboy center-folds that served as wall paper in many rooms. This somewhat casual minister was later replaced by a young skinny white Chaplin who immediately began to make changes.

108

It wasn't long before the new Chaplin placed a small sign in front of his church announcing that he would have an Afro-American study group on Thursday night the next week. All who read the little sign agreed that the 3rd Ord did have a large number of black soldiers billeted in the battalion area and that such a meeting might be worth the new Chaplin's efforts. We all watched eagerly on the first nights gathering and decided that all was well at the 3rd Ord Chapel.

The next week a much larger number of black soldiers attended the white Chaplin's Afro-American study group causing us to believe that some type of refreshment was the main attraction. Still all went well as the meeting disbanded before our main gates to the battalion area were closed for the night.

When the third Thursday rolled around Junior and I were late returning to the 3rd Ord from an off-post call and we were shocked to see that the new Chaplin's Afro-American study group had dramatically increased in size. We drove through a large number of black soldiers milling about the church and compound area. It was clear that there were far more attendees for the study group than were assigned to the 3rd Ord.

Being tired and hungry neither of us was concerned by the large gathering; after all it was a church meeting. But the block long drive from the main street to our building changed our minds. The members of the 3rd Ord E.O.D. appeared less casual in dress and action and the air felt charged with electricity. Our E.O.D. unit was the only personnel in the 3rd Ord Battalion who were allowed to keep our issued fire arms or for that matter allowed to carry knives. I say issued weapons because many soldiers, myself included, carried contraband or illegal firearms as part of our daily attire. We were instructed to keep our issued weapons close at hand and any explosives on hand should be moved to our holding area in the depot. Both of these orders were unusual in that our building often looked like an armed camp, what with all the B.A.R.'s, Thompson's, AK47's, not to mention M16's and Colt 1911 45 pistols normally within arm's reach. As to the explosives we often kept C-4 on hand in case it were needed during the night and procurement from the depot at night could be difficult and time consuming. Still everyone jumped to the tasks at hand for none of us had experienced just such a situation. Each team member had a different prediction as to the outcome of the group gathering for the Chaplin's Afro-American study group.

As the sun set the crowd around our building grew and became more threatening so we were instructed to use force if necessary to prevent any of the growing mob from entering our building. We had not observed any weapons, even among the group's more vocal individuals and we had no desire to shoot unarmed American soldiers. However the order had been issued to protect our files and classified publications. I never knew what happened next but the group became more agitated as they moved about the battalion area. This must have triggered security people to react because an armored personnel carrier suddenly appeared. The track vehicle began to chase people around the rubber tree grove and from building to building in an effort to control the rioter's actions.

The 3rd Ord E.O.D. occupied two buildings, neither of which would look out of place in the center of any slum in any third world country. Other than the material in the unit's safe, there was little of value to institute a gun fight. But when in the military, if you are ordered to fight for the possession of a dead skunk then you fight over a dead skunk. We were told to get in our

110

buildings and remain until the demonstration ended.
Tex and I were the only ones who slept in the second
building and it contained nothing of military or other
value, so we moved to the main building. We closed and
locked doors on the main building that I had never even
seen before, let alone seen closed and locked. By this
time large numbers of the Chaplin's study group were
running around the compound hoping to make a
statement without encountering the armored personnel
carrier. I remember the A.P.C. popped some tear gas and
it was reported that one of the protesters was injured by
the A.P.C. but after a couple of hours of yelling and bottle
throwing the crowd began to melt away. We truthfully
never knew what the whole uproar was about, but we
were damn glad that no one challenged the security of
our building. There was a unanimous feeling among the
members of the 3rd Ord E.O.D. that we did not want to
use deadly force on any U.S. military people even if they
were running amuck.

The morning after the 3rd Ord riot arrived as
usual with a beautiful fire ball in the southern sky. For
some reason at the 3rd Ord's rubber tree grove the sun
always rose in the southern sky and set in the north. In
any case, the morning after the outbreak found the
battalion area quiet with just a bit of nervousness in the
air. Our E.O.D. unit went about business as usual when
two of the local black ammo humpers came strolling by
our building. Big John always had the ability to strike
up a conversation with anyone even the devil himself if
necessary. John asked the two soldiers if they had been
involved in the previous night's activities.

"Of course." they replied with a dubious smile.
When he asked what it was all about the two men
couldn't give a factual answer. Then Big John stated how
glad we were that the mob didn't try to enter our

buildings and he explained how we had orders to protect our property.

"Oh no" one of the black soldier's replied. "We knew you guys are armed all the time and that you have all that explosive around." "We didn't want any part of that stuff." the other one agreed. These statements drew a good laugh from us because we had moved all of our explosives out of the area before the action started. Still we held our tongues until the pair had departed for we thought it best if everyone in the area thought we had explosives that we could employ to defend our buildings.

I don't remember if the young skinny white Chaplin was reprimanded but that was the last night for the 3rd Ord Afro-American study group. However in all fairness, many of the troops who worked in the depot served a pretty bleak year. They endured long hot or long wet hours moving ammunition; their food was fair at best. The Army did a poor job of providing any safe entertainment and little in the way of recreation. What remained and was easily accessed was drugs and trouble, many of these lonely homesick men found both. That is why I can understand how a harmless church group could develop in to a riot.

DRUGS & FRAGGINGS

The 3rd Ord living quarters were spartan at best, just an open bay that took up one side of the building and was filled with run down beds. The senior NCO's small room and the office made up the other half of our allotted space. A small bar/ day room had been added on the rear of the building, this addition provided much need space to entertain people passing thru or for official meetings. Of course the room's main function was for lounging and drinking. And although I didn't drink, I did lounge and witnessed a large amount of beer being consumed in that windowless little room.

Eventually Tex and I took over the building next door that had been the cook's quarters. We built a couple of rooms and turned the remainder of the space into a shop. Our shop until this time had been a duce-and-a-half truck that was fitted out with a metal box body and some work benches. The new shop gave us much needed space to work on weapons and inert ordnance. During the remodeling of the annexed building we discovered several drug stashes hidden in the walls and over head. One of the buildings former occupants, a cook named Ski, had been one of the local drug kingpins. It was strange how everyone in the battalion knew Ski dealt illegal drugs and had been caught with the goods on several occasions but for some reason he was never prosecuted.

People in the states never realized how large the drug scene was in South Vietnam. There again the media found fault with everything we did but for some reason failed to expose the drugs and black marketing that was so wide spread throughout the country. I stated before that our battalion had so much drug traffic and GI violence on each other that several of the GI's started an unarmed night patrol. They carried night sticks and moved about in groups for their own protection while at the same time trying to make it safe for a night trip to the outside latrine.

In some instances being on post could prove just as hazardous as being off post. The service clubs were a breeding ground for racial unrest that often led to fights. Fraggings were a common occurrence in Viet Nam and we were often called to assist with the investigation. A fragging is the use of a hand grenade or other explosive device used by an American to kill another American.

Support or noncombat personnel on large instillations like Long Binh were disarmed, their weapons kept under lock and key to prevent GI violence. It is my understanding that our unit in 3rd Ord Battalion EOD was the only men who were allowed access to their firearms at all times. We were also the only personnel in the battalion allowed to carry a sheath knife or bayonet.

One evening about sunset I heard a gunshot and I told the man with me that the sound had originated from somewhere within our small battalion area. Sure enough we learned shortly that some pot head returning from guard duty, by-passed turning in his rifle and walked directly to his barracks. There he found his best friend asleep on his bunk so he shot him in the head. He was apprehended, rifle in hand smoking a joint beside his dead best friend's bed. The killer made a statement that the friend had been bugging him so he simply shot the man. This kind of failed logic was common among GI's who resorted to fragging's and shootings.

VIETNAMESE SEGREGATION

Another subject that the national news media ignored concerned the division that existed in South Viet Nam. Of course everyone recognized the ongoing struggle between Communism and the Democratic factions, but I believe that most Americans through lack of interest or effort to understand the Vietnamese people never realized that other divisions were prevalent in the country. There were some definite lines of segregation that separated the people of this small nation. Of these lines of demarcation most obvious was religion, especially between the Catholics and the Buddhists.

The religious separation ran deep, often times affecting a person's political affiliations. Any information on this subject was difficult to extract from the locals but at times their feelings were openly expressed in front of we the outsiders. However I think the social cast system prevented the possibility of a unified front against the Communist. This and more hidden prejudice were based on skin color and nationality. The Vietnamese of a lighter completion looked down on those with darker skin to include our African American soldiers. People from Thailand and Cambodia were shunned whenever possible in social settings.

As I understand children of mixed blood such as Vietnamese and French or American soldiers became outcasts in their own land. I have been told that these mixed breed people were not true citizens and were not given the rights of other citizens. How true this is, I am not sure but I do know that the half American babies that became orphaned after the war were mistreated by the Vietnamese people and communist government.

115

But no matter what the reason there seemed to be many underlying problems that slowed the war effort. We werc forced to operate under restrictive rules that not only prevented successful operations but in some instances cost lives. Those who created such asinine policies must now accept responsibility for the failure of the war efforts and the lives lost in its futile prosecution.

DON'T GET OUT OF THE JEEP, BOYS

I had the honor in my unit of being known as a person who took great enjoyment from the demolition or destroying of almost anything. This passion for destruction was greatly amplified if explosives could be employed in any part of the operation.

One beautiful day Junior, Big John, and I were told to go to our demo range and demilitarize a duce and a half truck, a jeep and an Armored Personnel Carrier that had already been delivered to the site. It was just a coincidence that a large quantity of high explosives had been turned in to our unit also for disposal. It seemed prudent to combine the operations and use the condemned explosives to demilitarize the three vehicles rather than draw new C-4 from stock in the depot.

We three hurried around loading wooden boxes of explosives into our jeep and trailer in anticipation of what should be an entertaining job. Blowing up something was always fun and getting away from the building just doubled our eagerness to get off base to the demo range.

Our jeep hadn't come to a complete stop at the demo range before Big John bailed out of the back calling dibs on the APC. That left the truck and jeep for Junior and me but we conceded the honor of demilling the APC to Big John for he was as excited as a kid at Christmas when every package under the tree has his name on it. Big John in the mid sixties was a strapping youth who lifted weights and never shied away from anything including work. He fell immediately to the task at hand and began to carry box after box of explosives from our jeep to the APC. I paused in the midst of my own fun to ask "just how much explosive he thought he needed to destroy one big aluminum can", for that's about all the American APCs were. He explained in mid trip that we had to blow up all of these explosives so he would use enough to do the job right.

Big John, though younger than Junior and I was a proven EOD man with as much experience in demolition as either of us so we allowed him to continue setting his shot. We figured the length of time fuse needed to evenly space the detonations, then capped up and primed our shots properly. With everything in readiness we scanned the area for any approaching personnel, called "fire in the hole" and ignited the time fuses before jumping into the jeep.

The demo area at Long Binh sat well away from the perimeter bunker line and although I never stepped off the distance it must have been better than a mile between the two. We drove at a moderate speed across the flat land that was entirely denuded of all plant growth while keeping an eye on our watches in anticipation of the detonations. We had driven half the distance between the demo range and the bunker line when the first explosion came right on time; as did the second and everything appeared perfect until the third and last shot erupted with a huge roar. We all knew that this last detonation was Big John's shot that would send the honorable old track vehicle to where ever-faithful old war horses go.

The massive explosion was accompanied by the strangest whistling or howling sound that I had ever heard. Junior and I exchanged questioning glances then began to look in all directions for any sign that we were under attack. We had come under friendly artillery fire before but that had sounded entirely different. This new noise was not anything like the V.C. rockets that often roared over head nor did it resemble any aircraft we had ever heard. I can only liken the sound to that of someone blowing into a huge pop bottle.

"Might have been an echo." Junior quipped hopefully even though there was nothing for the sound to bounce off of for miles around. All three of us accepted in our own minds that the unusual noise was just one of those mysterious things that happen when one is in a war zone long enough. Now I'm the first to admit that we should have returned to the demo range to evaluate our handy work but the three shots had gone off right on time and there was no question in our minds that the vehicles had been completely destroyed. So with a feeling of a job well done we hurried back to the building to brag about the enjoyable afternoon.

"Don't get out of the jeep, boys". SFC Smith called out with a devious smile, rising from his lawn chair that set just outside the office door.

"Got another job for us?" We asked proud of the afternoons work.

"A job yes; a call no." He began, still wearing that same smile that indicated something was wrong.

"You boys get those vehicles destroyed?" He asked candidly.

"Sure did Sgt." We replied, beginning to wonder what he was leading up to.

"Good, now drive back down to the bunker line and police up your debris." His smile disappeared and his voice turned to a low snarl. "Seems you boys blew the side of that APC all the way from the demo range to the bunker line where it damn near hit someone!!"

A knowing look of shock passed between Junior and I as we suddenly come to the realization that the strange noise we heard driving back from the demo range had been the side of the APC passing over our heads. We naturally belittled Big John and hurriedly drove back to

119

the bunker line. He of course insisted it couldn't have happened. But when we arrived at the bunker line we found the greater part of the side of an APC imbedded in the dirt near an occupied bunker.

The three of us quickly loaded up the large piece of metal, made a lot of sincere but hurried apologies then made a rapid retreat. The errant metal scrap was quickly returned to the demo range and it was agreed that the less said about the matter the better. Still Junior and I often wondered why that piece of metal had separated from the rest of the vehicle and flown in the direction of the bunker line. We also wondered if Big John had planned this little joke; and if so, just how had he judged where and how to set the explosives to get the end results?

Now for those of you who are saying this scenario seems very unlikely; I recall an unsavory Sgt. who wanted a large teak tree blow down in such a manner as to make a foot bridge across a gully. The end results of that project found the tree blown down alright but it landed in the opposite direction of the impassable gulley.

If one asks the right people you just might find out who placed the explosive on that wayward teak tree.

ULTIMATE ACT OF BRAVERY

Many people, especially civilians are not sure just what to make of military awards, medals, citations and the like because in our society the public is grossly uneducated of their significance. Americans have become so jaded that anything less than being presented the Medal of Honor a body might just as well have remained in bed. They don't realize what all is involved in bestowing an award on a military person. The first step requires that the person perform an act so above and beyond the call of duty that it is noticed by others. Just because others take note of this act of bravery is not enough for they must take the time and trouble to write up what they saw and do so in such a manner as to place the nominee in the best possible light. Once the incident is written up it must be submitted through channels where a board decides if the action is worthy of recognition and to what extent. It suddenly becomes clear how important witnesses are to being rewarded for any act of valor. A person can save the world but if there are no reputable eyewitnesses, it just becomes a good deed. Of course some great acts of bravery would be best performed alone but that seldom happens as in this story of one such act of courage that should never have been witnessed.

The setting of this act of complete disregard for one's own well being was in a small non-sanctioned dayroom / bar that had been built on the back of our EOD hooch. The time was about noon on a typically beautiful South Viet Nam day. Several of the unit members were sitting at the small tables dinning on the rich delicacies from the hoagie bait truck situated just down the street. The units top Sgt. was reclining in his, and I repeat "HIS" chase lounge chair. The personal ownership of this particular chair was well known to one and all even to the point that the guests in the bar avoided setting in the chair out of respect for its owner.

The top Sgt. was laid back relaxing, his cap pulled down over his eyes when the unit's young commanding officer and an unknown major entered the day room. The C.O. nervously introduced the major to the top Sgt. before quickly explaining the reason for interrupting. The major had requested that this EOD unit clear a mine field.

The clearing of established mine fields falls in the job description of the engineers and the Top Sgt. patiently explained his strict policy of never allowing his personnel to be used for clearing mine fields.

Now remember the two officers were on their feet while the Top Sgt. remained reclined in his chase lounge, hat covering his face. For some reason this Major refused to accept the Tops firm "no", and anyone with the slightest bit of people-skills would have sensed that when this old Sgt. said "no" he meant "NO". The major asked the young C.O. "who runs this unit, you or this sergeant?" The C.O. wisely replied that the Top Sgt. did indeed make such decisions. The major made one more attempt to bully the two men into doing his will but once again the old man under the cap answered an emphatic "NO". The major, finally realizing he was not going to get his way, flew into a rage.

"Sgt..." the major bellowed. "When you speak to me you will rise to your feet and address me as Sir."

"F--- you Major" the Top Sgt. replied in a loud clear voice without rising from his chaise lounge or removing his cap from his face.

The young C.O. normally ruddy faced became a pasty white as he struggled to say the right thing to smooth over the situation. He needed to appease the angry major but at the same time knew that he could not apologize for his first Sgt's actions, at least not in front of the men. The distraught young Capt. did finally have the presences of mind to usher the irate major out of the room.

The room fell as quiet as a tomb for every man present had been a witness to one of the most courageous acts they would experience. Not only were these men witness to this conversation, each one knew they could easily be called to testify against one of the most respected Master Sgts. in the United States Army.

I often wondered thru the years when I recall this incident if the major had pressed the point and I had been questioned on the matter what my reply might have been. Possibly I would have asserted that working with explosive makes you deaf, or I was choking on my sandwich at that particular moment, I might have even tried the excuse that I had fallen asleep. But no matter what lie I chose, I would never have repeated Tops answer as long as I was still part of the green machine.

EMBARRASSING MEDAL PRESENTATION

The receipt of medals and awards can get a person in trouble in more than one way, as in the case of the award presentation made to Junior, Tex and me. We were informed that a full bird Col. would come to our building and make the presentation the next morning and that we should be prepared. I told our house girl what was happening and explained that the three of us would need clean ironed uniforms and polished boots for the ceremony.

This particular house girl was an old woman to us even though she was around thirty. Mammason as all of the older women were called was a small slender woman about 5 feet tall with straight shoulder-length black hair and a face that............ well, would never win a beauty contest. But the woman had a heart as big as all out doors and I can honestly say she was my friend. The house girls washed our clothes, made our beds, swept the floors and did all the menial jobs that we GI's thought we were too good to do. All of this activity provided my often idle and mischievous mind with many opportunities to play practical joke on these women and especially old Mammason. These were innocent little tricks like hiding or nailing down the woman's sandals when they were removed for one of their numerous foot washing.

On the morning of the presentation ceremony we found Mammason had honored our request for polished boots and clean pressed fatigues. We dressed and made our way to the dayroom where we were met by Mammason who seemed quite proud of the three of us. However the adulation was short lived for we received an emergency call forcing us to leave without changing clothes to meet a helicopter flight. The Col. was notified and the whole affair postponed until the following morning. We returned from the call late in the day, our fatigues and boots covered with dirt. I explained to Mammason what had happened and asked that she make the same preparations for the following morning. The next morning we three once again donned the especially washed and ironed uniforms only to once again be called out on an emergency but this time we quickly changed into dirty fatigues. The call was quickly completed and we rushed back to the unit to find the Col. not so patiently waiting in the day room.

We hurriedly changed uniforms and rushed to the dayroom and the Col. who did not appreciate the delay. Junior and Tex were already standing in front of the Col. when I reached the open door of the dayroom only to be stopped by Mammason. She insisted over my protest to check my uniform for loose threads and pocket flaps that were not buttoned. The old woman ran her hand up the front of my fatigue shirt as if checking the buttons then slapped my face with such force it produced a loud pop. At that point Mammason let out a loud high pitched girlish giggle and raced out the door. It was only then that I realized that the Col. and those standing in the dayroom could only see Mammason's petite back. No one could see what had really taken place but I'm sure it didn't look good.

I hurried into the dayroom to confront a rather irate Col. who was certain I had been fooling around with some cute little house girl while keeping him waiting. I also displayed a bright red hand print on the side of my face to reinforce his belief. I still have a photograph of the Col. with me standing at attention while Junior and Tex are ready to burst into laughter.

Immediately after the presentation ceremony ended I picked up the trail of the missing Mammason who I finally found watching me from behind the cover of a large rubber tree. She delighted in the fact that I had received my just deserts for all of my practical jokes that she had suffered through.

If you are wondering if I learned a lesson from this incident I can truthfully say "no" and poor old Mammason continued to be the target of my orneriness until I came home.

Old Mammason is the same woman who would carry watermelon on foot from the main gate, which was quite a distance to our hooch because she knew how much I enjoyed the delicacy. We often argued the pros and cons of life in the U.S. verses Viet Nam although she had never been more than a few miles from home; these debates often became very spirited.

I gave her ample opportunity to steal from me, especially the military pay script we received on pay day. This currency was like monopoly money that had illustrations of military hardware like ships or tanks or airplanes. This money was issued in all denominations including nickel, dime and quarter and added up in a hurry. I was very casual about this play money and it would become scattered all over my little room. Mammason would clean up the area and neatly stack this money in a pile before placing a weight on it to make sure it remained where she had left it. I purposely left many items laying about that the woman and her family could have made good use of but they never disappeared. The fact of the matter is, it was difficult to give Mammason anything as a gift including food items that her children were in dire need of.

I forcibly took her to an American doctor when she had injured her hand while working for us. This was the first physician she had ever seen and was terrified because of the horror stories that spread like wild fire among the poor in this country. She was amazed and grateful after the doctor's visit.

Still of all the things I recall about old Mammason, the one memory that is the strongest are the frequent warnings that she gave me about dangers in the area. She would strongly advise me not to go to certain towns or to avoid traveling a particular stretch of road or not to fly in helicopters for the next few days. As I recall now the woman was not just playing hunches for she was right more times than she was wrong.

As I recall now the woman was not just playing hunches for she was right more times than she was wrong.

I wish we could have taken her advice more often than we did but it was not always possible. I am sure that Mammason ran a risk of at least being reprimanded with each warning she provided. This may seem strange to most VN vets but I do want to say a thank you to old Mammason. As I have stated before there was nothing between us but friendship, no romance or affair, we were simply friends from two completely different worlds who found mutual respect for one another.

I often wonder the fate of people like Mammason who not only befriended us but often times defended the US military. Thank you, Mammason.

A SANITARY INCINERATION

The Mommason who I played pranks on is the same woman that reluctantly served as a go-between when I interviewed Old Pappason. This man made his living by burning human waste for our unit. This was another chore that the GI's refused to do so we followed suit of the ugly Americans before us and threw money at the locals to perform such tasks. This operation was essential to the war effort in Southeast Asia because the military built out-houses for our convenience but decided not to dig holes underneath to catch the waste. The military in all its wisdom thought it better to place half of a 55 gallon steel drum below the seat which filled up quickly and had to be disposed of frequently because of the intense heat and flies. The answer was simple, someone would have to pull the full drum out of the outhouse, mix in diesel fuel, and set the entire mess on fire. This burning produced a black odorous smoke that hampered the worker from the constant stirring that was required to do a complete job.

The average GI considered this a repulsive detail and all but the most miserly soldier was willing to pay out of pocket to avoid his turn at this duty. Our unit employed Pappason, a Vietnamese man who seemed more than willing to provide this vital service that we were much too important to do ourselves. This man we referred to simply as Pappason or if in doubt "Big Pappason or Old Pappason" and then everyone knew without further question who was being discussed.

Old Pappason was a big man for a Vietnamese, taller than normal with a very muscular build that he proudly displayed by wearing nothing but shorts, sandals and a coolie's hat. The man truly had the physique of a body builder but his seventy odd year old face betrayed his true age.

Old Pappason would show up intermittently at our outhouse and willingly performed his unsavory duty before retiring to the covered porch of our hooch. This small porch was the house girl's favorite place to chatter while polishing our boots and performing other domestic tasks. But Old Pappason's arrival marked the end of the house girl's conversation and they usually disappeared as quickly as possible. We noticed that few of the V.N. spoke to this old man and if possible they avoided all contact with him.

Old Pappason would set in the shade of our porch then while begging a beer he would break out a small opium pipe and take a few puffs. He never seemed to over indulge in either the drugs or the beer but they did give him a loose tongue and a great sense of humor.

Most Vietnamese being proper hosts knew some words in English while we GI's as good guest managed to pick up a smattering of Vietnamese. But Old Pappason never learned or at least never used any words of English even when mooching beer or extending a good natured challenge to fight one of us. He simply smiled and made hand gestures to communicate.

I was always intrigued by this mysterious old man but because of the language barrier I had never been able to get more than a smile and a laugh in reply to my questions. One day when the house girls were unable to sneak away and Old Pappason had finished his pipe and beer I began to ask questions. The old man seemed receptive to being interviewed but communication quickly lagged so in frustration I enlisted the three house girls present to serve as interpreters. These normally warm smiling women refused to speak or even look up at me. I began to beg the women to do this minor chore but the only response I could get was "Tam Biệt, Tam Biệt" which is the phrase the Vietnamese would repeat over and over when they didn't understand or more often than not they **didn't want** to understand. One of the young house girls remained head down and was clearly shacking with fear at the idea of speaking to Old Pappason. I realize that my only hope was to convince old Mammason to act as a go between.

I offered the woman money or food but she refused all my offers and remained silent, head down looking at her work. Suddenly it became clear that these women feared Old Pappason so much that no material inducements would entice them to interpret for me.

I then promised Mammason that I would not let this old man hurt her while on base but I could not protect her off base except to warn Old Pappason that if anything happened to her I would find him and even the score.

I also told her to be sure that Old Pappason understood the questions to be asked were all mine and that she was serving me against her will. This finally won Mammason over and she consented although reluctant and extremely nervous to be a go-between.

Once again I made certain that Mammason explained her position to Old Pappason and that if he took offense with anything asked that I was solely responsible. The old man agreed and laughed a lot and I wondered if the beer and opium had loosened him up a little more than usual. I began by asking his age as well as other minor question concerning his past. He replied that he was 74 and that he was originally from what we called North Viet Nam. The old man went on to explain that he had severed with the French Army and had been captured with the fall of Dien Bien Pu. Then without being asked Old Pappason freely divulged that when Viet

130

Nam was divided into two countries, north and south that he had left his family and walked to South Viet Nam.

Mammason was fairly proficient as an interpreter and we exchanged questions and a few laughs when I asked the old man if he had fought against the Japanese in W.W. II. "Oh yes" he replied proudly, a large smile on his grey beard stubbled face.

"Well." I concluded. "If you were in the French Army you must have learned some of their language.

"Yes, of course." He smiled.

"Then did you learn Japanese when you fought against them?" I asked.

He smiled a bit and answered. "Yes, of course."

"Then if you learned French when they were here and you learned Japanese when they were here why is it you haven't learned a word of English?"

A mischievous little boy smile flashed across Old Pappason's craggy face before he gave a rather lengthy reply just before breaking into howling laughter. He slapped his bare muscular thigh repeatedly with his hand and rocked back in forth in fits of laughter. Old Mammason eye's fell to the floor and she refused to repeat Old Pappason's answer no matter how much I insisted nor how much he laughed. I promised no matter what had been said that I would not be mad, still it took several minutes of cajoling before the obviously frightened woman agreed to reveal Old Pappason's answer. As Mammason reluctantly interpreted it seems that Pappason explained.

"I learned French and we kicked their ass out." "I learned Japanese and we kicked their ass out." "And I'm not going to waste time learning English because we are going to kick your ass out next." Old Pappason broke into a new fit of laughter as Mammason delivered the

131

punch line leading me to believe that the old man did have some knowledge of our language.

Somehow I remained calm, not showing any surprise but I did manage to sooth everyone's nerves by admitting that the old man was probably correct. I have often wondered if Old Pappason lived long enough to see his prediction come true or for that matter if Mammason was still around to witness the fall of Saigon.

HOUSE GIRLS ON STRIKE

The government paid a minimal fee for Vietnamese day laborers to do menial jobs on post. The 3rd Ord Battalion EOD like most units paid house girls additional money to do much of the domestic work around our area. They washed our clothes, made our beds, swept our floors and polished our jungle boots. All of this cost one dollar per day for each of the two or three girls who were in our full time employment. The best part of this arrangement derived from the fact that this money did not come directly from our pockets. We operated as small bar and the profits from it paid these day workers' wages. It was a perfect setup for a bunch of busy GI's who for the most part felt they were above such menial tasks.

Now before I go any further with this story, I must explain the monetary system that existed in Viet Nam at that time.

In the first place, the GI's were paid each month in cash not by check. However this cash was not the familiar green-backs that circulated in the United States which in fact was illegal to possess. The medium of exchange was either Vietnamese piaster or military pay script. The Vietnamese piasters were nearly worthless so no one wanted to accept these notes in payment. The military pay script however was gladly received by everyone in country. The military pay script or MPC as it was known was a slip of paper the U.S. Government printed up with a number value and some patriotic picture rather than famous faces. All MPC was in paper; even the nickel, dime and quarter denominations were paper. Secondly, in an effort to control crime and the black market, a GI could not spend more than $200.00 a month without a letter of consent from his commanding officer. This presented a problem since our monthly pay was over $400.00 tax free. Now understand not only were there restrictions on how much money a person could spend, there was very little to buy. The large Post Exchanges had occasional shipments of high quality cameras or electronics but little else. Today's Super Wal-Mart or Target stores would have been a bit of heaven to the GI in country. Also the MPC we received in pay was subject to a surprise wholesale exchange at any given moment. Once again a person could only exchange $200.00 old MPC for $200.00 new MPC. During these exchange times, military bases were locked down for the few hours of the conversion. If you had money saved up and were caught off base say TDY on exchange day, your savings might very well be lost. Our little bar always got caught with too much cash on these MPC exchange days even though we made deals with people to change it for us. Now with those facts in mind, I will tell you about the house girls going on strike.

A new man transferred into the 3rd Ord one day who had a burning will to cause trouble and spread dissention wherever possible. Needless to say he and I never saw eye to eye from the first minute he walked in our door and our relationship went downhill from there.

One bright sunny day this new man (let's call him Sgt. Flower) decided that we should not pay the house girls for their labor. After a couple of days of arm twisting and complaining, Sgt. Flower badgered a couple of other men into agreeing with him. Suddenly a decree comes down that the house girls would no longer be paid, at least not with our illegal slush fund. The house girls were good, honest, poor hard-working girls who counted on our pay to feed their children. Obviously no pay meant little work and suddenly our boots went unpolished and our fatigues lay dirty on the hooch floor. The girls' warm friendly smiles disappeared and they moped about the area whispering curses and death threats behind our backs.

The situation worsened by the day until one day all the work ended and the girls just sat around refusing to speak to any American.

Finally the 'powers that be' called in some crisis management type who professed to speak Vietnamese. When the Army linguist arrived the girls had formed a caucus in one corner of our shop where Sgt. Macksey and I were working on some of the unit's firearms. This Army trouble-shooter came in and confronted the house girls and spoke for several minutes about the situation then departed without a reply from the girls. I can't speak Vietnamese but I knew enough to realize this trouble-shooter was not getting thru to the girls. Sgt. Macksey had a very good working knowledge of the native tongue and he confirmed my suspicion that the Army strike breaker was getting nowhere fast!

Sgt. Macksey encouraged me to speak to the girls in hopes of ending this foolishness but I insisted he speak to them being much more fluent in their language. He argued that it was a matter of trust. The girls didn't know him well enough yet and they certainly didn't trust the stranger who just departed. He was certain that the girls trusted me and would listen to what I had to say. Well, I for one wanted to end this dispute quickly because I am one of those who felt this housework was beneath my current station in life.

I approached the girls' huddle and asked if I could set down and talk for awhile. The negotiations were simple and straight forward; they needed the dollar a day to make ends meet and we wanted the work to be done. Their demands sounded simple enough to me and in desperate fear that I would have to do my own chores, I agreed to pay the girls myself a dollar a day for their work. It was agreed they would clean for me and a few of the others but not for Sgt. Flowers. The girls dried their tears and hurried back to the cleaning and polishing.

I thought the strike was at least semi-settled until we had a meeting that night in the bar. Sgt. Flower found out how I handled the strike. He then adamantly demanded the house girls do his chores as well. I reminded him that I and some of the other unit members were now paying the house girls wages and that neither he nor the unit was paying so he had no right to demand services. That started another heated discussion where Sgt. Flower stated some rule that if the house girls were in the building they must clean the whole building. I tried to explain the girls were originally paid from our bar's profits and were expected to clean the building, but now that I was responsible for their payment, they would follow my orders. Once again tempers flared and demands were made. I countered the demand by warning that I would keep my ration card. This card, issued once a month allowed enlisted men to purchase beer, liquor and cigarettes. There were no stores that sold spirits so we were forced to obtain these goods through the government. These cards helped to supply our bar with goods. A couple of the other men agreed and warned that they would also withhold their ration cards. Our threatening to withhold our ration cards was like throwing gasoline on a fire and the debate continued.

The whole matter ended with the house girls' pay coming from the bar's profits. In other words the whole fight was for nothing, other than Sgt. Flower's little ego trip. This was just one of many petty points that Sgt. Flower used to instigate discontent in the 3rd Ord.

MAMMASON AND THE TEAR GAS

It was a late night call on the Long Binh Depot perimeter road that led me to receive an unexpected beating from an unexpected person. Daniel from depot security called pleading frantically for our unit's assistance. It seems a fork lift driver had, while operating in the dark, dropped a plastic fifty-five gallon drum of powdered tear gas and then proceeded to run over the container spreading the fine talcum powder-like substance all over the area.

This particular grade of tear gas might best be described as a super industrial strength irritant that not only attacked the eyes and respiratory system with a vengeance but even the slightest contact with bare skin would produce an intense burning effect. It is easy to understand Daniels urgency to have the tear gas mess cleaned up for the dogs of his K-9 units were suffering intensely. The canine olfactory organ is of course much more sensitive than we humans and this powdered tear gas was driving them wild. The poor dogs were out of control, snarling and growling; they were dragging their handlers around while refusing to obey any commands. The loss of these valuable sentry dogs' talents left a big hole in the depots perimeter security so it was the EOD to the rescue.

SFC Smith roused me out of bed well after midnight and asked if I would go on an emergency call in the depot. I hurriedly dressed while he explained the situation and our need for gas masks, gloves and long sleeved shirts.

On arriving at the incident scene we decided our butyl rubber chemical suits would have been more appropriate for the air was filled with the insidious white powdered tear gas. While the security people trained head lights on the area, Sgt. Smith and I donned gas masks and gloves and proceeded to clean up the spill site. We lasted for better than an hour before Sgt. Smith suggested that we run back to the unit to take a shower and change uniforms. I'm either super sensitive to tear gas or a pansy but I jumped at the chance to be rid of those tormenting burning clothes.

We rushed back to the unit to a welcome shower that we had just built from abandoned and casually appropriated materials. We followed our chemical training in that we undressed outside the building, showered then took a deep breath before removing our masks and washing our hair. We dressed, returned to the incident site, and completed the clean up then rushed back to the unit for one last through shower. Once again we piled our tear gas contaminated clothes outside knowing that the house girls would come along in the morning and gather them up for their hand laundry. This seemed like a good idea in the weary early morning hours but the plan had one major flaw.

As it was the custom in the 3rd Ord to sleep in the morning after a late night call, I was sound asleep when someone struck me a heavy blow to the head. This first stunning attack was followed by strike after strike, each directed at my head and each impact was accompanied by a liberal and loud amount of yelling.

I struggled wearily to gain control of my senses in order to muster a defense against this sudden violent cunning sneak attack. It was at that moment that I discovered the weapon crashing against my skull was a large wooden broom handle and the assailant wielding the broom was dear old Mammason, my friend. Startled, I finally managed to wrench the broom from the dear old lady's hand which ended the physical attack but not the verbal abuse. Old Mammason cut loose with a long

138

enraged string of Vietnamese, some of which I understood and all of it I'm sure by the tone of her voice was not very lady like.

At the end of the tirade Old Mammason ran out of my room leaving me to wonder just what I had done to deserve such a beating. It was in this moment of thought that I realized Tex had been leaning very nonchalantly in my doorway thru the whole affair. He wore a very amused expression but remain silent until I asked what had taken place.

"Your clothes." He laughed.

I still didn't understand until Tex explained how Mammason being the ever dutiful house girl had scooped up the innocent looking piles of tear gas cover fatigues in her arms in order to wash them. The action of gathering up the clothes in her arms puffed a large quantity of the powdered tears gas into Old Mammason's face, eyes and nose, all of which immediately began to burn. She threw the offending clothes on the ground while making a quick search for the name tags worn over the shirt pockets. Well she found my name and was sure this was another one of my practical jokes, one that she took great offense to. Needless to say the broom handle beating of my head followed directly after the discovery of my name tag. I am sure that on the balance scale of justice this punishment was equal to my past crimes even though I was completely innocent on this occasion.

I spent the better part of the next two days trying to convince Old Mammason that the tear gas was simply a mistake but she was convinced that I had master-minded a fiendish plot to trap her. SFC Smith and the other members of the unit enjoyed seeing me stew in my own juices and managed to reinforce Old Mammason's believe in my guilt.

139

When I asked her why she didn't give Sgt. Smith an equal beating Old Mammason explained that he was too important and far too nice a man to mistreat a lady as I had done.

Old Mammason and the other house girls held a grudge so long that I had to wear dirty fatigues for a few days with the threat that if this ever happened again I would be doing my own laundry for the remainder of my tour. This was not a pleasant thought, so of course I did a lot of groveling and a lot of bribing until the girls finally relented and began to wash my clothes again. But from that day on I was always careful to stay out of striking range of those tiny little house girls when they had a broom in their hands.

DANIEL & THE BACK GATE GUARD

Long Binh post was blessed with many an unusual character, aside from those in the 3rd Ord EOD, one of which was the Sgt. in charge of depot security. We will call him Daniel, not out of any inclination to protect his reputation or identity but because I am a feeble old man and it's just possible he is still alive and might read this at sometime. Daniel was a large ruddy complexioned man who did his best to buffalo all of his men and anyone else that came in contact with him. In my younger and much more foolish days Daniel and I shared a lot of enjoyable time toe to toe in yelling matches that never ended in violence or in rectifying the subject of the argument. In all fairness I will concede that Sgt. Daniel had a huge responsibility managing a large security force trying to protect a very large depot that the V.C. would have loved to destroy.

Long Binh had a remote back gate that was seldom used and of course this lonely gate had a security guard. This sentinel was blessed with a small guard shack that was little more than a roof to block out the blistering sun or torrential rains. The man who drew this post enjoyed a tour from sunrise to sunset with a view of nothing but defoliated ground and an expanse of concertina wire. This rear gate was the loneliest post on the depot, what with no one to talk to or traffic thru the gate.

As head of security Daniel had assigned one timid young man to this chunk of emptiness seven days a week for months on end. This particular young soldier was for the most part illiterate but he managed to pass the long weary hours by carving the names of American cities on pieces of scrap lumber. He then posted these signs as is a common practice of home sick G.I's everywhere.

141

Junior and I learned that this mild mannered private had not had a day off in months, nor had he ever been to Saigon. So the next time Sgt. Daniel came into our private bar and asked for a beer I told him this one was on me but it was the last until the man on the back gate was given a thee day pass to Saigon and at least one day off a month.

Daniel as was his nature, exploded in rage, cursing and ranting, telling me I could not tell him how to run his unit. I agreed but I told him I could keep him from drinking in our bar. That brought on another string of profanity and the warning that he would go over my head and get permission to drink in our bar from the First Sgt. or the C.O. I tried to explain the rule of our bar allowed any member of the unit to ban any guest. When this still didn't dissuade Daniel, Junior, who I might add was not afraid of Big Daniel, backed up my ultimatum. This brought several other members into the fray and it became unanimous that Daniel was banned until the gate guard was given time off.

It should be explained here that the military clubs, especially enlisted men's clubs on post were not safe places to drink. Many clubs had fist fights and fraggings and were considered unsafe by a lot of soldiers especially those who had a talent for making enemies and Daniel was not blessed with people skills.

Since Daniel was not a regular in our bar the incident was nearly forgotten until one night the side door open and the big man quietly slipped in. He planted himself on a stool at the bar and asked for a beer as if nothing had ever happened. Big John who had never succumbed to Daniel's bulling ways was behind the bar and extended a polite greeting to Daniel but stated firmly that he was banned from drinking at the 3 Ord bar. Big John could be the sole of tact when the situation called for it and often times our contacts with the rest of the world called for just such discretion. Now Daniel, like most of the world, never recognized that below Big John's rough tough exterior, beats the heart of a truly sympathetic, compassionate do-gooder and champion of the down-trodden. He insisted on writing letters home for any illiterate in the battalion; he counseled the grieving, preached to the drunks and druggies and attempted to protect anyone lacking the ability to do so themselves.

In any case Big John made it quite clear that the ban positively stood until the man on the back gate got proper time off duty. Daniel snorted and bucked but he knew he was up against a brick wall and quickly conceded that he had already issued the three-day pass.

Big John let out a bear type howl and extended both his hands to Daniel, the left contained a cold can of beer on the house and the right was to shake the man's hand to seal the deal. That was just one of the many disputes that I managed to instigate with Daniel but fortunately for me they all ended just as peacefully.

DANIEL- DEPOT SECURITY

Big Daniel was a true character in every sense of the word. He was a product of the war and the military system, what he was like in civilian life was in all likelihood considerably different. Still I considered the man an antagonist and I truly enjoyed hearing stories of his misfortune. The one that gave me the most satisfaction began when Daniel appeared at our bar with bandages and scratches on his head and face. Of course such injuries to a man of Daniel's importance and bravado could not be ignored and our questions came fast and furiously until the complete story was revealed. I said in all honesty before that Daniel carried a heavy responsibility in managing the security personnel in Long Binh depot. This was a massive facility that was vital to the war effort in S.V.N. and it required hundreds of soldiers to make it function properly. Of course not all of these troops were under Daniels direct control but he did have a good deal of sway over their daily lives.

Long Binh depot was laid out in a grid of semi permanent roads that gave the ammunition personnel access to load and unload from large storage bunkers. This whole area was encompassed by a perimeter road just inside the bunker line. This road was patrolled after dark by K-9 units who were on the alert for sappers or infiltrators.

The rules of this perimeter road required that all vehicles use black out lights at night which were much more difficult for Charlie to see and use as an aiming point for his rockets or mortars. While these lights prevented us from being seen they also prevented us from seeing as we tried to negotiate this long dark road. This poor visibility greatly reduced driving speeds making the vehicles occupants an easy target for any unseen attack.

144

The use of black out lights on the perimeter road also made it nearly impossible to spot the dogs and handlers of the K-9 teams who often took up a position on the inside edge of this road.   It was common knowledge that one particularly big dog who stood this guard duty at night would alert on every passing vehicle. It was also well known that the smallish handler could not control his charge; that the animal would bite any appendages extending from the passing vehicle.

The savvy traveler of this foreboding stretch of dark road would count each of the K-9 teams as they were encountered in preparation for the snarling attack that was sure to come. Driver and passengers made sure that all arms and legs were tucked deep inside the vehicle in anticipation of the big dog's ambush.

I hope you have gotten the picture, a pitch black road with no lighting, a huge German Sheppard dog with a real attitude problem and a small handler.

As Daniel told the story of his injuries that night in our bar, he was making his rounds driving the depots perimeter road to check on the K-9 units. He followed the standard practice of counting each team as they appeared like a ghost beside the jeep before slipping silently into the night. Everything was going as usual and when Daniel's lacksadazial count brought him to the area where the big dog should be he took all the standard precautions to protect his body but the dog never alerted. He drove even more slowly not wanting to miss the K-9 team while at the same time he was concerned about the handler's welfare.   It was at that very moment that Daniel felt a small bump in the rear of his jeep which of course caused him to turn to his right to look in the back seat. Daniel's face impacted with the hairy muzzle of the famous big dog. The big dog snarled and Daniel decided it was the proper moment to jump out of the still moving jeep. He landed hard on the rough road while the unmanned jeep and big dog proceeded on down the road finally running over a dirt berm and landing in an ammo pad.

Daniel roundly and soundly cussed the handler out, all the while accusing him of releasing big dog on purpose but the handler maintained his innocence to the end claiming the animal just got out of his control. Daniel of course did not have a leg to stand on but I know that thereafter he made absolutely sure of his counting of the K-9 teams when driving the perimeter road at night.

The story about how he got all the scratches and bandages earned him a free drink and howls of laughter from everyone in the bar.

SMITTY TAKES A DIP

Late one night shortly after my arrival in country, SFC Smith woke me from a sound sleep to inquire if I would like to go on an interesting incident. Being new in country I had been requesting to be taken on off-post calls. Actually I had been a nuisance trying to wrangle call assignments so I knew better than to refuse Sgt Smith's offer even if it was late at night.

SFC Smith or Smitty as everyone called him had a very unique leadership trait that made it nearly impossible to refuse when he asked rather than ordered some task to be undertaken.

We quickly dressed, loaded in a jeep and headed off for parts unknown. The night being so dark and I being new in country had very little knowledge of the area but I am certain we ended our drive at the Mekong River docks at Saigon. At the dock we grabbed our gear and stumbled through the dark to load on board a Navy Swift boat. These brown water Navy crafts known as swift boats resemble the famed PT boat of WWII fame.

The helmsman wasted no time in casting off before slowly motoring to the main channel of the Mekong River. Once the swift boat reached open water the helmsman pointed the bow downstream and threw the throttle wide open. The powerful motors roared to life and the large boat's bow reared out of the muddy Mekong water like a switch blade knife opening.

I will confess this ride was a bit unnerving yet somehow very exhilarating. The Asian night was very dark, as was the very wide Mekong River. The swift boat was also very dark and showed nary a running light as we raced over the turbid water. How that helmsman could see what lay in the waters ahead I will never know but he never backed off the wide open throttle until we neared a very large boat anchored some distance from the river bank. Smitty and I quickly transferred from the swift boat to the deck of the larger boat where we were lead from the dark deck to the well lighted bowels below deck.

It was here that I learned the nature of our incident. The all South Vietnamese boat crew explained in broken English that this craft was a river dredge. Its job was to keep river channels clear of mud and debris. This cleaning of the river bottom was accomplished by employing a large pump to suck the sediment off the bottom of the river. This MUCK was passed thru the pump then deposited on the river bank. Our problem centered on an artillery round that the huge pump had suctioned off the bottom only to become jammed in the large pump's impeller.

The South Vietnamese crew had opened up the pump far enough to determine the blockage was an artillery round but made no attempt at removing it. I questioned where the South Vietnamese EOD were but never received a straight answer. We got the usual double talk from the crew saying they could not understand us but at the same time insisting the round be removed immediately. Smitty reluctantly agreed that we would remove the round since we were already on sight. A brief discussion ensued as I quickly volunteered to go into the pump but Smitty insisted that it was his place. I stated that being younger and single that I should go but Smitty remained firm, not believing that married men should be exempt from dangerous calls. It was obvious I had lost the debate when Smitty began to strip down to his underwear.

I quickly reminded him that the pump was filled with river water that he would have to swim through in order to retrieve the artillery round. It went without saying that if the round should detonate while SFC Smith was inside the pump, he would have no chance of survival. After stripping down to his Army issued OD colored boxer shorts, Sgt Smith turned to me and whispered. "Chamber a round in your rifle and if you see any of these crewmen make a move to start this pump, I want you to shoot them." "I don't want to be chopped up and spit out in some mud pile". He said firmly looking me straight in the eye.

"I got you covered." I whispered back hoping to relieve any anxiety he might have on that point. He smiled and walked down to the opening on the pumps top. The muddy Mekong river water's smell and appearance would have detoured many people from submerging their body into the pump, but Smitty settled in as if he were entering a hot soapy bathtub in some plush hotel. The Mekong River was a multi-use facility; the natives fished and bathed in its waters, but they also used it as a laundromat and a free flowing public toilet. I have witnessed South Vietnamese squatted at the water's edge brushing their teeth while just a few yards up stream another person was defecating in its contaminated waters.

Then without a word, Smitty took a deep breath and disappeared down through the blades of the pumps impeller. A few seconds later he reemerged only to take another deep breath before sliding into the interior of the pump again. Suddenly Smitty hands clutching the 105 mm projectile broke the brackish water's surface. I gave a sigh of relief when Smitty's face wearing a wide smile of pride also appeared in view. I left my vantage point to hurry to the pump to take possession of the muddy 105 and to prevent any mishandling by the South Vietnamese crew members. I remember the crew did thank Smitty and praised his bravery for making their boat safe once more. I completely agreed with the Vietnamese crew but Smitty passed the whole affair off as a minor incident.

Now, if you share in Smitty's modesty then think about this; find an open septic tank and try diving 8 or 10 feet to its bottom and pull a 50# weight back to the surface. That is, without the chance of the pump starting up or any one of a thousand other dangerous things that might have been concealed inside the pumps murky water. Now imagine the 50# weight you are recovering could possibly explode with any movement or the slightest impact.

We quickly secured the 105 mm artillery round and made our way topside of the dredge where we found the Navy swift boat was returning out of the black to give us a ride home. The ride back to the docks was a repeat of the trip out except now I had more time to consider that this boat and crew were sitting ducks for ambush from the river bank or a floating mine in the water. I was glad to return to the 3rd Ord building and glad that SFC Smith pulled rank on me when he decided that he would dive to the bottom of that pump.

BARGE SEARCH

Shortly after this call I had the opportunity for another night ride on the Mekong courtesy of the Brown Water Navy. It had been reported that a satchel charge had been set on a large barge in the Mekong River.

Junior and I responded to the call by jumping into a jeep and heading off-post where we met up with an MP escort. We all raced with lights and sirens blazing down toward Saigon in the dead of the night. We exited the highway through a small village before coming to the Mekong River barge sight. As we slid to a stop another swift boat approached out of the night in a hurry to pick up its two passengers. Here we also learned the facts of the call that lay ahead.

Someone had reported that a satchel charge had been set in a large river barge that was delivering 750# low drag bombs. The officials in charge of the docks had the barge in question moved far upstream to the center of the Mekong River channel where it was anchored. Once again the swift boat commander didn't spare any horses while ferrying us to the barge. Not only that but he quickly disappeared out of blast range the instant our feet hit the barge's steel deck.

We found the crews quarters but they had abandoned ship leaving us without any further explanation or directions. Junior and I stumbled around in the dark until we found the hatch that lead to the lower storage area. Time seemed important to everyone and we questioned if the satchel charge was controlled by some type of timing device. If so we were not informed of this limitation.

Climbing down the ladder to the hold we were dumbfounded to see litterly hundreds of 750# low drag bombs that were stacked in loose piles. We had no idea

151

what we were looking for or how to find such a device. The only thing we knew was that a very small charge could have destroyed tons of explosive and of course us along with it.

Fortunately each of us was armed with a good flashlight so we split up and began to search the endless piles of steel cased bombs. We could have used a lot more help but there wasn't any way to communicate with our unit. We also figured that in the event of an explosion there would be no chance for escape and it would be foolish to lead anyone else into this situation.

A couple of fruitless hours of searching among the bombs and other likely places led us to believe the whole call had been a hoax. Still we searched on until satisfied the area was clear of explosive charges. We climbed on the deck and signaled the swift boat for our ride to the dock sight. All Junior and I could do now was wait and see if the barge and its cargo was safely unloaded. We never got a report of an explosion and we both hoped that there would not be any more calls to the barge sight. If so, we hoped experience would not count in choosing who responded next time.

HUEY'S IN THE RAIN

It was a beautiful South East Asian day when my partner and I were given an incident call in the Delta. Because of the distant location travel by helicopter seemed the only practical form of transportation. We hurried to the Medivac hospital where a huey helicopter waited to whisk us to the incident sight. It was all planned out that we would have a pleasant flight out, get to set off some high explosives and then fly back to the Battalion area in time for supper.

And that is exactly what happened until half way through our return flight; a hugh monsoon rain developed as we approached Bear Cat fire base. This particular fire base had a good helicopter landing pad and the pilot and crew discussed landing there for the storms duration but since I didn't get to vote they elected to continue on to Long Binh. I, (being a person in possession of a lifetime string of bad luck and one who knows that even things that can't possibly go wrong will go wrong for me), would have chosen to set down at Bear Cat just a couple of minutes away.

In inclement weather like this pilots would often follow a road, train tracks or canal to prevent getting lost in the storm. This pilot chose to follow the highway back to Long Binh. The farther up the highway we flew the heavier the rain became and the clouds were black and hung low in an ominous manner. I should explain the monsoon rains in South East Asia have a season when they strike nearly every day at about the same time, day after day. The monsoon rain fall can be and often is a deluge that makes one wonder how the lowlands can possibly handle any more moisture.

As the rain clouds lowered so did our little helicopter. The pilot was now following the highway to make navigation easier. We were now only a couple hundred feet off the ground flying through rain that appeared to be a solid wall of water. I always liked to sit near or in the side door of the Huey helicopter in order to view the scenery and to facilitate taking aerial photographs of the countryside. On this particular afternoon I had planted my carcass in the left hand seat in the huey's open side door. As I said the rain and visibility grew worse by the minute. Both the passengers and crew strained their eyes trying to detect anything that might pose a hazard to the little aircraft's forward movement.

Suddenly out of nowhere we all spotted another huey helicopter coming from the opposite direction. The other huey was also following the highway and was at the same altitude as we were. The two crafts were mere feet from crashing into one another when both pilots became aware of the other aircraft. The pilot in our huey made a hard right turn as did the pilot in the oncoming huey. Both hueys were laid over to an extreme angle as the landing skids on the bottom of the aircraft passed only a couple of feet beyond. I, sitting in the left side door had a ring side seat of the near miss. I also had a good view of the face of my counterpart seated in the left hand door of the southbound huey. I turned and asked my partner if the expression on my face displayed as much terror as the guy in the other huey's doorway. He answered over the engine noise with a huge nod of his head.

I knew we had experienced a very close call when the highly trained and somewhat jaded flight crew was excited about the incident. Everyone on that flight exhibited a new found appreciation of mother earth when we touched down at Long Binh that evening.

WORKING WITH THE THAIS

Many people do not realize that the U.S. military forces were not alone in South Viet Nam. The Australian, Korean and Thai maintained large contingents of troops in country. I never got the opportunity to work with the Koreans but I did spend a good amount of time with the Australians and Thais. The Aussies were great and loyal friends that could be counted on in any situation. The Thais on the other hand while friendly, could be unpredictable. One of the Thais companies that I worked with was made up of men from the Bangkok Circus. Many of them juggled or were talented acrobats. One Thai soldier from the circus had been a kick boxer. He was very strong and had muscles that any body builder would envy. This boxer always wore a wide smile which was very pleasant but he also wanted to fight me and that was not pleasant. The man would follow me around all day hoping to pick a fight. Now I have never claimed to possess much intelligence but I'm smart enough to know fighting this Thai would be a foolish mistake.

One fine beautiful South East Asian day this group of Thai soldiers managed to blow up much of their artillery base while firing projectileless propellant charges out of the 105 mm artillery piece. The ensuing fire and detonation spread ordnance all over the compound. We were called upon to clean up the hazardous items to make the base safe for operations again. This small artillery base provided a wide array of damaged ordnance and loose explosives. We found white phosphorous in the soil that would begin to smoke from the slightest disturbance. There also were large piles of loose propellant often times intermingled with the buried white phosphorous. The Thai soldiers loved to stir the soil with their hands which produced clouds of white smoke that

155

is until the white phosphorous gave them a good burn. Since I hadn't any authority over these men and I had warned them repeatedly not to play with the WP, I allowed this horseplay until a couple of them received minor burns.

I discovered shipping pallets of unfused 105 mm and 155 mm high explosive shells that had been burned and now were buried under piles of dirt and debris. I tried to get the Thai soldiers who were standing around to load these damaged projectiles into the back of a 2 ½ ton truck, but they refused to be part of the work. To illustrate I picked up a 105 mm projectile and loaded it into the back of the truck bed, but the Thais still refused to load the projectiles. It was at that moment I recalled Mark Twain's story of Tom Sawyer tricking his friends into painting his Aunt Polly's fence, so with that thought in mind I picked up one of the much larger 155 mm projectiles and made quite a show of grunting and groaning while loading it into the rear of the duce-and-a-half. This little act triggered something in the big boxer causing him to run to the 155 mm rounds where he snatched one up and threw it the length of the truck bed. I then repeated my charade with another 155 mm but this time I just barely managed to load it into the edge of the truck bed. The over-muscled boxer laughed out loud and began heaving projectiles, one after another into the truck bed. Suddenly the scramble was on and every man standing around raced forward for his chance to throw a 155 farther than I could. The fact that men half my size could out-work me became a badge of honor as nearly every man in the camp lined up for his turn to outdo the big fat American.

I reverted back to loading the smaller 105 mm projectiles and again I made a dog and pony show of struggling to load even these lightweight shells. It was only a matter of seconds before I was pushed out of the way so that all the Thais could have room to work. Now I know throwing these unfused projectiles is not advisable but we managed to get the truck loaded without exchanging any heated words. In fact, I think they caught on to my little trick because there was some sort of challenge involved in every piece of work we undertook for the rest of the day.

THE CAPTAIN LEARNS THAI MANNERS

The 3rd Ord received another call from the same Thai fire base to assist in clearing some unsafe ordnance. I was given the job as well as the honor of taking our new commanding officer on his first real off-post call. We helicoptered to the Thai Fire Base where I introduced my Captain to the camps commanding officer, a man who I had dealt with on several occasions. We then split up and went to work.

The Thais always assigned an interpreter to assist us in translating orders to their men. I had become accustomed to the interpreter following me about but I quickly realized the man was always with the Captain in respect to his rank. At noon the camp commander as I had come to expect invited us to eat with the officers. These people always did their level best to provide proper meals for their guests. It normally consisted of a large bowl of sticky rice, small pieces of meat of unknown origin and two types of sauce. On the way to the bunker where the officers ate I pulled my Captain aside and warned him that the red sauce was hot as fire and the yellow sauce was twice as potent. He said not to worry he loved spicy food. I told him this stuff was beyond hot and to blend in just a little of red sauce in a lot of rice until he got the feel of the thing. My last word to him was not to offend these people at dinner because they had gone to a great deal of trouble for us. The Captain reassured me he could handle it.

We took our seats at the narrow wooden table inside the underground bunker just as the food was served. I always teased these officers by removing a small piece of the mystery meat from the platter and smell it before guessing if it were monkey meat, or water buffalo, or could it be dog?? Whatever it was they just laughed and refused to identify what animal the meat came from. I took some meat and a lot of rice with just a few drops of the milder red sauce on my plate. The Captain however took a lot of rice and a lot of the yellow sauce before tasting his meal. Just as I feared, he could not eat what was on his plate. I also began to realize the Captain was being ignored during our lively and usually jolly conversation. We returned to work and I found that the Thai interpreter was suddenly at my side. Soon our work at the fire base was completed and the helicopter returned to give us a ride home. As the Captain and I prepared to depart the camp commander thanked me for my efforts and bid me to return anytime. Then his smile disappeared and he added earnestly "You are always welcome but never bring that man back again!" I explained that was not up to me but the Thai officer merely repeated his decree not to return with the new Captain. We shook hands and parted with friendly smiles on our faces.

On the walk to the helicopter the Captain asked what we had been talking about. I repeated in the commanders exact words.

"But why?" the Captain inquired.
"I warned you not to waste these peoples food." "You broke the first rule of being a good guest because you left food on your plate."

I know the Captain went on to reach great heights in his life and hope he remembered this valuable lesson. Always treat people, whoever they are, in the manner they expect not how you expect to be treated.

DICK RECOGNIZED FOR DRINKING BEER

Many unusual things happen in the confusion and chaos of war; some of these things are important while others are insignificant but still can be irritating. One such trivial incident began when SSgt. Dick and I were sent down into the delta to assist the Thai Army with some explosive devices.

As the story unfolded we learned the explosives were in the bottom of a collapsed bunker on the perimeter of the Thai compound. These items were not just explosives abandoned underground but were in fact rigged as booby traps of unknown design.

SSgt. Dick was always quick with a smile and a glib tongue that appealed to the Thai personnel while at the same time he managed to convince me that he could not possibly squeeze his body thru the small bunker's collapsed opening. I foolishly agreed to do the dirty work while he would remain outside safing the items handed out of the bunker. In the time it took me to crawl into the collapsed bunker and begin to locate the explosive my partner outside had removed his shirt, found a chase lounge and a can of cold beer. He lay back in the recliner soaking up the hot tropical sun while chattering away with our hosts who were supplying his cold beer free of charge.

I gave up the effort after a couple hours of crawling around in the dirt and dark of the bunker and immerged to find SSgt. Dick imitating a rich play boy at a beach resort. I won't say he was drunk but he was unable to help clean up the explosive items or tools. We returned to the unit with little said about the call for I was use to SSgt. Dick's over indulgence.

160

Soon after this incident SSgt. Dick transferred to another nearby EOD unit and I hated to see him go for we had served together in the states and he was indeed a character to be reckoned with. I was glad to see my old friend come racing into our units drive way a couple of months later. He was all excited about something while insisting that I change to clean fatigues so we could get going. As it turned out SSgt. Dick was being given an award by the Thai Army for our work in cleaning up the explosives in their collapsed bunker. It seems that SSgt. Dick had neglected to give my name to the officers in charge so I didn't even receive an honorable mention.

I reminded SSgt. Dick every time we met thereafter that he had gotten a medal for sun bathing and drinking beer to which he always smiled and patted me on the back just before saying "Thank You".

JOINING THE GREEN BERET

Thinking back over the intervening years maybe I should be grateful that SSgt. Dick neglected to mention my name. At this time there was a Special Forces Unit on Long Binh and SSgt. Dick decided that he needed a change and that joining the Green Beret was the answer. He courted and cajoled the members of that team until they were willing to accept him in a demolition man spot.

All this excitement was not enough and as everyone knows misery loves company so SSgt. Dick began to badger me into joining the band of elite fighting men. I guess I'm easily led so I finally agreed to be interviewed. We had very little trouble getting permission from SFC Smith to visit the Green Beret unit because he felt it was a grand opportunity to be rid of two trouble makers.

SSgt. Dick and I jumped in a jeep and headed for the land of the men with silver wings on their chest, fearless men who jump and die in hopes of finding adventure and glory. I was driving when we reached the Green Beret compound, whose front gate was a copy of the war wagon from the John Wayne movie of the same name.

Our boisterous conversation lagged as we neared the impressive Special Forces fortress and I asked SSgt. Dick if we had completely lost our minds. But before he could answer I drove thru the gate made a sharp 'U' turn and roared back out the gate.

"Where are you going?" SSgt. Dick demanded.
"They are waiting to interview us."

"They are going to have a long wait to interview me." I snapped back. "And if you have any sense it will be just as long before they see you again."

We argued back and forth on the way back to our unit, SSgt. Dick felt bad they had his name and might think him a coward. I for once was glad that my old friend had not spread my name around with the Green Beret staff because they did contact him wanting an explanation of his absence.

There is an old saying "no guts - no glory". That may be true but you still have to ante up the guts in order to win the glory and I thought the price to buy into this game of chance was a bit too high for my taste.

PROFESSIONAL PRANKSTERS

While I am on the subject of SSgt. Dick, it's only fair to say that he had a zest for life that many times led to trouble. He also liked to pull pranks and practical jokes, some of which should have caused him great trouble but his broad smile and quick wit usually defused the situation.

The 3rd Ord had so many visitors that we became cramped for space so we finally managed to take possession of the hooch next to our building which had been occupied by a bunch of cooks who were heavy drug dealers. Tex and I moved into the newly annexed building, threw together a couple of rooms out of packing crates and made beds out of plywood. We found several drug stashes while remodeling the remainder of the building into a workshop. These hooches had plywood floors and side walls that came only half way to the ceiling while the upper walls were made of screen wire. The roofs were corrugated tin that roared under the heavy monsoon rains to the point of preventing normal conversation. But we were dry and that's more than a lot of troops could say in that tropical paradise.

Not being a consumer of alcohol while in country I was not usually a late night patron of our bar as were some of the other members of the unit. Late one night not long after we had moved into the old cook's hooch I was awakened from a sound sleep by the sound of something hitting the tin roof directly above my bed. I passed it off as an accident but this startling late-night interruption became a nightly event. I would get so irate that I would storm over to our bar next door and soundly cuss everyone present and usually offer to fight the perpetrator. Of course everyone would deny all knowledge of the crime to the point that they swore no one had left the bar.

Sometime later SSgt. Dick, who had by that time been transferred to another EOD unit, stopped by for a visit. After a couple hours of drinking he needed to urinate and demanded that I accompany him outside. I of course refused but he insisted that if I would go along he would tell me a big secret. After several minutes of wrangling over the subject I decided it would be easier to accompany him than to continue to argue. I should explain that it was not safe to wander around outside of the buildings on post after dark so most men avoided the outdoor latrines and just urinated in close proximity of the building. SSgt. Dick paused very close to the bar's door, did his business then stepped to one side and bent down to scoop up a handful of gravel. He then lobbed the handful of gravel high in the air causing it to land with a terrible clatter on the tin roof of the hooch next door. That particular spot on the tin roof happened to be directly over my bunk.

SSgt. Dick laughed out loud and declared he didn't think I was so stupid that I could not put it all together, that these rude noises happened only when he was in the bar and that they had stopped when he transferred to the other unit. I'll have to admit that in my blinded furry I never suspected the one person who I should have accused from the very beginning. When SSgt. Dick and I went back into the bar I was greeted by a lot of good natured ribbing because the whole unit had been in on the prank and had enjoyed my little displays of temper.

We all had a good laugh and I promised to get even with the whole crew but it never came to pass. They were all too cunning and usually stayed one step ahead of my meager jokes for I was a rank amateur living in a group of professional prankster.

165

RECAPTURING FIRE BASE

A call came to the 3rd Ord requesting our assistance in the planned recapturing of a fire base somewhere in the three corps area. The date and time for the kick-off was given and SSgt. Dick and I were given the assignment. Our First Sgt. at the time, one of five or six we had in the year that I was in country, decided to go along on this job. This particular First Sgt. and I had never hit it off from the moment he arrived causing SSgt. Dick and I to regret being chosen for this detail.

The night before we were to depart for the fire base our unit got an emergency call from the compound of the outfit we were to join in the morning. Since SSgt. Dick and I planned to leave early the next morning we remained at our building not knowing how long a team would be needed on that site. A team whose member's names I can't recall responded making a fast red light and siren run to the incident sight. They returned later that night explaining what had taken place in the compound. As the team told the story, the soldiers were having one last bash in the Enlisted Men's Club before departing for the fire base assault. This E.M. club was shaped like a large igloo with a long tunnel serving as the entrance. With the club packed with merry-makers someone pulled the pin on a live hand grenade and dropped it in the middle of the clubhouse floor then ran out the tunnel before it detonated. This would have been bad enough but the fiend dropped a second grenade in the tunnel then a third grenade just outside the tunnel's entrance.

A person can only imagine the terror of being trapped inside that building when a grenade detonated. Of course the frightened troops automatically ran for the exit where they were caught by the explosion of the second grenade. The explosion caught the attention of the men on duty in the head quarters building who came running to the aid of those soldiers already injured by the first two blasts. These would-be rescuers were caught in the blast of a third grenade dropped near the headquarters building. I would hate to quote the number of men killed and injured that night but it was substantial. The preliminary investigation pointed to this act of cruel terrorism to have been the work of an American soldier. I never knew if the murderer was ever discovered or caught but it was very demoralizing to the troops.

When our team joined the assembled convoy early the next morning it was clear that these men were in a bad state of confusion and fear. It was bad enough that someone had tried to kill them the night before and that many of their friends had been victims of this senseless attack; but they all realized that this murderous fiend was most likely among those in this convoy. The men of this unit were understandably nervous, for when going into the field it is comforting to know that you can count on the men with you in times of trouble but now every man had reason to doubt every other man. This turned out to be one of those exceptional times when the troops were anxious to leave the comparative safety of the base to take part in a potentially dangerous field operation. That very sentiment was often heard repeated that morning as we joined the ranks of the convoy.

We meandered out through the beautiful Asian countryside until I was completely lost. In the distance we could see a small lone mountain protruding high above the surrounding area. The lush green of the mountain side was in contrast to the deep blue of the cloudless sky and I thought it a very unusual yet pretty scene until we were informed that this was our objective.

The fire base was on a flat area part way up the mountain and it gave a commanding view of the deep valley below. This seemed like a precarious place for an army installation for the base butted up against the steep over grown mountain, giving Charlie the perfect perch where he could look directly down on the camp. The opposite side of the base fell away into a deep valley and the whole area was heavily over-grown with foliage providing Charlie with perfect cover to conceal his movements.

Upon arrival of the deserted base, the three of us immediately began to work on potentially booby trapped and abandoned ordnance that was scattered all over the compound. The combat troops secured the perimeter and at the same time tried to strengthen these positions. SSgt. Dick and I were in the process of loading some 105 mm artillery rounds when I was stung in the palm of my left hand by a nasty black scorpion. It was an extremely painful sting that rapidly spread through my hand then began to climb up my arm. Everything below this band of pain became numb until I lost use of my hand and arm. SSgt. Dick and I thought it best if I found the medic but the First Sgt. insisted that I was being a baby and refused to let me find any medical aid. As I stated before this particular First Sgt. and I did not get along for a number of reasons and this was just one more thing to add to the list.

I should explain that at this point in time the First Sgt. and I were having an ongoing dispute because I had refused to take a promotion to Staff Sgt. Now it may seem strange that a soldier would turn down a stripe and a raise in pay but there were many reasons for my decision but the most important one dealt with protocol. That is, I had a few less days' time in grade than Junior who should have been offered the stripe first. Junior had a family while I was single, he was a highly proficient EOD man who kept his head in all situations and possessed good leadership skills. Besides I liked the man and enjoyed working with him and I felt he had been slighted by the decision to approach me first.

Junior did not want the promotion for his own reasons and this aggravated the higher ups including the battalion XO who lectured us for not accepting the promotion. The First Sgt. thought it would be interesting for Junior and I to fight over this honor but I explained to him that I had too much respect for Junior and that the middle of a war where we handled explosives daily was not the place to feud over a promotion that really meant very little to either one of us. In any case this matter came up several times on this job, which led to more ill feelings. I never could understand why this First Sgt. who seemed to dislike me so much would push so hard for me to be promoted. In the end neither one of us accepted the Staff Sgt. slot with no regrets from either one of us. We worked together on many calls after that without any problem and I for one was always glad to have Junior at my side no matter what the situation.

Back at the fire base our First Sgt. kept disappearing leaving SSgt. Dick and I to fin for ourselves. As the morning wore on and the heat increased we ran low on water so we began to search for water or pop. As it turned out we were refused not only pop but water and food. This came as something of a shock to us for our teams were usually treated as guest by everyone we encountered irregardless of service branch or country. The standard in the military was share and share alike. In situations such as this where plans had been made and we were requested to provide our services the requesting unit supplied everything we needed.

169

As night approached we were informed that the V.C. had surrounded the fire base and that the road out was not safe to travel. This was not welcome news for we were out of water and our work on the base wasn't completed. The only place that we could find for shelter was a small building in the center of the base that smelled like its last occupants had been hogs. Still the little building was better than nothing if rain set in or Charlie decided to attack the base over night.

We found our vanishing First Sgt. and asked for food and water but he stated that the company we were with would not supply us and we would have to wait until we returned to Long Binh. He then wandered off again and I have always suspected that he had made personal arrangements for his provisions while ignoring his men's welfare. SSgt. Dick confidently announced that if I would remain in the hog house with our tools and explosives he would return shortly with supper. As I have said, the man had a winning way about him and I was certain we would soon have something to eat and drink. The sun had set and as darkness enveloped the fire base Charlie became bolder and began to harass us from the mountainside that loomed above us. When some time had passed and SSgt. Dick had not returned I began to worry about him or more truthfully suspected that he had managed to find a banquet for himself and forgot to return.

Now anyone who knows me very well will testify to the fact that I have little patience when it comes to food or the lack of it. As time drug on and I became more hungry after a day's work without food my temper soared at a brisk rate. Just as I was about to explode SSgt. Dick returned from his scouting trip empty handed and confessed that he had failed to get not only food but any sympathy from our hosts.

170

I, of course, unloaded my feelings on SSgt. Dick to which he said if I could do any better I should give it a try. I have never been a trader or wheeler dealer type and couldn't talk a person out of something they were trying to give away. But I was bound and determined not to go hungry when there was food to be had here on the fire base. The base was alive with activity; flares filled the air over the base as the nervous GI's fired at shadows or noises while Charlie passed the night taunting the new neighbors.

Still in a fit of rage I told SSgt. Dick that I was not about to go hungry and that I was going out to find something to eat. He refused to stay behind so we pick up our equipment and explosives and headed out. We tried the head quarters and were given a less than polite "no". After several attempts to buy or trade for food I asked SSgt. Dick where the supply Sgt. was located. He explained that he had tried the supply room where a very large Sgt. had used a long profane way of saying no. Still I insisted on giving the supply room one more try so SSgt. Dick lead the way to a large wooden building that sat very near to the perimeter wire.

The firing was really beginning to pick up as we approached the big old supply Sgt. who was standing just outside the make-shift supply room watching all the action and flares being fired. We addressed the man in a warm polite respectful manner but were quickly dismissed. I, as is my nature continued to talk, trying to explain our situation and that it was their responsibility to meet our basic needs. My arguing with the supply Sgt. only angered the big man further causing him to break into a rant of profanity and physical threats directed at me. This of course was not the thing to say but he thought he was man enough to bully us.

I calmly asked the man if he recognized the bag hanging from my right shoulder. He glanced down and replied it was a demo pack. I agreed and stated that at this very moment it contained 40 pounds of C-4 plastic explosives. Then I warned the Sgt. that his supply building was very near the perimeter wire and a prime target for V.C. sappers. I then promised the Sgt. that sometime before daylight sappers would blow up his building and all the supplies in it.

The big supply Sgt. turned to SSgt. Dick and instructed him to get control of me or there would be real trouble. SSgt. Dick just smiled and replied that he couldn't do a thing with me, and then leaned very nonchalantly against the supply room's outer wall.

SSgt. Dick not only out-ranked me, he was a good deal larger and his response drew a strange look from the Sgt. I saw it was time to strike so I gently patted the bag full of C-4 and said **"if I don't eat, nobody eats."** I repeated that before daylight sappers would blow up this building and spread his valuable C-rations all over this mountain side. The big Sgt. swallowed hard, looked both of us in the eye, to which I smiled and SSgt. Dick shrugged his shoulders.

"How many men do you need food for?" He asked timidly. But before we could answer - "three men", he grabbed a full case of C-rations and asked if this would be enough. I grabbed the box of 24 rations and replied it would do for supper but I would be back for breakfast. SSgt. Dick and I turned and casually walked out of the supply Sgt's sight before we broke into laughter while running to the security of our hog house.

Once inside the hog house SSgt. Dick and I divided up our spoils, with the ham and lima bean meals being the first meals to be set aside. In the dim light we went thru those plain brown card board boxes picking

172

and choosing the cans of food that appealed to us most. SSgt. Dick and I ate until we were stuffed then put some food aside for breakfast fearing that we would never be able to pull off that same stunt in broad daylight. Later that night the First Sgt. reappeared and being generous humane types, we offered him some of our culled out meals but he had very little interest in our meager fare. I knew he had been drinking and could never determine if it was the alcohol or a full stomach that dulled his appetite that noisy night.

SSgt. Dick and I ate our reserves of food the next morning and again we offered the First Sgt. a meal as we felt obligated to do so. The C-rations are far from gourmet food but say what you want, the contents of those ugly brown cans often prove to be very filling in an emergency.

With the sunrise SSgt. Dick and I decided to make a tour or the fire base to make certain we had not overlooked anything that could be considered our responsibility. As we neared the perimeter opposite the base of the mountain we got our first good look at the deep ravine just beyond the wire. I was admiring the view and a cute little 57 mm recoilless rifle that I just knew the 3rd Ord EOD could make good use of when a B-52 strike began to roll down the valley floor below. All of us had experienced B-52 strikes from near and far but I had never witnessed one from so high above. I was so intrigued that I forgot all about the 57mm and kept my eyes fixed on the massive destruction below.

I believe it would take a poet of Edgar Allen Poe's dark talents to accurately describe the incredible power of a B-52 strike. I do not have such word skills but I will try to report what I saw that sunny morning. Our attention was drawn by a sudden loud eruption at the lower end of the valley of such a magnitude that no one could look away. There weren't any warning sounds on the beautiful sunny morning, just the rolling detonations of uncountable 750 pound bombs as they destroyed the lush green valley below. The earth shuttered and trembled like an earth quake had struck the little lone mountain but it wasn't nature that made the ground shake beneath our feet, it was merely man's wrath against man. The clear morning air was filled with black smoke and dust that helped conceal the debris that flew in all directions from the bombers path.

We looked into the clear blue sky overhead for any signs of the massive B-52's but they were undetectable with the naked eye. I must confess our concentration was confined to the awesome devastation being unleashed on whatever or whoever had been unlucky enough to have been caught in the innocent stretch of mother earth. I could only imagine what must go thru the mind of anyone caught in that fiery maelstrom. I had by chance been much closer to a B-52 strike than this mountain side perch and I can report that the ground under us shook so violently that it was difficult to walk. Dust and smoke filled the air that day and the sound of the detonation was unbelievable.

It was a well known fact that at 10 to 12 miles distance B-52 strikes would rattle walls and shake objects off of shelves. The aftermath of such attacks had to be seen for the human mind to comprehend.

All of these facts raced thru my mind as I stood on our lofty perch all the while harboring the selfish hope in my heart that all this effort would make my tour in country safer. We left that fire base shortly after the bomb strike so I never knew the fate of any of those soldiers but I often wondered if that supply room ever got hit by sappers.

CUE BALL AND THE B-52

The instance in which we were too close to a B-52 strike occurred when I and another EOD man, I'll call Cue Ball were being guided by a grunt to a large booby trap out in the middle of nowhere. Our guide was the perfect image of a Viet Nam era ground troop, he wore a battered jungle hat, dirty fatigues, unpolished jungle boots and nearly worn out web gear. He had an M-16 slung over one shoulder while two bandoleers of ammo criss-crossed his chest.

I thought I knew the roads in that area but the laid-back young soldier led us down back roads and trails that I had never seen until I was convinced we were both lost. He almost began to question himself and was nearly ready to give up the chase when suddenly a familiar corner came into view. From this point of recognition we drove down a very narrow trail that ended in a wall of bamboo. It was clear that we would have to leave the jeep and proceed on foot to find our objective that was hidden somewhere in the forest of woody grass.

As we loaded up to traipse off into the boonies we noticed that the driver's side front tire was going flat so I asked Cue Ball to change it while the grunt and I went on to search for the booby trap. The guide and I wandered around for awhile following different trails until it became obvious that he did not know the exact location of the explosive device.

I began to worry about leaving Cue Ball alone out in the middle of nowhere knowing that he was a bit flighty. The grunt and I had just begun to discuss giving up on the search when the big B-52's began to unload ton after ton of ordnance just ahead of our position.

Needless to say the question of leaving or staying was not debated further.

The roar of the bombs was horrendous and the ground shook so violently that it was difficult to walk. I had images in my head of Cue Ball being trapped under the jeep after it fell off the shaking jack. However I must admit that my bigger concern centered around our being overrun by a bunch of V.C. fleeing the B-52 strike. I figured that those bombs were being dropped on an enemy target, which meant we were probably close to a V.C. compound. My mind compared it with a good bird dog flushing a covey of quail from a patch of tall grass; the bombs were the dogs and Charlie the quail. I just didn't want to be in the path of anything those planes flushed out.

When we arrive back at the jeep Cue Ball hadn't changed the tire and I'm sure he didn't know how but the ground pounder and I made short work of the job. In just a couple of minutes we were racing down the rough dirt road that led away from the bomb's target. I never did know if that booby trap was taken care of but I can guarantee you that I never went back in search of that particular device.

Cue Ball hadn't been in country long and like everyone else he had to learn to adjust to a new way of life. Lessons had to be learned and mistakes were made but never repeated. The art of bomb disposal especially when practiced in a war zone is very intolerant of mistakes. I had noticed that Cue Ball not only made mistakes, they were simple errors that any novice EOD man would have avoided. What was worse, the man repeated these same mistakes even after being called on them. I began to think that Cue Ball either had too much on his mind or that his brain was never engaged.

I found out a few days after the run-in with the B-52's when I took Cue Ball on a call to a small fire base in the delta. Cue Ball was driving, something I questioned but still foolishly allowed because we were in a hurry for some forgotten reason. We needed to get to the opposite side of the fire base and I knew of a short cut that required traveling on an abandoned road.

I told Cue Ball to turn onto the closed dirt road which he did without any argument. The road was flat as a pool table and just as barren. In fact the entire area was defoliated and cleared of all trees and brush. Immediately after turning onto the deserted road I spotted a large dirt pile that served as a speed bump about two foot in height some quarter mile ahead. Cue Ball kept increasing speed as if the road was clear ahead. I glanced at Cue Ball's face then back at the bump then once again at his face feeling certain he had seen the dirt pile and planned to simply drive around it at the last minute. By the time we reached the speed bump we were running a good forty miles an hour and judging from the force of the impact and how high the jeep flew into the air we could have been moving a good deal faster.

The M151 jeep landed with a crash throwing up a large cloud of dust and nearly ejecting me out the right side. Cue Ball calmly looked back in the rear view mirror and asked what had happened. I explained that he had driven over a large pile of dirt. His only response was "Oh". I guess I should have warned him that he was rapidly approaching a second and taller speed bump but I decided to see if he would remain unconscious enough to repeat that stunt.

Well he was; for in less than a minute Cue Ball struck the second higher dirt pile at an even greater speed than the first impact. Again the little jeep vaulted into the air only to slam down on the dirt road with an impressive crunching sound.

After he had regained control of the vehicle Cue Ball again looked in the rear view mirror and expressed his disbelief at what had happened. I asked him if he had seen those two bumps and he readily admitted that he had not seen a thing. I knew there was no use in yelling at him but I did drive back to the unit and seldom if ever worked with the man again.

I don't mean to dramatize the EOD mission but when you are traveling around in two-man teams in a war zone it behooves a person to keep all senses working.

Several of the men I worked with were excellent drivers and I can assure you the term "wheel man" was applicable in their cases. I took many rides with these men and while we got into some unnerving situations they always managed to calmly handle the problem. I mean this with the greatest of compliments for the M151 jeep was a notoriously ill-handling piece of equipment. As a matter of fact the property disposal yards on Long Binh Post were filled with dozens of these vehicles, some with very few miles on the odometer that had been wrecked. The Army even required all M151 operators to attend a special school for this vehicle in order to obtain a military drivers license.

OLD MAMMASON WARNED US

I saw many examples of fool heartedness but this tale is one of the better examples. An example of keeping a cool head and being able to handle a vehicle came late one night while returning from a party at the Bien Hoa EOD unit. We all had been invited to a party at the 42nd but as it turned out only Junior and I were available to go but both of us were scheduled to catch an early morning helicopter flight. We agreed to go to the party for a short while and return early without any drinking in order to have a clear head the next morning.

First Sgt. Mud, the one I could not get along with had been drinking that afternoon and decided he would ride along to Bien Hoa fearing that he might miss some good food or free booze. He decreed that we could not take any fire arms even though we would be off post after dark. I being a devout coward had a personal rule to never be off post at anytime unarmed but somehow I was shamed into breaking this rule.

The three of us arrived at the 42nd in the late afternoon where Sgt. Mud made his presence known by drinking heavily and being obnoxious. Junior and I tried to keep to our plan of no liquor and leaving early, but Sgt. Mud wouldn't hear of it, continuing to drink he refused to leave the party. We and our good host tried to make Mud see the logic of our plan but he steadfastly refused even to the point of giving Junior and I direct orders to remain at the 42nd. Finally around midnight, SSgt. Dick who had transferred from our unit to the 42nd and some of our other friends kept Sgt. Mud occupied while Junior and I made our escape. Since we were unarmed our comrades offered to loan us weapons but

179

because of foolish bravado I refused and we departed leaving an inebriated Sgt. Mud to spend the night at the 42nd.

The Bien Hoa gate guards were surprised to see us leaving the air base unarmed late at night but I was sure we could sneak the several miles back to Long Binh without any trouble. The next question was which route we should take on this midnight jaunt. We could take the road that swung out thru the open country or drive thru the town of Tanhiep. Junior told me to decide but I threw it back to him since he was behind the wheel. As it turned out we decided it would be safer to drive thru the town, unwisely reasoning that population meant safety. Of course this was after we laughed off Old Mammason's warning not to be in Tanhiep at any time.

It was a nice evening for a ride and all was fine until we topped a small rise and started down the other side. When our head lights came to bear on the bottom of the hill we spotted several armed Vietnamese men scurrying across the road. We were driving at a moderate speed on the dark unmarked city street that was lined with dark dwellings and the VC were about 100 yards ahead. This was not anything I had foreseen happening but it was time to make a snap decision. Junior called out. "What'll we do?"

The whole thing played out in my mind in an instant. We could not stop in time to turn around and we could now see several armed VC on each side of the road taking up defensive positions while bringing their weapons to bear on us.

I answered Junior by calling out. "Floor it." He had already come up with the same answer and had already stomped the foot feed to the floor.

Now if you have ever driven an M151 jeep you already know that an asthmatic on a bicycle with a flat tire can out run this ill designed vehicle. In any case we took the only action open to us and defenselessly waited for the inevitable clatter of the Chinese 7.62 cartridges being discharged in our direction.

But to our amazement we sailed right thru the impromptu ambush without a shot being fired. The VC on the roadside was close enough that Junior and I could easily see their faces and the bores of the firearms they had trained on us. Junior kept the foot feed on the floor and we both expected to be fired on from behind, instead we climbed the next little hill and rounded a corner and disappeared.

Junior made one of his usual casual off-handed comments. "Damn that was close." He seemed unconcerned about the whole incident while I on the other hand needed to make a potty stop. Junior and I quickly discussed what had just happened. It became clear that our not being armed probably saved our lives. We knew if we had been armed the natural instinct to fire on the VC in the roadside ditch would have precipitated a heavy gun battle that we surely would have lost.

The two of us dissected the whole affair and reasoned out that Charlie was trying to move thru the village undetected was their reason for not firing on us. And while I cursed Sgt. Mud roundly and soundly for leaving our weapons at the unit, Junior reasoned (probably correctly) that if we had been armed our reactions would most likely have been entirely different with the outcome questionable for our side.

There was one other occasion that I found myself unarmed off post and once again Junior was driving the jeep. We had responded to a simple on-post call which lead to another then another and by the time we finished we were on the far side of base. Long Binh post was a very large complex that was scattered over quite a large area. Much of this area was divided into battalions and was fenced off from one another with gates that were closed at dark for security reasons.

The calls had caused us to pass thru several of these gates that at dark were closed off behind us. We were left with the choice of spending the night in the jeep or exiting one of the main gates and return to the 3rd Ord by rural round about routes. The gate guard warned us that security was on high alert and that we might not be able to re-enter the base gate nearest our battalion area.

Once again it seemed imperative that we reach our unit in order to take part in an operation the next day so we opted to take a chance of leaving the safety of the base to drive unarmed thru the dark with the hope that we could pass thru the main gate.

Junior steered the little jeep thru the high chain link gate that closed quickly behind us as we headed down the dark highway. I leaned back in the vehicles spartan passenger seat and began to rethink our situation.

Junior was pushing the little jeep along near its top speed which was about 55 mph but it felt like 95 when I blurted out how stupid we were for making a second such drive. I will never forget his reply. "But you are the envy of every little kid back home reading a Sgt. Rock comic book." He laughed.

Now I'm sure he thought this comment to be reassuring or at least a confidence building statement, but to tell the truth at that moment I would have gladly traded places with the little kid back in the world reading a comic book. This was Junior's usual casual attitude in any given predicament, no matter how crazy or serious the situation, he remained laid back and fearless thru it all.

V.C. BODIES AT AMBUSH

Junior and I were working together one day when we got a call for assistance at an area near Saigon. A convoy had been ambushed and some VC had been killed; we were needed to search their bodies for booby traps. We realized when arriving on the scene that some time had passed since the attack as a crowd of local's had gathered. These good citizens had tied scarves over the faces of the dead for some religious reason and were determine to remove the bodies. A couple of the South Vietnamese White Mice or police were providing crowd control but they were less than enthusiastic about the job.

As the scene played out it was obvious that this was a very poorly planned ambush if it were planned at all. I say this because the first body I came to had been struck in the left wrist by a 50. cal. bullet that traveled down the length of his forearm and exited out his elbow. The one 50 cal. round had killed him instantly. This man had fired a PG 2 at a truck that was loaded with Fanta cola, a soda drink that you could not give away in country.

The PG 2 is a shoulder fired anti-tank weapon, sometimes known as a rocket propelled grenade that is the forerunner of those shown daily on the news being brandished about by Mid-East terrorist. It is a formidable weapon when properly employed, however in this instance it caused more damage to Charlie than to us.

When the first VC fired his PG 2 it blew the right front tire off of the soda pop truck and the blast also killed his accomplice who was hiding in the road ditch just a few feet from the trucks wheel. This man still had two full bandoleers of 40 mm M79 rounds on his body so I doubt if he ever got a shot off.

Junior and I made a quick inspection of the area; made a plan then set to work. I began to examine the first man for any booby traps under his body which was now stiff with rigor mortis. Just to be safe I tied a long line around the dead man's arm, gave Junior a heads up then rolled him over from a safe distance. This procedure exposed his cloth-covered face that I reasoned should be removed. I pulled out the sharp sheath knife I carried and easily split open the red handkerchief material in order to check the man's mouth for any explosive devices.

Now you must realize that I was and still am an ignorant farm boy who grew up on a dead end dirt road. I had very little of what is known as worldly experience so I did not anticipate what would happen next. However, even if I had known I would still have removed the cloth from the dead man's face. In any case this simple act infuriated the crowd of onlookers causing them to protest my actions in threats and gestures. There was no mistaking the resentment and hostile feelings raging through the crowd that was suddenly turning into a mob.

Junior walked over and asked what I thought we should do. I explained that I had no intentions of being ripped apart by these people for doing my job and that if push came to shove I would stand my ground and defend myself. He agreed that it was too late to run and force seemed to be the only response left to us.

As the mob grew more violent the White Mice Police became less and less concerned about our safety and more and more concerned over their own well-being until they scurried away. It looked very much like we would be forced to fire or flee, neither option was very appealing. But Junior and I readied ourselves and tried to look as fierce as possible in the hope that it might defuse the situation. We never knew just exactly what happened but the crowd had just started to move forward when something changed their collective mind and they paused. My male ego would like to think it was the menacing front we presented but these people had witnessed a great deal of war and bloodshed and were not easily bluffed. But for some reason they did refrain from causing any serious trouble and grudgingly allowed us to finish our work.

Junior and I both breathed a deep sigh of relief when we were able to get back in our jeep and depart the area. It would have been a very low disturbing moment in our lives if it had become necessary to use terminal force against a group of people who, though probably our enemies, were grieving family and friends of those men killed in the foolish attack.

I say foolish attack because Charlie was in an open grassy area with no cover or concealment when they opened fire destroying a grey soda pop truck, which is not a vital military target. For some unknown reason they had focused their wrath on a soft target while passing up a two and a half ton truck with a quad 50 in the back.

The quad 50 is four heavy 50 cal. machine guns mounted on one revolving pedestal, it is a devastating merchant of death. This weapon should have either deterred the assault or been struck first in an attempt to neutralize its tremendous fire power. They were killed while killing their own man. As I said it was a foolish poorly planned attack that made us wonder why. But Charlie's lack of training and experience was a blessing for our troops; it definitely saved American lives that day.

185

BUDDHIST MONK

There was one other occasion when Junior was driving and I was a passenger when we crossed swords with a mob of civilians. I can't after all these years recall what was our intended destination but our route lay thru Saigon, I believe the Cholon district. Whatever the address we encountered an unusually large number of vehicles and people beyond the normal everyday traffic. All this activity should have given us reason to doubt our safety but we continued on down the street curious to see what the big attraction was.

Because of all the bicycles, motor cycle and cars in the street Junior was forced to slowly thread his way through all of these obstacles until coming to a large group of people milling around something we could not see. Suddenly we saw thru the crowd; there was a Buddhist Monk setting cross legged on the side walk. Suddenly the monk poured gasoline over his entire body then without hesitation lit himself on fire as a form of protest over the war. He was instantaneously engulfed in flames in what must be a horrible way to die. The milling crowd suddenly became an excited mob and it was clear that we were the object of their hate.

Junior wisely accelerated thru the crowd and it looked like we would escape with nothing more than a few insults and some serious threats. But just as we broke into an open area a large car pulled across in front of our jeep forcing Junior to turn to the left and at the same instant a large black Citroen car full of men stopped on our right side preventing us from going in that direction.

The mob of screaming protesters were rapidly catching up to us and it was clear by the actions of the men in the cars that they intended to hold us there until the mob caught up. Junior in his usual laid-back way asked what we should do now. I replied, "be ready to move" then I jumped out of our jeep and took a couple of steps to the driver's side door of the black Citroen that had cut us off. The driver had his window rolled down and you could tell by the smile on his face that he was in the height of his glory until I rammed the flash suppressor of my M 16 up his nose and strongly suggested he back up or die.

It's amazing how fast a person can back up a Citroen when given the right incentive. I stayed with the Citroen driver until Junior managed to maneuver our jeep into the small opening between the vehicles then I leaped into the passenger seat and we sped away. Our get-away was just ahead of the screaming mobs arrival and I am convinced that they did not intend to give us the key to the city. That mob had hate in its voice and murder in its heart! This would have been a very inopportune time to kill the jeeps motor or for a nervous partner to drive off without me. I have always praised Junior for his driving ability but more than that I admired the man for his unwavering calm collected attitude.

TO REST & RECOUPERATION – OR NOT

One of the supposed perks of serving in country was a few days off known as R&R.

As you can imagine R&R was a much anticipated trip that meant good food, a lot of rest and most important of all a change of scenery.

A person could choose from such exotic destinations as Hong Kong, Bangkok, Hawaii, or Sydney, Australia with the latter being my choice. I was probably influenced by the Aussie EOD team that often visited the 3rd Ord; who of course continually bragged about their homeland. I had been well schooled in what to do and see in Sidney along with how to get invited to stay on one of the large ranches in the out-back.

I could hardly wait knowing that at the end of the flight I would be able to get a meal other than the hot dogs being served three times a day in the mess hall or the C-rations or freeze-dried food in a plastic bag.

When that long anticipated day finally arrived, a couple of the men from the 3rd Ord provided transportation from Long Binh to Ton Son Nhut Air Base in Saigon. They obligingly dropped me off in front of a typical long dreary looking wooden building used to process the lucky R&R bound soldiers. I quickly found that the atmosphere inside the building was just as depressing as the outside had indicated.

Going on R&R anywhere should be a joyous time but just as my luck usually runs the NCO in charge of the processing was a real ass. He immediately began to make us jump thru hoops if we wanted to board the plane. Trouble was I had early on discovered that my rotund body wouldn't pass thru a hoop very easily. The

188

NCO began showing his authority demanding that we stand with our backs to a wall and empty the contents of our pockets on a long table. He ridiculed everyone, especially those soldiers that he judged too weak to resist his verbal attacks.

Just my luck, there was a small meek little guy standing beside me who the NCO picked as the main target of his wrath. The abuse went on and on until the little fellow was visually shaken and actually broke into tears. I had never seen the little man before and have no idea of his MOS or what he may have gone thru. The NCO seemed to be having the time of his life wielding his power knowing that no one was about to challenge his authority and take the chance of missing out on R&R. Of course the man had never had a rock head like me to deal with.

As the airplanes departure drew near the NCO became even more aggressive for he had found someone to bully that would not fight back. In desperation I told the NCO to leave the man alone, but this of course just diverted his attention to me. Several comments were exchanged, each one becoming more violent in nature until I was challenged to step outside. I not being very bright accepted his threat and gladly headed for the door. By this time the crying young soldier had been completely forgotten as the situation had escalated to a war of wills between me and the belligerent NCO. When we reached the front door I stepped outside but the bully refused to come out. He tried to order me back inside saying that I had orders to be on that plane or their bookkeeping would be off.

I explained calmly that I really didn't have to do **anything** and I didn't really care that my not being on the plane would mess up his books. I felt he should have thought of that before he started the trouble. Once again he ordered me back in the building and I could see the other men were filing out the back door of the building on their way to Australia. I still refused and demanded that he come outside where we could settle the matter but he steadfastly refused while trying his best to get me on the plane.

When I saw that the NCO was not going to fight I walked over to an M.P. jeep that was parked nearby and asked if I could use their radio because I was sure I could contact our jeep through them. The M.P.'s had sat quietly witnessing the verbal exchange between me and the NCO and were not quite sure what to make of it. They thought I was foolish for missing out on my R&R but to me it was the principal of the thing.

In just minutes the 3rd Ord jeep returned and without too much surprise or questions transported me back to the unit. I, of course, explained my early return to everyone including the C.O. who had already received a call as to my whereabouts and the fact that I had disobeyed orders to go to Australia. Fortunately he explained as I had that I didn't have to go and that the NCO should receive a reprimand for his actions that day.

I did feel bad about missing out on my R&R but as it turned out I was needed that week, for it was during the next couple of days that Junior, Tex, and I had to remove a 40 mm grenade round from a dead soldiers head. That is another story but I was glad I was present to serve with them on that ticklish incident.

SURGERY ON THE SIDEWALK

Late November 1969 Tex, Junior and I were called from our sick beds in the middle of the night to respond to an explosive incident. We three were members of the 3rd Ordnance Battalion ten-man EOD team stationed at Long Binh, South Viet Nam. Though normally only two men responded to such calls we decided because of our illness all three should answer the call. The remainder of the team were either incapacitated or assigned to other calls.

Our only instructions were to report to a remote section of the perimeter bunker line where an explosion was reported to have taken place. Night bomb disposal calls, even if on base are much more difficult and dangerous to handle than those attempted in daylight. For security reasons many compound gates and interconnecting roads on Long Binh post were locked and guarded at night. Our compound for example, the 3rd Ordnance Battalion was one very small part of Long Binh post that had two gates that were closed at sunset. It was difficult even with emergency lights and sirens operating to make our way across the large base and through the massive ammunition depot to the incident sight.

On arrival at the incident site we were blocked access by the MP's depot security and the military investigators. When finally allowed near the sight, we found a dead American soldier who had been on bunker line duty that night. The large man's body lay face down in the dirt, his feet still inside the open doorway of an outhouse or latrine. A large hole in the right side of his head just above the ear, combined with the M-79 40 mm grenade launcher laying inside the latrine told us what to

191

expect. The military investigators allowed us to open the M-79 in order to ascertain by examining the empty 40 mm shell casing, which of the many projectiles this weapon could fire was lodged in the deceased man's head. Our findings were what we had feared, that the round was indeed a high explosive grenade type that Army regulations state **will never** be moved after firing. This regulation is due to the very sensitive fusing employed in the M-79 high explosive projectile. Standard render safe procedure calls for this item to be remotely detonated in place. However, there is another military regulation that requires any explosive object that is embedded in the body of a U.S. personnel must be removed by a qualified U.S. medical doctor.

We then had no alternative but to transport this dead soldier with the high explosive projectile still buried in his head to the Medivac hospital. This required loading the body into an ambulance then attempting to negotiate several miles of rough rutted roads while driving with only black-out lights.

We loaded the body containing the explosive round into the ambulance and climbed inside the enclosed metal box that served as the rear body of the vehicle. We thought it best to support the body on top of our own hoping to cushion any shock caused by transversing the rough roads from detonating the M-79 explosive round. This trip from the bunker line to the Medivac hospital locked inside the small confines of the bouncing hot, dark ambulance while holding a highly explosive dead body was a never ending experience from hell.

After a very trying ride from the bunker line we arrived at the hospital only to be greeted by what I would term hostility. The facility commanding officer, a Col. made it quite clear that he would not allow the dead soldiers body inside the building nor would he allow any of his personnel to touch the man.   We attempted to explain our position and the Army regulations that demanded a doctor had to perform the operation but he would not listen. We were finally allowed to carry the body inside for x-rays before being forced to return the deceased to the sidewalk outside the hospital's door.

Even though it was after midnight a crowd of medical personnel began to gather around to listen to the on-going argument. However we remained in a stalemate for the Col refused to perform the operation and we were prevented from completing our mission. We became inundated with questions and suggestions from those gathered around, none of which were productive. This stand-off continued until a Lt. Col wearing ordnance insignia materialized out of nowhere and began to ask questions. This officer seemed very knowledgeable about ordnance in general and the M-79 specifically and to our good fortune he backed up our statements concerning risks and regulations. The hospital's commanding officer finally began to listen to reason and finally relented to the surgery, but refused to assign a doctor to perform the work. He insisted that whoever did the surgery would have to volunteer.

Fortunately for us, a doctor we knew was present in the crowd and he bravely came forward against the advice of his colleagues to volunteer for the surgery. He asked us to tell him the real risks involved and we admitted there was no way of knowing the condition of the projectiles fuse. It was made clear to the doctor that if there was a detonation during the procedure that we all ran the risk of losing hands, eyes or even our life. To our surprise the doctor remained willing to perform the medical part of the procedure. The hospitals commanding officer demanded the operation be performed outside of the building and that helmets and flack vests be worn.

This started another argument because EOD teams at that time never wore protective gear. The Col won out in the end when we allowed the doctor to wear a helmet and protective vest. Our team worked bare headed and in tee shirts.

We moved the body to a more remote section of sidewalk where we dismantled part of the hospitals sand bag wall to build a barrier around the deceased's head and shoulders.

We then pulled an ambulance nose-first up beside the body and directed its headlights onto a large mirror that we mounted on the hospitals exterior wall. We adjusted the mirror to reflect the light from the ambulance so that it would illuminate the dead man's upper torso.

When everything was ready the doctor knelt down just outside the low wall of sandbags at what would be the top of the deceased man's head. Our team took up positions on top of the body in an effort to hold the head and upper body motionless and to provide instructions to the doctor as the surgery was being performed.

I had my right hand on the dead man's face when we realized his eyes were protruding grossly between my fingers. In a reflex reaction I gently placed my left hand over my right in an attempt to force those huge haunting eyes back in their sockets. At that instant the doctor's helmet fell from his head and impacted directly on top of both of my hands and the dead man's head. The big steel pot impacted with a loud thud that made all four of us freeze in place and no one breathed for the next few seconds as we awaited the possible detonation. Out of anger and frustration I stood up and with all my might, skipped the doctor's errant helmet across the black asphalt helicopter landing pad. My temper flared to the boiling point as I screamed profanities for all to hear that just such accidents were exactly why we warned against wearing helmets.

The operation itself required splitting the scalp and holding it out of the way while we used a pair of pliers like tool to break off pieces of the skull in order to enlarge the wound opening. We then took great care probing the inside of the skull in order to locate the exact position of the explosive projectile. This involved inserting our fingers inside the skull and feeling about the destroyed brain matter until we were certain of the position and condition of the projectile.

Once the item was located we quickly devised a plan for the projectiles safe removal. We discussed the proper tool to be used in grasping the projectiles metal base and that it was imperative that once grasped it not be dropped. The doctor pulled the projectile to the edge of the skull opening where our team took over. Once the explosive round was clear of the body it was carried to the middle of the parking lot and placed in a pile of sand bags to await being transported to a safe area for detonation.

Just moments after the procedure was completed medical personnel descended on the area and began taking photographs of the dead soldier's body still laying face up on the sidewalk. The military has strict rules against taking pictures of dead American service personnel with private cameras. We protested this activity to both the people involved and the hospital commander, but he refused to take any preventative action. In the midst of this early morning excitement and reverie one of our unit members arrived offering his assistance. This man was well known for his deep sympathy for our soldiers, especially the wounded or dead. His verbal protest of photographing a dead man soon escalated into a shoving match with several officers

195

becoming involved. We were warned to intercede or charges would be filed against us. We managed to quiet the EOD man and to load the 40 mm projectile into the back of our jeep.

Our team returned to the building, wrote up the incident report and thought the matter closed. However a few days later a number of officers arrived at the 3rd Ord demanding that our incident report be changed. It seems the investigators had ruled the young soldier's death a suicide while we had reported an accidental death.

Our decision came from examining the M-79 grenade launcher at the bunker line latrine the night of the death. We found the spring loaded swing-away trigger guard flopped from side to side exposing the trigger and that the manual safety was of questionable operation.

The young deceased soldier came from a poor black family who would be denied his life insurance if the suicide ruling stood. Not only that, but the deceased memory would carry a questionable stain forever. We had witnessed other cases where soldiers had been seriously injured or killed themselves because of horse play or senseless acts and they were given a medal and an honorable discharge.

In any case these officers gave us direct orders to rewrite our incident report, which we refused. They then ordered our commanding officers to change the report but he could not because he was not present at the time. When all else failed the orders became threats and bullying but we stood our ground and our original incident report remained as written. "Accidental Death".

DUSTER COMPOUND

Sundays and holidays usually came and went in the 3rd Ord unnoticed or at least with very little fan-fare except for one particular Sunday morning when SFC Smith asked if I would like to go on a job with him. He explained that this would not be the run of the mill call and that he was sure I would enjoy myself. Smitty was a highly respected EOD man and a fine person that I seldom had the opportunity to work with so I jumped at the chance without knowing just what I was getting into.

We loaded a bunch of explosives into a jeep and headed off base driving into the bright early morning sun. We circled around the perimeter of Long Binh base until we came to a duster compound that I knew existed but I was not familiar with. The camp commander, a young Capt and his First Sgt. were eager to extend a warm welcome as we pulled thru the gate. Smitty obviously knew this officer and they exchanged warm greetings before introducing me.

A duster is a twin 40 mm cannon that fires high explosive rounds on full automatic. They can deliver an impressive and accurate load of explosive that Junior and I witnessed firsthand one sunny afternoon. We were racing down an abandoned dirt road when this very same compound laid down a string of 40 mm shells right across the bow of our jeep. Junior who was driving slowed for a second, declared it was a duster strike then sped up so we could fly thru the cloud of dust caused by the explosions. I never knew if he thought they might just fire again or if he hoped to race by before the gunners could reload.

In any case - back to the story. Smitty and the Capt. had come up with a plan to drain a large stagnate water hole that lay just within the compound. They explained that the road leading into the compound served as a dam that prevented proper drainage and we were going to breech that road using explosives. They had chosen Sunday morning in hopes of having less low flying air craft traffic to worry about. The main low flying air craft they most hoped to avoid was that of the Long Binh Provost Marshall who liked to personally fly over back roads in an effort to stop drug trafficking.

A plan was made to place some explosive charges in holes in the road in an attempt to break up the hard packed soil. We set some shots of C-4, cut a 30-second time fuse then Smitty backed the jeep up to the edge of the proposed ditch. I looked all around for any traffic, bent down, pulled the fuse lighter then yelled "go" as I jumped into the back end of the jeep. When Smitty heard my body thump into the back of the jeep he peeled out and we raced down the road just as fast as that pathetic little four cylinder jeep motor could run.

We realized after a couple of shots that while this was great fun our C-4 had little effect on the soil and that we needed an explosive more like dynamite that heaved rather than shattered. Somewhere in all this revelry a bunch of Bangalore torpedoes came to light and they sounded like the answer to our problem. Of course this presented a new problem in that with C-4 we could keep the strength of our shots to a minimum which helped prevent any brass from discovering the good time we were having. The Bangalore torpedoes are three feet long tubes that are pre-packed with an explosive that is made for blasting but their configuration made controlling the size of the shots much more difficult. Still it sounded like fun so we decided to give them a try.

198

Smitty and I placed a Bangalore torpedo in the ditch, cut a couple of 30 second time fuses and again I pulled the fuse lighters before jumping into the jeep for a hasty get away. Of course now that we were using more explosives than before we got a much louder report plus being covered with debris from the blast. It was obvious that a 30 second delay was not long enough for us to drive clear of the fall out. Returning to inspect the blast site it was obvious that we had made some progress using one Bangalore but a little dust was not enough to discourage a couple of fools so we set a second shot. The results were the same, a lot of noise and dust, but the ditch grew which was enough encouragement to think that if one Bangalore was good two would be great. On the next shot, two torpedoes were set and the 30 second fuses were definitely too short but for safety reasons we continued to use 30 seconds.

After a couple more shots using two Bangalore's we thought it best to try to finish the job before we were reported so it was decided to use three of the powerful sticks for one last shot. We tied three of the Bangalore's together, placed them in the hole then capped up a couple of 30 second fuses while briefly discussing that if anything went wrong, such as the jeep stalling or any number of other things we would be in a world of trouble. At 30 seconds it would be difficult to get out of the blast range even in the jeep let alone on foot and nowhere near enough time to cut the fuses before the detonation. It was clear that everything must go exactly as planned on this shot but as is often the case with EOD men we decided to leave matters to the Gods. Smitty backed the jeep up close as I scanned the area and the sky for any aircraft then pulled the fuse lighters. Just as I yelled go and Smitty peeled out a small helicopter appeared at tree top height coming down the road in our direction. We were beyond the point of no return and far too late to do anything except hold our breath and wait for the inevitable. I was so absorbed with the potential tragedy unfolding before my eyes to worry about our own safety.

Now remember that we had not set off three of these Bangalore torpedoes before and we were not sure just what to expect other than the report would be very loud. I can't recall the military model of the fast helicopter that suddenly appeared out of nowhere but they were commonly called a Loch and resembled a large green egg with a tail. The helicopter fortunately was just off to the side of our shot but it was very low when the detonation wave caught it. The little Loch was blown sideways and upward by the force of the blast and you could see the pilot fighting to control the fragile little air craft. The big fear of setting off an explosive charge below a low flying aircraft is not so much the debris that might strike the craft, rather the danger in the blast of air below the wings or in the case of a helicopter the rotor becomes rapidly displaced causing the aircraft to plummet to the ground.

The helicopter pilot either through luck or skill managed to prevent crashing into the ground; however he did land in a big hurry just inside the duster compound. The Capt. we were trying to help quickly deduced that someone would have to go over to the helicopter and explain what had taken place. Smitty and I refused to go telling the Capt. that we were cowards and besides it was his compound and he out-ranked us so it was his place to go. Well, I guess he was a coward too because he ordered his fearless First Sgt. to face the indignation of the offended pilot. The three of us stood nervously by as the brave Sgt. confronted the helicopter pilot and passengers. It was obvious even from a distance that he was receiving a real dressing down. But in a few minutes the little chopper started up and flew away. The now demoralized First Sgt. slowly dragged his buttless body back to our position.

The duster compound Capt. began to shout questions to his Sgt. before the poor man had cleared the front gate. "Who was it?" "What did they say?" he demanded but the First Sgt. remained silent until he was standing beside us. The dismayed Sgt. shook his head and then replied. "That was the Provost Marshall of Long Binh Post and was he mad!" came the report.

"Did you explain what happened?" The distraught Capt asked.

"I really wasn't given much of a chance to speak." "The Col. did a lot of yelling and threatening and then he asked me who had set off the explosive charge." "I told him it was Sgt. Smith and Specialist Pool from the 3rd Ord EOD."

"What did the Col. say about that?" Smitty asked knowing full well we had broken several post rules.

"That's the part I don't understand," the Sgt. replied with a mystified shake of his head. "When I told the Col. that you two had set off the explosives, he let loose a string of swear words then ordered the pilot to take off." "They just took off leaving me standing there."

I have to say that when I learned that the helicopter was the Provost Marshall's, I let out a loud sincere groan because he and I had crossed swords before and I'm sure I would not be on his party guest list.

I am surprised that I can't recall the Provost Marshall name for I heard it enough times but to categorize him as a hard man would be a gross understatement. The Long Binh Provost Marshall position would be equivalent to the chief of police in New York City only he had much more power over your destiny than any civilian police chief. In this situation, he could have thrown the book at us and even if the charges didn't stand up the man could have made life very miserable.

I never knew why the Provost Marshall merely cursed and flew away and even though we met several times after that I was smart enough not to bring up the subject in his presence. I just thanked the Powers That Be that no one was injured and that one of the most powerful officers in South Viet Nam had a much more forgiving nature than anyone ever expected.

TEX AND THE PROVOST MARSHALL

One of my first encounters with Long Binh's Provost Marshall came on a bright summer day that Tex and I had somehow managed to come up with a good enough excuse to get permission to go to Saigon. I never did care to hang around the building, I always wanted to be out and doing something. I still to this day have a phobia about working in the same place day after day.

On this particular day Tex was driving our fastest jeep as only he could at well over the 35 mph speed limit when he flew by a Military Police jeep at about 50 mph. I recall telling Tex that he had just passed the Provost Marshall. That was just before the red lights came on behind us. We pulled over to the side of the road and the M.P. jeep stopped behind us. To our surprise the driver who was alone waved for us to come back to him. We hurried back to the jeep where the Col. sat smugly in the driver seat knowing that he had us for speeding.

"Going a little fast weren't you?" the Col. asked in a firm manner.

I tried to make up some excuse about hurrying to our unit in Saigon to do some research on unusual piece of ordnance because they had more army publications than our unit. By the look on his face it was clear the Col. wasn't buying my story. He asked if we were in EOD but of course he knew we were for we were wearing our badges, but the real give away was our jeep's bright red fenders, sirens and flashing red lights. Then the Col. asked if we knew who he was and I playing dumb replied "No Sir". He then told us to go around behind his jeep and read his spare tire cover.

Custom personalized spare tire covers were very popular in country and of course this one said Provost Marshall Long Binh but we already knew that. Tex and I walked back around to the driver's side of the jeep where I reported as if surprised that the tire cover identified him as the Provost Marshall. He then informed us that EOD men were supposed to be observant and aware of their surroundings at all times. I replied "Yes sir!"

The Col. had remained seated in his jeep throughout this little charade but suddenly the man struck out hitting Tex with a solid blow in the stomach. "I expect men who are addressing me to stand at attention." He roared. Tex who had been standing in a casual manner with both hands in his pants pockets doubled over from the punch to his stomach. The Col. then declared Tex was out of uniform because he was wearing a Marine jungle hat, air force zippers in his boots and a long shaggy moustache that covered both of his lips. The Col. was an unhappy man and he made his feelings well known. We took a good dressing down and I feared that article 15's were going to follow but after promises were made to be better soldiers and to stay out of the bars in Saigon the tough old Col. told us to be on our way. I believe his last words centered on driving slower.

We drove the remainder of the distance to Saigon at the posted speed limit with the Provost Marshall of Long Binh right behind us serving as an M.P. escort.

JUNIOR AND THE PROVOST MARSHALL

About this same time Junior and I were assigned to help provide security for President Nixon's wife Pat who was scheduled to make a visit to the wounded in a local Medivac hospital. This was easy duty that we had some experience with in the states, although it is a big secret that during the 1968 presidential election the Army EOD personnel were employed to back up the secret service in protecting the candidates. This was a unique opportunity for us commoners to gain insight into the workings of a powerful government agency and the candidates as well.

When Junior and I arrived at the Medivac hospital we were surprised to find a very nervous Provost Marshall scurrying around trying to make a plan for Mrs. Nixon's arrival. With a nod and a wink we began to share our vast knowledge of security which the Col. greatly appreciated. A couple of our recommendations included enlarging the perimeter restricted safety zone, placing a sniper on the top of a concrete water tower, and restricting the number of people allowed in the area. We then swept the area for any explosive threats and waited for the dignitaries to arrive by helicopter. In the meantime we were surprised to see our suggestions were implemented and the First Lady's inspection came off without a hitch.

Sometime later Junior and I were asked to respond to a call at Long Binh's south gate. It was evening when we arrived and we were lead to a supposed satchel charge buried in the ground just outside the perimeter fence. We began to carefully exhume the buried object that was wrapped in green rubber rain coat material. Green was the national color of S.V.N; while this green rubber material was used for everything from food storage to make-shift body bags. The rubber covered object we uncovered was about 18 inches long and square in shape. We knew that much of the explosive that the VC used was cast in the shape of bars of soap and that is exactly what this package looked like in the fading light.

We immediately began to look for booby traps that would set off the blocks of explosives if they were disturbed but we found nothing of the sort. The package felt soft to the touch and once safely out of the ground the green rubber was cut away to reveal packages of cigarettes. As I recall there was 20 packs of Viceroy's, a less than popular brand of smokes. Each pack was in new condition with the clear cellophane and little red zip strip still intact. A close inspection of the bottom of these packs by flashlight revealed marks where the seal had been tampered with.

This we knew was a common ploy of the drug dealers who would buy up undesirable brands of cigarettes then carefully open up the bottom of the packs in order to remove the contents. The tobacco was gently removed then replaced with marijuana before the cigarettes were returned to the pack and the cellophane on the bottom resealed with a hot knife.

The contraband smokes could then be resold at a great profit and the purchasers could pass thru the M.P.'s on the gate with new unopened cigarettes. This should have been a dead give away to the guards but for whatever reason they often failed to question the altered packages.

I could write several pages on the drugs in country and the lack of enforcement by the military on their usage for it was everywhere and usually ignored. In any case Junior and I had a problem on our hands. We could not just leave the package there and we could not put it in our holding area to be destroyed and we were not about to sell these drugs. We quickly decided to drive straight to the Provost Marshall's office and turn in the illicit weed so it could be handled in an official manner.

Junior, on second thought questioned the wisdom of our plan to go directly to the Provost Marshall thinking it better to place a little C-4 on the package. He argued correctly that if the contraband were destroyed with explosive no one would know what had happened. Junior was behind the wheel when we arrived at the Provost Marshall's office where he elected to remain outside while I delivered the goods. I recall Junior calling after me that if I didn't return in 15 minutes he would go for help. I laughed at his fears for I was sure there wouldn't be any problem.

And there wasn't, until I placed the green rubber wrapped package on the M.P. Sgt's. desk.

"What's this?" He demanded with a snarl.

"I think its marijuana." I told him before explaining where it had been discovered. I then turned around and headed for the door.

"You're under arrest." The M.P. Sgt. yelled. I attempted diplomatically to explain what had taken place and that I **was not** under arrest.

The more the M.P. Sgt. tried to arrest me the more I objected until he called for assistance. Several more M.P.s materialized and I became even more determined not to be taken into custody for doing the right thing. I felt especially strong on this point when I had witnessed drug dealers being caught red-handed but were released because they stated the drugs were not theirs. Just as things were looking the darkest and my arrest looked emanate the same bird Col. that I had encounters with before appeared from some distant office and demanded to know what all the commotion was about.

"Oh it's you." He said with a frown.

"I found this stash just outside the south gate and came here to turn it in and your men want to arrest me." I blurted out angrily.

"What?" The Col. roared but the word was not really a question. "Get out of here; I have more important things to do!" With that he turned on his heels and disappeared. I took him literally and hurried out the front door while the M.P.'s watched with a strange expression on their faces.

Back in the jeep I related the story to Junior who was very glad that he had not accompanied me into the building. He also gently reminded me how much better his plan to blow up the package would have turned out. I often found his reasoning and logic far ahead of mine; if only I would have taken his advice more often I'm sure life in country would have been less stressful.

Welcome to Hotel California

House girl polishing our boots

Day laborers raking rubber tree leaves

**One of the comely day labor women.
Background SFC Robert Smith talking
to Mommason**

Chinese mortar, notice house girl's nonchalant attitude.
They probably knew more about this mortar than we.

Leopard dog – the Vietnamese painted
these pups & sold them to gullible GI's

Walter Gee ready for action

**Mike Nichols getting slicked up
before we build a shower room**

John Claffey, Art Macksey & Gary Pool

**Radio Da Nang just across the street
from Da Nang Army EOD**

**Army EOD Villa – Da Nang where we
spent the night on the roof top -- Tet 1969**

Gee, Nick & I trying to keep a straight face after Mommason slapped my face.

Walter Gee, Mike Nichols & I after award presentation

Dick Hause – 3rd Ord EOD Clerk

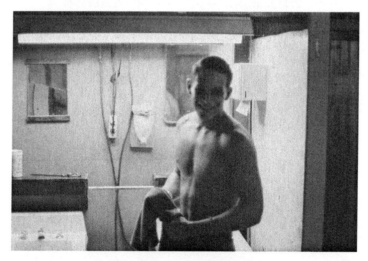

Dick Hause getting slicked up in our new shower room

Gary Pool
VC modified 107 mm rocket

**Hershel Jackson & Walter Gee
setting a shot to destroy 2.75 rocket**

**Walter Gee ready to pull
fuze lighter on demolition shot**

**One of many VC arms caches
we had to search**

ARVN APC in Delta jungle

**View of our holding area after
self-destruction**

View of our holding area after blast

Borrowed 2 ½ ton truck in our holding area after blast

Everyone had to inspect the holding area blast

Typical demolition shot of mixed ordnance

Split Bridge on QL 1

Thia artillery base after they blew it up while firing propellant charges for fun.

Thai artillery projectiles rowed up for destruction

**Catholic Church at the old
French Fort in the Delta**

Statue and hut at the French Fort

Tenants & shacks at the French Fort

Bailey Bridge that provided access to the French Fort

Vietnamese women willowing part of the rice harvest

Vietnamese farmer threshing rice by hand

**Vietnamese woman irrigating
vegetable fields.**

Vietnamese Gas Station

**Bob Hope doing warm-up for show
Long Binh Post**

**The Gold Diggers
part of the Bob Hope Show**

AIR HOLE IN DEPOT

On another sunny day (there are only two types of days in South Viet Nam, hot and sunny or hot and rainy) Junior and I were asked to respond to a call in the new part of Long Binh depot. This area of the depot had just been built so the ground was denuded right down to the bare soil.

On arriving we were met by several officers who led us to a hole in the ground that was about 4 inches in diameter. The officers were convinced this hole was the top of a camoflet which is a cavern produced by the detonation of an explosive underground. Camoflets leave little disruption above ground but result in a concealed crater that is often full of carbon monoxide or other toxic gases that could be deadly if a person should fall thru the thin soil crust.

Junior and I inspected the small opening and came to the conclusion that it was in fact an air hole for a V.C. tunnel. Charlie was famous for his tunnel work, so much so that most GI's thought the Vietnamese to be part gopher. The officers on the scene immediately rejected our opinion and demanded that we do something about the situation. We suggested that a back hoe or some other piece of equipment should be brought in to dig up the area. They refused but insisted the camoflet be caved in before someone was injured. We then suggested that water should be poured down the hole, which if it was indeed a camoflet the carter would fill up and the top would cave in. They thought this idea workable and called for a tank truck full of water.

Shortly a straight tank truck filled with water arrived and pulled down close to the small round hole.

A hose was strung from the truck to the hole and the flow of water began with great promise but ended shortly after a couple hundred gallons of water disappeared down the hole without a sign of filling the crater.

Not willing to accept the theory of this being an air hole, the officers then radioed for a semi trailer of water. The tractor trailer rig followed suit of its little brother except that this time the hole swallowed several thousand gallons of water without leaving so much as a muddy spot on top of the ground. At this point I reiterated that if this were a true camoflet the crater would have filled with water by now but if this was an air vent for a tunnel no amount of water would ever fill it up. At that moment one of the officers looked at his watch and declared it was mess time and they all piled into vehicles and departed.

Junior and I had just spent the entire afternoon helping some misguided officers pour water down a rat hole; something my mother always advised was the pass time of fools.

NITRO BASED DYNOMITE

When it comes to the subject of tunnels under Long Binh depot, a half hearted search for the elusive passages lead to a disagreeable detail for the entire 3rd Ord EOD team. One bright sunny day Junior and I were on a call in the bowels of Long Binh ammunition depot when we came across some small sandal tracks near an explosive bunker.

I always enjoyed reading sign and tracking; of course this was a bit more intense as the game we followed was our enemy. We trusted that the trail would not lead to an armed encounter with any V.C. foolish enough to be loafing around the depot in broad daylight, but there was always the chance of encountering a booby trap or a delayed ignition device.

These particular sandal tracks led us to a bunker full of ammo that had been decorated with Cho Hoi leaflets that Charlie had used for toilet paper.

These leaflets were written in Vietnamese and were illustrated as well. The dollar-sized papers offered payment for surrendering as well as for any ordnance or ammunition turned in. Though Cho Hoi leaflets were dispersed by the thousands from aircraft and were commonly encountered, in this case they were purposely placed as a taunt to the GI's.

Junior and I after a short debate, decided to leave the soiled leaflets for the ammo humpers to deal with. Giving up on the sandal tracks we started to leave when one of us foolishly asked why everything in this berm was covered with tarps. As everyone knows curiosity killed the cat so we just had to look under the covers because the lumps underneath looked vaguely familiar. We threw

231

back the tarps to find box after box of dynamite. This was quite a find knowing that nitroglycerin based dynamite is not allowed in combat areas because of its sensitivity to any impact such things as a bullet. I will admit that we tried to convince ourselves that it was not commercial dynamite and that it was safe to store in a combat zone.

The printed words on the boxes read "nitroglycerin base dynamite"; but we still refused to believe that someone had shipped in hundreds of pounds of this hazardous stuff into Viet Nam. What was even more surprising to me, having been through ammunition storage school, was the fact that the shipment had been received, unloaded and stored for what appeared to be a considerable amount of time in one of the largest ammunition depots in the world. If this stack of boxes had been struck by any type of fire, or bumped hard, or if it had just decided to go off, it would have resulted in one hell of a big crater. Not only that but someone would have had to do a lot of fast talking to explain just how it come to be stored in Long Binh.

A quick cursory inspection of the heavy cardboard boxes showed no signs of leaking nitro which we took as an encouraging sign but deep down we knew that was too good to be true. There was no doubt in our minds that we must open up some of the boxes and inspect the condition of the contents.

Nitro based dynamite is a mixture of an inert base like saw dust or clay with nitroglycerin mixed in which makes it relatively safe to use if a few rules are followed. The first rule is that each case must be turned over about every thirty days to prevent the nitro from exuding out. It was obvious that these boxes had not been touched in a long time. It's also a good idea not to let nitro-based dynamite to be exposed to extreme temperature - the countries high heat was extreme. There was a short discussion regarding the condition of the explosives. After setting so long in the intense tropical heat, its sensitivity was a grave concern.

When commercial dynamite gets old and has not been stored properly the liquid nitroglycerin begins to exude thru the paper walls of each stick. This exuded nitro looks like thick oily beads of sweat that are extremely sensitive. The exuded nitro also takes the form of crystals that may appear as fine as sand or grow into large delicate shapes that are arguably more hazardous than the liquid form.   Handling old nitroglycerin in either state is a task that normal people would avoid at all cost. However not being normal, Junior and I felt compelled to open some of the boxes to determine just how unstable this pile of illegal explosives would be.

We hoped deep in our hearts that the dynamite would be in "like new" condition; if so, the disposal of the problem might fall to other hands. Of course Junior and I both knew this was wishful thinking for experience had told us what happens to commercial dynamite when mistreated as badly as this had been. I'll be the first to admit to committing episodes of bravado when on calls, such as misleading authorities about the danger of a specific procedure so that we might do a job without interference. I will confess to using the utmost care when opening these boxes of old dynamite. We looked and listened very intently for any signs of resistance or sudden loud noises but the cover slid off without a problem. Inside we found the sticks of dynamite were inside of heavy plastic bags. At first glance this plastic bag didn't pose any problem until we noticed large crystals of nitro had formed in the folds of the bag.

Perhaps it was plain foolishness but we were not to be deterred at this point so the plastic bag was unfolded and we peered in like two kids expecting to find a monster. As it turned out, that is exactly what we found, for the top sticks of dynamite were covered with nitro crystals that ranged in size from that of the head of a pin to large complex formations. The bottom of the plastic bag held a lot of nasty looking liquid nitroglycerin.

This was not a good scenario for we had a large number of boxes full of dynamite that had both free flowing liquid nitroglycerin and crystal formations and to make matters worse it was stored in the middle of a large ammunition depot. It was obvious that we would not be allowed to blow it in place, (the EOD man's favorite render safe procedure) although for an instant the idea did have the floor and nearly won the voting.

Aside from the danger, handling nitroglycerin can induce severe headaches in some people and I knew from experienced that I was numbered in that group. I had suffered a terrible headache from a minor exposure to some nitro fumes so I was not thrilled at the thought of wallowing in the stuff.

Junior and I mulled over the problem; both being very reluctant to report the hazardous material, knowing full well what would happen and that we would certainly be a party to the solution. I would have given anything to throw the tarps back over the dynamite and hope it was not rediscovered during our tour in country.

After a discussion involving a lot of "what if's" and "maybe's" we reached the forgone conclusion and returned to the unit and reported to SFC. Smith. He was the only man of authority I trusted to make the right decision.

I must take the time to state that I always felt SFC. Robert Smith possessed more common sense than any man I have ever met and he also had the knack of leading men to do unsavory tasks that other NCO's would have ended up with a revolt on their hands. This was one such instance; Smitty saw our duty clearly and he easily cajoled everyone into taking part. I never saw the man pull rank to accomplish anything; rather he employed humor and personality to make his point. I often wondered if this was a product of his being raised at Boy's Town or if he had read Mark Twain's tale of Tom Sawyer painting Aunt Polly's fence too many times. Whatever the charm was it worked and we all willingly agreed to move the dynamite out of the depot.

All the preparations were quickly made; clearances, trucks signed out, routes of travel laid out and demo range area approval. There was some serious discussion on the proper render safe procedure of the badly deteriorated dynamite. The often suggested disposal of aged dynamite is to carefully split the sticks open, place each one on wood and light remotely. This normally works well but can result in a detonation. Of course in this case we had far too much explosive to work with and that would not have disposed of this liquid nitro. The nitro itself can be mixed with acetone to desensitize it and oil poured over the crystals helps prevent stressing them to the point of detonation but once again we had far too much dynamite to process and the mere act of processing the material could have caused an explosion.

As strange as it may sound, many decisions in the Army EOD are often a consensus of opinions and not a command made order. This is one field where it may save a lot of lives including your own by listening to a little advice. It is also a field where few orders are issued, jobs are weighed pro and con until an obvious course is determined. At that point everyone accepts the plan and without orders go about performing the task to the best of their ability. This was one of those situations.

235

The final decision was to load the intact 50 lb boxes into the back of two 2½ ton trucks known as duce-and-a-half's to be hauled to a safe area for detonation. There seemed little else we could do to prepare except to get a professional mind-set and get to the work.

It was an unusually hot sunny day but we started the operation early in order to avoid doing the physical labor in the heat of the day. Every member of the team pitched in but the loading process was slow, hot, and sweaty work that required serious thought and patience to prevent a mistake that could cost not just a team, but the whole squad.

When both trucks were loaded we followed a route that presented the least chance for loss of life or property if one or both of the truck loads should detonate. I had an Army truck driver's license so I volunteered to drive one of the duce-and-a-half's and while I can't remember for sure, I believe we conned some poor truck driver into operating the other one.

As we started to pull out Junior brought me a can of pop; I thanked him and told him to jump in the passenger seat. He smiled and replied he would ride in the jeep following behind. I remember telling him not to follow too close. That was the first and only time that Junior turned down one of my hair brain ideas. But I knew he was right, for there was no reason to chance the loss of another EOD man in light of the fact that we were always shorthanded.

The road to the demo area was rough so we traveled at a very slow pace to prevent having any accidents and so that we could avoid any large bumps or holes in the road. Since this was to be a controlled detonation it would have to be limited to the size of each shot; it would require more time and space than our usual demo range provided. We had received permission

236

to set up the shots nearer to the bunker line than was normally allowed, thus giving us a confirmation of each explosion through both sight and sound. Also we could have visual control of the blast area hoping to prevent anyone from wandering into harm's way. Being so close to the bunker line would also discourage the ever-present V.C. from attempting to sneak into the shot and cut our time fuses and steal the explosives.

We placed, as I recall, seven boxes in each stack forming roughly ten stacks. C-4 plastic explosives were placed on top of the top box with the whole thing being fired non-electrically. With everything in readiness we called "fire in the hole" three times and began pulling fuse igniters, then retired to the other side of the bunker line.

The whole unit eagerly awaited the first detonation; each successive one was spaced two minutes apart, and was in my estimation disappointing. The detonation produced a dull roar and a passable fire ball. I had hoped for more excitement but it might have been a case of too little too late. Three hundred pounds of explosive detonating at a time in the states would have been impressive but we had all worked on large shots while clearing ammo dumps and similar operations that had made us all a bit jaded. Still an explosion is an explosion and I was Johnny on the spot to get a good view of the fireworks.

We counted each shot and briefly reconned the area to make certain that we had not produced any low order detonations with the badly deteriorated dynamite. The blast site looked clean and we headed back to the unit to clean up our gear.

As I stated earlier this happened to be a very hot day and the whole crew was exhausted from the physical labor and mental stress not to mention missing a couple of meals and being too busy to drink enough water. It was mid-afternoon by the time we settled in for a rest, each man looking for a quiet hole to crawl into.

Shortly after laying down I became ill and headed to our luxurious outdoor latrine, but half way there I was struck down by the most God-awful pain in my head. And I do mean struck down, for I collapsed right there as if hit by a hammer. I called for help. The effort only doubled the pains in my head so I didn't try again; besides no one responded. I had the bad luck of hitting the ground out in the direct rays of the tropical sun instead of in the shade of one of the many rubber trees in the area.

I lay there for some time and finally become resigned to my fate, fearing that the combination of the nitroglycerin poisoning and the exposure to the sun would kill a weakling like me. But then I thought of how it would look back home when word arrived of my death while serving in Viet Nam.

I could just hear the folks in my small Iowa home town saying things like: "Ain't much of a war, the damn kid dropped dead walking to the outhouse" or "I always knew he was a weakling, I heard he died of overexposure while sun bathing" or "I've said a hundred times that Pool boy was worthless, here we spend a lot of tax dollars to get him over there and he just up's and drops dead, most likely from fear" or "You'd of thought he would have been considerate enough to get killed in combat if we are going to have to foot the bill for his funeral." The thought of all those folks talking that way about me gave me enough incentive to get up and make my way back to my bunk. None of the folks back home would have been surprised to hear that I died in bed.

I found out the next morning after doing a lot of complaining that I would receive little sympathy from this bunch for they had all experienced the same effects from the nitro and the heat. I think back now so many years later and realize just how fortunate we were to have passed the day with nothing more serious to report than a headache but what a headache it was!

I should add that we eventually learned that Pacific Architect and Engineering, a large contracting company was the guilty party that imported the commercial dynamite and then abandoned it in the middle of Long Binh depot. You don't suppose someone explained the hazards of using nitroglycerin based explosives in a war zone and they abandoned the dynamite there?

THAI ARTILLERY FIRE BASE

This story concern's a heavy piece of steel from an artillery shell just missing my head after a stack detonation. The flying piece of steel drew many chuckles and a couple of scoldings from the other team members but that is like closing the barn door after the horse got out. We naturally photographed the errant piece of metal before policing it up and placing it with some other metal remains of the shot.

I was part of a three man team that was sent to a Thai artillery fire base in the delta to destroy a large quantity of artillery rounds. The Thais had already designated the projectiles to be destroyed so we supervised separation and loading of the various types of rounds into trucks. The trucks were driven to an open plane and unloaded for us to make up the shots following the proper safety procedures.

We laid out two long rows of artillery projectiles, added a layer of C-4 then decided to run a second course of projectiles on top of the C-4. It was then that someone asked the age old questioned "what would happen if". Strangely enough it sounded plausible and knowing that we had a lot more projectiles to destroy and a limited amount of time "IF" became the answer not the question.

We capped up, called "fire in the hole" and pulled the fuse lighters. We then drove one of the duce-and-a-half's to a safe distance at what would have been the end of the rows of projectile. The projectiles had been carefully laid out alternating fuse to base which gave us a view of the sides of the munitions.

We crouched down behind the truck and awaited the detonation from our vantage point; that is everyone but yours truly. I had taken up a position near the trucks front bumper and had rested my camera on the hood hoping to get a good photograph of our handy work. I was warned it would be best if I got down behind the truck but I argued that only my head was exposed above the hood.

The explosion was indeed colorful and I managed to get a relatively good shot of the resulting smoke and fire, but just as the shutter on my camera clicked shut a large piece of steel buried itself in the ground just behind me. It was the base plate of a 155 mm high explosive round that must have just missed the top of my head.

I don't know what that circular piece of flat steel weighed but being struck by it would have been equivalent to a cast iron skillet traveling at the speed of sound. That base plate must have made a ninety degree turn to have landed where it did and it was the only piece of metal that came near our truck.

The EOD team thought the whole thing very humorous and you would have thought this was a lesson learned, but I must admit to being a slow leaner for I often exposed myself to take a picture of an explosion.

I would like to state at this point that the incident of the flying piece of steel put an end to our experimentation with explosives. I would like to say that but that would be an outright lie.

There were the usual experiments with primer cord; you know, like how many times you had to wrap this explosive cord around a tree or post to cut it off cleanly. There was the test to find out why civilian electric blasting caps would fail to initiate C-4 plastic explosive and the flip side of the question was how many of these caps were required to achieve a complete detonation. Of course, it seemed essential to ignite military propellants to determine how fast they burned and at what depth they would begin to detonate rather than burn. The powder in photo flash cartridges usually won the powder train races or free standing detonation contests. It's truly amazing what a fertile brain can think up when surrounded with tons of material to work with. However, I am quite certain that my simple day dreams did not hold a candle to some of the more experienced men's adventures in refining the field of explosives in everyday life.

Of course there was other less hazardous diversion at times when the war slowed and the men became bored. Tex and I enjoyed inerting explosive ordnance, especially weapons employed by the V.C. The communist ordnance ranged from sophisticated multinational factory produced weapons to very crude homemade items. Some of the explosive items of local origins displayed a cunning ingenuity that required extra effort on our part in order to be safely inerted. The wooden handled Chinese stick hand grenades were one of our favorite projects. Since we had a full case of new factory-fresh potato mashers nearly everyone in the unit had a chance to disassemble at least one of these sought-after war trophies. Many of these Chinese stick grenades were presented as a memento to officers returning to the world. The demand for these items was high but it was our rule to reserve enough inert grenades so that EOD men could also be awarded this honor upon completion of our time in country.

THE DELTA – A VERY MEMORABLE DAY

Towards the end of my tour in Viet Nam I was down in bed with some unknown illness. This problem had been on-going for over 60 days and the military doctors suggested I either go home or lie down and die.

There was one doctor that I knew and in fact he had worked with Junior, Tex, and I when we removed the M 79, 40mm grenade from a dead GI's head. I trusted this doctor because he was the only one in the Medivac hospital that night who volunteered to help us. I looked him up and his recommendation was the same, go home because the medical facilities in country were set up to treat gapping flesh wounds. It seems they were not equipped to diagnose illnesses.

Anyway I was laying on my bunk about midday when the First Sgt. came in and asked if I felt up to flying down into the delta on a call. He explained that everyone else was out on calls and that left only him and me. Just to make matters more interesting the First Sgt. confessed that a bottle of Crown Royal had attacked him earlier and that he was in no condition to do any work. He freely admitted that I would have to do all the work and that he was just going along as a witness.

I would have loved to say no, but what can a person do when asked by the First Sgt. to help, after all he could have just as easily ordered me to go. So I grabbed my gear and we rushed to the chopper pad where a warmed up huey awaited our bidding. It was just about this time that the thought stuck me that maybe I should have asked just exactly where we were going and what type of call we had.

We traveled by air enough to know some of the flight crews but I didn't recognize any of these men. The pilots and door gunners were friendly but stated they had a lot of traffic that day so they appreciated our being on time. We climbed in thru the wide side doors and took off immediately heading south in the direction of the vast delta area.

The four corp. area was a wide flatland created by the silt from the Mekong River. On the map this area is marked with many canals and water ways but few roads. From the air the canals looked like long straight brown lines that cut thru the green rice paddies and fields. These waterways seemed to stretch to the horizon and were used for irrigation and transportation. The lack of roads and bridges over the waterways as well as impenetrable forests were the reason we were traveling by helicopter.

We landed in a hastily prepared L.Z. or landing zone that the local engineer company had cut out of the brush with their bull dozers. Not feeling well and hoping to return to Long Binh that night I asked the huey's crew chief if they would be able to wait for us or at least pick us up later. The pilot turned around and told us that he had to ferry a Col. somewhere but promised with a wide smile and a thumbs up that he would not leave us stranded out there over night.

An officer from the engineer company was waiting to greet us and led the way to our assignment. Everyone ducked from the blades and debris caused by the huey taking off and for some reason all eyes watched as the chopper tipped nose down trying to make top speed as it flew back out on an exact reverse heading that we had approached the L.Z. on. It was common knowledge that this was a bad practice because Charlie would watch a helicopter land then hurry to the area of that flight path in hopes of catching them returning on the same heading. If the chopper returned on the same path and Charlie had enough time they would set up an ambush for the low flying bird. That happened to be just the case on this flight, for the pilot in his rush to make everyone happy chose to retrace his path. Suddenly we heard an explosion and the huey fell from the sky.

We all stood in stunned silence for a moment before the engineer officer directed some of his troops to go to the downed crews' aid. It sounded good but we all knew that it was a waste of time. We hadn't gone far when the rescue team reported back to the officer that everyone aboard the huey had died.

Even though we expected as much, the word of the helicopter crew's death came as a shock. I had just enjoyed a long flight with these men and had even spoken to them just minutes before they met their fate. I have always carried a feeling of guilt over this incident, because I knew they were busy and yet for foolish selfish reasons I asked them to do a little more. I have no way of knowing if that pilot would have flown out the same course if I had not asked a favor of him, but in any case several good men were dead.

Our little group exchanged silent glances, possibly out of respect or possibly in a silent prayer of thanks that we were not numbered with the dead. Still it's amazing how military training and dedication to duty takes hold and we all turned to face our objective. We walked a short distance to a waiting APC that would transport us thru the engineers company bivouac area. Their living quarters consisted of wide deep trenches they had dug out of the sandy soil with their own equipment. The trenches were covered with tents or pieces of steel, all this may sound dismal but living in a hole in the ground was much safer than in tents above ground.

At this compound we joined up with more track vehicles, part of which were metal shielded bull dozers. As I have stated before an APC was a large metal box on tracks that most soldiers considered a death trap if you were attacked while riding inside. It was standard procedure to ride on the flat tops of these APC's, the idea being it was better to be killed out in the open than trapped inside.

In any case we were given our choice of riding inside the APC or outside as the little slow moving convoy proceeded out onto a wide open plain bordered by heavy jungle. The offer was made because the engineers traveled this route twice a day and always received at least small arms fire from the tree line. We chose to ride on top of the APC but were fortunate to receive only light small arms fire and then most of it was directed at the lead bull dozer. These engineers had become so used to a few bullets ricocheting off of their vehicles that no one bothered to return fire. I gathered from the talk that if the firing was light and no one was hit it was better to ignore the whole matter.

This joy ride ended in what would be considered a jungle area that the engineers were busy clearing with their heavy equipment. Of the area that had been cleared, it was easy to spot the numerous air holes and openings to a vast V.C. underground tunnel complex. I suddenly had a vision of me crawling into one of these forbidding tunnels to dispose of some booby trap or cache of explosives. Now I am not claustrophobic but I am certainly not a tunnel rat and made up my mind before the APC rattled to a halt that I was not going to enter a V.C. tunnel.

For the uninitiated, the South Vietnamese people must be part gopher for they built large tunnel systems that were multi storied, some even had hospitals and ammo bunkers in them. They also had some home protective devices in the form of booby traps and pungi sticks, and poisonous snakes, not to mention Charlie waiting to spear or to shoot you. No, a V.C. tunnel was not the place for a little fat man like me. The military had people known as tunnel rats who were trained in the suicidal art of inspecting these subterranean hell holes. But my worries were wasted for the engineers had called us all the way down to the delta to handle one 175 mm artillery round that was obviously a booby trap. I was so thankful that I would be staying above ground that I didn't care what sort of item I would have to work on.

The 175 mm artillery shells are very large and heavy and contain a good amount of high explosives. This particular 175 had obviously been set up as some type of booby trap for it sat on the edge of its base with the nose and fuse leaning in the crotch of a small tree. The round had been fired but the chances of it landing in such a configuration would have been one in ten million. I presumed it had some type of anti-lift or anti-disturbance device under its' base for I couldn't see any trip wires or remote detonation devices.

I told the officer in charge of the engineers that I would have to get closer in order to determine just what we were dealing with and that his personnel would have to pull back to a safe area and stop shaking the ground with their heavy equipment.

Just at that time a company of South Vietnamese soldiers, known as ARVNs came rolling in on an APCs supposedly to provide security. I questioned the logic of this for the ARVNs were often more of a hindrance than a help and there were few Army engineer companies who needed anyone to protect them. This green clad band of merry men and their American advisor deployed in the same cleared area that the engineers had settled in. I

247

began to think that, being bored, many of those present were there for the show that they hoped I would put on.

I took stock of the audience then told my First Sgt. that I thought it best to take a closer look at this 175. He agreed to allow me to make a good recon of the situation. This sounded like a good plan for he was still a bit wobbly on his feet.

There were a couple of different paths leading to the 175 mm artillery round, one was a straight line while the other branched off in a semicircle and terminated at the far side of the leaning round. I was of course, alert to anything out of place or of an irregular nature. I paused at the fork in the trail to take stock and decide on which approach was best. One would think a direct line the best but I could see impression in the dust where small hands had attempted to rub away some sort of sign.

The first thing that comes to mind was that some V.C. had planted another mine on the obvious approach route to the 175 but on second thought it could be a ruse trying to divert me to take the longer trail which could have also been mined. O.K. which trail do you take or is making a new course a viable option. I only knew that it was hot and miserable and I didn't feel good and my teammate was not up to the task at hand. I looked over the roundabout trail very closely and couldn't see any sign of disturbance, or trip wires, not even sandal prints. It was time to decide and I chose the longer undisturbed trail that led to the far side of the 175mm. It was with great trepidation that I stepped onto this path that eventually brought me to the side of the artillery round. I made a quick inspection but without doing a lot of probing and moving around it was not possible to determine exactly how the V.C. had intended to initiate this device. I took great care on my return to the APC to step in the same tracks as my jungle boots made coming in.

Why I bothered to ask the First Sgt. his opinion of my plan to blow up the 175 mm artillery round is a mute question. The man was standing alone in the middle of the clearing with both hands stuffed in his fatigue pants pockets and was swaying to and fro even though there wasn't any wind that day. I explained to him and the engineer officer as well as the Sgt. who was the ARVN advisor that I planned to gently place a block of C-4 on the big shell and destroy it in place. I also advised one and all to move out of the fragmentation range. I tried to stress that placing the adhesive backed block of C-4 on the projectile could be a touchy procedure, hoping they would curtail at least some of the noise and activity coming from the ARVN troops.

I capped up two equal lengths of time fuse and picked up a 2 pound block of C-4 that now came wrapped in green cellophane with a strip of sticky tape on the back side. I once again stepped in my old tracks until I arrived at the far side of the 175 where I inserted the blasting caps into the plastic explosive. The plan called for sticking the C-4 on the projectile at the junction of the nose fuse and the body of the shell casing. This particular spot was chosen because it is one of the most vulnerable places on such a projectile, that and the fact that the nose fuse was well supported by the crotch of the little tree.

I looked back at the First Sgt. who still had his hands in his pockets and was swaying back and forth like a drunken sailor. There was no sign of recognition from the man and I wondered for a brief instant if he knew just what I was doing. It would have been reassuring to know that if anything went wrong my

249

witness would have been able to state what had taken place.

I took a decp breath and gently touched the C-4 block to the steel body of the artillery round. It had just made contact when a sudden explosion ripped thru the jungle area. I paused for a second trying to judge how badly I had been injured or to determine if I might be dead. But I hadn't any pain and the 175 mm shell was still leaning in the same place and my hand still held the block of C-4. Many, many thoughts raced thru my brain in the split second after that detonation. I of course, thought the 175 had detonated, or the block of C-4 had gone off or that I had triggered another mine or that possibly Charlie couldn't resist all of those troops gathered in one spot and had started dropping mortars on us.

Whatever had exploded, I was still able to set the shot so I pressed the C-4 securely to the projectile, pulled the fuse lighters and began to make my way back to the APC. It was at this point that I got a good look at my First Sgt who was now standing erect, hands out of his pockets looking sober as a judge. I chuckled to myself thinking the whole thing was worthwhile for that explosion had scared the hell out of the First Sgt. and most of the other onlookers. We moved to a safe area and watched as the 175 detonated right on time; its powerful blast was followed by some secondary explosions which reinforced our belief that the area around the projectile had been mined.

The entire group, Americans and ARVNs enjoyed watching the 175 mm artillery round explode harmlessly except for destroying the little tree. Wearing a smile, I have to admit to being a bit proud of the outcome of this relatively simple call. I was just turning around to speak to the First Sgt. when I realized that some kind of a disturbance had erupted among the South Vietnamese troops and their American advisor.

I watched in amazement as the American advisor and a couple of his ARVN troops began to rough up a small South Vietnamese army private. They pushed and prodded this little fellow all the way across the clearing, finally ending up directly in front of me. The American struck the ARVN private several times about the head and shoulders with a long wooden bullet tipped swagger stick. The victim seemed resigned to taking the physical abuse, only flinching under the blows of the hard wooden stick.

The American advisor then explained that this little man was the person responsible for the explosion while I was trying to carefully set the C-4 on the 175. This led to further humiliation of the private and an offer was made for me to beat him or shoot him or whatever I thought equaled his offense. The poor fellow stood head down ready for whatever punishment I decided to dole out. I have to admit that I pretended to be upset by the man's disregard for my safety but truthfully we were trained to ignore such outside distractions. I also have to admit I secretly enjoyed the prestige and power suddenly thrust on me to determine this man's fate. So in keeping with the role I demanded an explanation as to why he had set off an explosion at that critical time.

The man mumbled out a lengthy excuse in Vietnamese and broken English, part of which I managed to understand. I gathered that he had fired an M-79 40 MM grenade for some reason. That was not good enough because we were not under attack at the moment and I could not see any targets that called for such a weapon to be employed. The advisor and some of the other ARVN soldiers began to explain that the man had shot a small deer. Well, I didn't see any deer carcass lying around and scoffed at the weak excuse. The guilty man now all smiles motioned for me to follow him and the others to an APC. The little man scampered on top the vehicle and quickly returned with the absolutely smallest deer I had ever seen. The American advisor explained that they called these mouse deer and that the man was something of a hero with the other troops for supplementing their normally meager rations of plain rice.

The smile on the young ARVN soldiers face reflected his pride in taking this miniature antlerless deer. You would have thought that he had just made a record book kill, when in fact most Americans eat more meat in a single day than this tiny creature would provide. Still these hungry troops would stretch this meager meat to feed ten or fifteen men.

The American advisor still demanded to know what I wanted to do with the errant soldier who stood so resolutely before us. I didn't feel it was my place to dictate his punishment for he was not under my command nor was it my orders he had ignored. Besides, I came from a poor family and grew up on a dead end dirt road which for most practical purposes put me out of reach of all but the most understanding game wardens. Under my father's excellent training I became a year-around substancy hunter and can well appreciate the pride of returning from a long days hunt with nothing more to show than a cotton tail rabbit or a skinny squirrel. While there is not much meat on either animal, an ingenious cook can make a feast of such game as in a rabbit pot pie; a dish I relished as a youth.

I guess I saw a lot of myself in this hungry ARVN soldier and considering no harm had really been done; it was easy to dismiss the matter. I gave the skinny ARVN soldier a playful blow to the mid section then laughed and shook his hand. I glanced at the American advisor and I could tell from the expression on his face this was the results he had expected.

"I guessed you right." The American Sgt. laughed. "Somehow I just knew you were a hunter at heart." He added. We laughed and talked for a moment, and then he suggested we load up on his APC because some V.C. were moving in to the tree line just behind us.

This seemed like a good idea as we would be without transportation. The ARVN soldiers sitting on top of the APC made room for me on the left side of the vehicle right next to the then new .30 cal machine gun. I have been a life-long weapons enthusiast and thought this a good opportunity to observe this machine gun up close.

The American advisor directed the APC driver to move up to within about 30 yards of the tree line and then stop parallel to it. He then ordered the new machine gunner beside me to fire into the area where the V.C. were thought to be hiding. In all my interest in this new weapon, I had failed to notice that the operator had not released the catch that locked the muzzle pointing down and rearward in what is considered a safe travel position. The advisor was seated directly behind me and when the machine gunner failed to follow his orders and fire the Sgt. struck the man over the head with the same stick he had used on the private earlier. The frightened gunner jumped forward tripped the trigger and fired a short burst into the ground beside the APC. The biggest problem I could see with this foolishness derived from the fact that my feet were in line with the muzzle of the new machine gun. The muzzle blast struck my right foot with such force that I was certain I had been shot. It was just dumb luck that my feet were not hit by a bullet and that the machine gun mount and lock had held the weapon securely in place. I know that if the terrified ARVN had

253

been able to move the machine gun's barrel he would have surely shot me. The American advisor reassured my belief in this theory as he took up beating the dimwitted machine gun operator once more. He suggested I move out of the way as the gunner unlocked his mount and made it quite clear that this man had better fire at the designated target this time.

The second attempt did go much smoother with the machine gunner throwing a lot of lead into one particular unfortunate tree. The advisor then called for a recon by fire, which means everyone is to fire their weapon into the jungle in hopes of killing or driving off any V.C. hiding there. I refrained from this order for it always seemed to me that if every weapon is fired until empty at some unseen target then what happens if the enemy begins to fire back. I always envisioned a picture of a bunch of soldiers suddenly receiving fire without loaded weapons to use in defense. I held my fire and waited for the game to flush but nothing moved until we started to move away and then Charlie began to fire back.

Those in power decided it was time to pull out of the area so the little slow moving parade formed up for the return to the engineers camp. Once again Charlie remained hidden in the surrounding jungle firing harassing shots as we rode confidently and definitely out in the open. This whole affair seemed like a tradition where our side was determine to clear all the foliage in South Viet Nam while the other side felt obligated to shoot at those defiling the jungle.

We returned to the engineer's compound in late afternoon with no idea of what we would do next. I felt these engineers would be more hospitable than some of the units we were forced to stay within the past. Still when you are not part of a unit it's easy to get lost in the shuffle and this particular camp was not an ideal place to be lost.

We checked on truck transport but there wasn't anything going by this late in the evening, nor were any M.P.'s nearby and it seemed that air transportation was out of the question. Then suddenly we heard from a huey pilot heading north who offered to give us a lift if he could get into the little hastily made landing zone before dark. We hurried out to the landing zone in time to hear the beautiful sound of a Huey helicopter approaching from over the jungle. We said quick good-byes and jumped into the side door of the huey the instant it touched down because it was understood that this bird was not going to roost here that night. It was one of those touch and go landings where the copter's skids hit the ground, bounced once and was back in the air. This short time frame on the ground prevents Charlie from materializing out of the dark and attacking the chopper.

Our EOD teams frequently traveled by helicopter, in all kinds of weather and times of day but this was a unique experience for me because the flight was made in total darkness. South Viet Nam was a country devoid of lights at night owning to the fact that the V.C. liked to rocket or mortar such easily defined targets but it was still interesting to search the blackness below for signs of life. I watched the illuminated gauges and dials on the pilots console and wondered just where we were.

Everything that goes up must come down so they say and hueys seemed to come down all too often and in the wrong places. Being forced down in broad day light is not considered a good time but at least you know where you are and you can see any threats coming your way. I began to wonder just how terrifying a crash landing at night would be. You would have no way of knowing where you are or where to go. Your survival would be a matter of luck and I felt I had pushed my bad luck too far that day. As I stared into the ocean of blackness below in an effort to get a fix on anything that might give me an indication of our location, the other passengers were nodding off. As we flew north out of the delta area I began to pick up points of light that I recognized from day light flights and felt more confident about the situation. We landed safely at Long Binh in the middle of the night and I admit to saying a little prayer of thanks, although I doubt if many people ever said a word of thanks for being delivered safely back to that particular post.

I must add after finishing this insignificant little tale that I nearly erased it on several occasions. Some of it is troubling to me; some parts I find a bit humorous still other parts are a little bit exciting. But the reason I decided to leave it intact is that it was a representative day in our lives, and I am sure that every active EOD man had many such experiences. Now after several decades have passed, many of my days in country have blurred or are completely forgotten, some admittedly by choice. However this particular day is clear in my memory due in part to the many varied experiences that were packed into just a few hours.

ELEPHANT SNOT

Of course I can recall only portions of some days and have absolutely no idea of what occurred before or after that memorable hour. An example of this would be the day we explosive experts were called to the main gate of Long Binh depot to handle a report of an explosive spill.

On arriving at the incident site we were shown a truck loaded with clear tube shaped plastic bags that were about three feet long and eight inches in diameter that weighed 50 pounds each. We discovered that some of the plastic bags had ruptured and leaked out their contents, a thick greenish yellow liquid that had the consistency of corn syrup.

Neither I nor my partner had ever seen this particular liquid explosive but as experts, we were not about to admit to our ignorance. Our training had told us that most liquid blasting explosives were not very sensitive so that became our diagnosis.

We cleaned up the sticky substance and permitted the load to move on into the depot for storage. We hurried the short distance back to the unit to question the rest of the team about this unknown item when it became apparent the liquid which became known to us as 'elephant snot' was highly corrosive.

Our skin began to burn and soon our uniforms and jungle boots were deteriorating. I would compare the stinging to that of coming into contact with battery acid.

It was soon discovered that no one knew of this new explosive and we had to do some in-depth research to get any information on it. Our unit had additional occasions to handle this nasty burning substance and word quickly spread to be prepared when called to recover any of the spilled elephant snot.

As I said before I cannot recall anything about what happened before or after this particular incident.

CIA MAN'S DANGEROUS JEEP

Another such incident that I have no recollection of what happened either before or after the event began in the middle of a bright sunny day when we received a call from depot security that a strange looking booby trap device had been spotted in the middle of the main depot road. The whole thing sounded peculiar from the start, causing everyone to question how such a device would suddenly appear at this time of day in the middle of a very busy depot. Still it was not our place to question such calls but merely to respond. The loss or even major damage to Long Binh ammunition depot would have been very detrimental to the war effort and our unit took great pride in trying to prevent such catastrophes.

As it often happened we had company in our unit bar that day in the form of a civilian CIA man, who as I recall posed as a contractor. This man drove a jeep that was painted grey and was shod with conventional car tires rather than the tactical tread tires that were standard military issue. The tactical tread tires had a zig zag center lug with heavy rubber cleats that slanted in from each side. This design worked fairly well in off road situations whereas the street tread tires on this man's jeep worked much better on hard surfaced streets.

When the call came in, three of us jumped up and headed out the back door of our bar. As we exited the CIA man called out for us to use his jeep because it was parked behind ours. This offer made us hesitate for a second because our jeeps had bright red fenders plus red lights and sirens that the depot security would immediately recognize. We looked for a way to get our jeeps out but time was wasting so the grey jeep would have to do. Just as we began to climb into the grey jeep the CIA man appeared at the door and yelled out not to get in his jeep. He paused a second then called out again to go ahead and take the jeep. With that he disappeared back into the bar and we headed for the depot's main gate in his jeep.

The gate guards who were unable to recognize an EOD team in a grey jeep, not only failed to stop traffic for us but tried to stop us as we flew passed them. This required us to dodge heavily loaded semi truck traffic while trying to negotiate the rough dusty dirt road. Not far inside the depot was a 90 degree corner that was deep mud during the monsoon season or deep powdery dust in the dry season. I was driving the grey jeep as we came into the sharp dusty corner; a corner we had all taken before at high speed in our tactical tired jeep.

It has been said that most EOD people drove at a high rate of speed even when not responding to an emergency call and we were no different that day. Perhaps a prudent person would have been a little more conservative when driving an unknown vehicle but I figured that one M151 jeep would handle just like any other M151 jeep--lousy. Of course I didn't take into consideration the street tread tires on this grey M151 and when we hit the deep talcum powder dust on that 90 degree corner all hell broke loose. The little jeep jumped straight in the air and turned sideways causing us to cross the road backwards. We slid to a stop amid a dense cloud of blinding dust, while the other two guys cursed me soundly for what I considered a good piece of driving. I shifted into low and tore back out on the depot road as fast as possible for there was no time to relive or dissect my driving abilities.

We raced on down thru the depot until spotting some of the security people parked in the middle of the road. Sliding to a stop we three grabbed our tool pouches and jumped out, moving quickly to the suspicious item protruding from the middle of the hard packed dirt road. This unknown item was a tube about 1 inch in diameter and about two feet long that tapered at each end. The ends appeared to have wire sticking out of them and the body's exterior looked to be made of a flexible black plastic.

I searched my memory but couldn't recall anything from EOD school or my field experience that even vaguely resembled such an item. Then someone said it looked a lot like the splices that the communications guys used to repair broken phone lines. It was clear that someone had just buried half of the device in the ground so we took care when digging it up to be sure the bottom was not attached to a booby trap. We found nothing hidden and declared our find to be a phone line patch. We placed the item in the back of the jeep then climbed aboard for a more leisurely drive back to the unit.

On the short trip from the depot to our unit the subject came up of the CIA man's strange behavior when we were departing with his jeep. It was agreed that one way or another we would get an explanation as to the CIA man's actions. Back at the unit, I parked the grey jeep by the bars rear door, and then headed inside to speak to our guest. The man was well into his drink and he laughed when we related the story about spinning out in the dusty corner. He admitted that he should have warned us about the jeeps peculiar handling problems, then added that he had other things on his mind at that moment. When we asked why he came to the door and told us not to take his jeep and then said it was alright to use, he laughed again saying that was what he had on his mind when he forgot to warn us about the handling problems. I said that I didn't understand what he was talking about but wished he would explain. He laughingly agreed to tell all for one more drink. I bought the man a drink and he led us all outside to his dusty grey jeep. He leaned in took a quick look then rocked the driver's seat forward to expose a two pound block of C-4 tucked up inside the seats frame work. I might add that the driver's seat sets right on top of the gas tank, not that it would make much difference if two pounds of C-4 detonated under your butt. The C-4 was wired with an electric cap and the wires disappeared in the wiring harness that ran up under the dash.

"See that toggle switch?" The CIA man asked pointing to a small switch on the dash. "That switch arms this block of C-4 so if a person turns the starter switch when that toggle is in the armed position it blows the jeep and occupant to hell." "I've had a couple of jeeps stolen so I began to rig this little surprise for the thief and it has worked great every time." He laughed again. "When I stopped you from taking my jeep I couldn't remember if the switch was in the armed position or not."

A serious discussion broke out over the merits of such a serious anti-theft device and the fact that if one of us had thrown that switch out of curiosity or if it had gotten accidently bumped when we slid off the road we would all be dead. He conceded that is exactly what would have happened but it didn't so in his mind everything was alright. The discussion continued a bit more heated than before. The result was that we all agreed not to take any other vehicles on emergency calls except our own and to never ride with this particular CIA man in his jeep.

This sort of individual creativity was quite common in country. It behooved a person to inquire and carefully examine any situation before taking any rash action.

262

OPIUM PIPE

One unusual call I responded to concerned a reported homemade Bangalore torpedo. I'm ashamed that I cannot recall who accompanied me on this call but at this point the 3rd Ord was blessed with good experienced men who could be entrusted to handle any given situation. I felt comfortable working with any member of this team of professionals and as such this man did nothing notable to aid my memory.

The directions lead us off base to a small unit where we were shown a bamboo tube about 30 inches long, 2 inches in diameter and painted bright blue. The tube lay within some concertina wire that prevented us from getting close enough for a good visual inspection. Still we could see that one end of the bamboo tube was closed by a crude hand whittled wooden plug, while the opposite end had a can forced over it. The can had a small tube running out of it while two thirds of the way down the pipe was a small funnel shaped piece of metal poked into a hole in the bamboo. We immediately recognized this as an opium pipe, an item commonly reported to us as an explosive device. A pretty simple item to handle except that it was placed in concertina wire as a Bangalore torpedo is normally employed; that and the fact this pipe was painted bright blue.

My team mate and I began to out-think ourselves by wondering if this opium pipe might have been converted into a Bangalore torpedo serving as a booby trap. We reasoned it could be filled with explosives with some type of anti-disturbance switch hidden inside or it could be placed on some type of booby trap. Many ideas were bantered about until it was decided that we must move it remotely by use of a rope just to be safe.

We tied a rope around the piece of brilliant blue bamboo and backed off a safe distance. The big pull was anti-climatic for nothing happened and a resulting dismantling of the bright blue opium pipe revealed nothing but drug residue. The whole thing was disappointing and a waste of time but it was typical of the foolishness that some calls turned out to be.

The "why" and "how" a bright blue opium pipe was placed inside the protective concertina wire we will never know but I'll bet some bored GI thought it would be fun to watch us disarm this item. Although we appeared to be too overly careful in disposing of this device, it's stupid stunts like this that lead EOD personnel to become complacent and lax in their safety procedures.

PULLING RANK

There were calls that resulted in nothing more than a hand full of live small arms rounds or empty hand-held flare tubes. When mortars are used to light up the night sky, they are fired to a preset altitude where the tail section separates from the main body. At that point the flare is expelled and with the aid of a parachute drifts slowly back to earth while the mortar shells two body parts plummet back to the ground. These two body halves are quite harmless but people often call in EOD units to dispose of these inert items.

It was not unheard of when responding to a call to have an inexperienced officer try to prevent a mere enlisted man from performing his duty. The lower the enlisted EOD man's rank, the more often this happened, with the objecting party demanding an officer perform the render safe procedure. This sort of unreasonable objection usually centered on some relatively mundane piece of ordnance like an inert hand grenade or a belt of machine gun ammo. I always found a little pleasure in explaining that any person who wore the EOD badge regardless of rank was completely qualified to perform any and all render safe procedures or they would not be wearing the insignia. Of course there were instances where the objecting party would not listen to reason. It was at that point we would bid them a pleasant good day and turn to leave. This often resulted in permission to dispose of the item or an irate call back to the unit where the facts of life were thoroughly explained to the caller.

Many military people and it seemed young officers especially became very nervous in the presence of even the simplest piece of ordnance. I have often thought that their basic training must have been lacking or that being inexperienced had no idea what to expect in a war zone. I am certain that some of these people thought they were still back in the world, walking down a quiet city street and not in the land of an armed enemy.

We refrained from looking over anyone's shoulder or trying to second guess a man's action. There were times when the lowest ranking man would draw the more difficult or dangerous items. Never once did I encounter a lower ranking EOD man ask a higher ranking NCO or officer to handle a hazardous situation or vice versa.

We had a major over all Army EOD who would show up at the 3rd Ord unannounced and make himself a team member. The major would usually remove his shirt and once on site would not assume command but rather insist that my partner and I were in charge. The major would ask what he could do to help and then begin filling sand bags or help in digging a hole. He might make a suggestion or ask if we had considered an alternative but he never took command. I had a great deal of respect for this man because he really understood the EOD traditions of that time.

ACED OUT OF A CALL

Most people in the states never realize the amount of on-the-job training a new person in Viet Nam had to endure. Everything from uniforms to chow on base was unfamiliar. Everything from language to traffic rules was different off base. We had an unwritten rule that new personnel in country could go on off-post calls only in the company of an experienced man.

One of our many First Sgts forcefully implemented several new rules after he attained leadership of the 3rd Ord. Most of the new rules were based on a need to hurry, a word the locals didn't understand and the men of our unit refused to live by. This man demanded that our phone be answered in three rings or less and radio response had to be immediate. I am a firm believer that only a fool hurries when working with explosives not to mention explosives that were intended to end your career.

One beautiful south East Asian day Junior and I were scheduled to catch a chopper to the delta on a booby trap call. We also received a call on the phone that only rang twice before Dick Hause answered asking for our help at one of the local Medivac hospitals. We had plenty of time to respond to the hospital and return in time to catch the helicopter flight, but when we arrived back at the building we learned that the new First Sgt had talked our new commanding officer into taking our flight.

I have to admit being aced out of the call did get under my skin, but more importantly I worried about two novice men going on a flight to the middle of nowhere. It was irresponsible not to mention dangerous for our two top ranking rookies to take an off-post call together.

The phone may have rang more than three times per call that afternoon but somehow we managed to keep the unit running. However one of those calls reported that the little observation helicopter that the C.O. and First Sgt were on had crashed in the delta. There was little information on the condition of their injuries or the outcome of the call.

We later learned that the C.O. had several injuries and would be sent home, the pilot also had received broken bones, while our First Sgt had sustained some back damage but would be returning to the unit. We were all relieved to know that no one had been seriously injured or killed in the crash and that some good people in the field had taken care of our men. I never saw the C.O. again but the First Sgt returned to us that same day.

Now it should be obvious to even nonmilitary people that an E-5 seldom wins an argument with an E-7 but I initiated one with the First Sgt, right after his not-so-triumphant return. I scolded him for taking what was supposed to be our call and for going off base with another new man. I told him that we were not here to set speed records but rather to do the job and hopefully survive. Naturally the man did not like my opinions but he reluctantly agreed he should not have been so anxious.

When I had said my piece, Junior and I walked out of the office toward the mess hall where he reminded me how stupid I was for complaining about the First Sgt. stealing our call. He reasoned correctly that the First Sgt and the C.O. had done us a great favor in taking the flight, because it would have been us that received the injuries and they might have been much worse. This was something I had never considered but then Junior was always more level headed than me.

I never heard about our new C.O. again and I am told the First Sgt died not long after returning home. They were both good men that made the mistake of being in a hurry, which can be dangerous in a land where time has little meaning and the enemy is all about you.

RACING THE MP'S

One bright sunny day my partner and I headed down the highway south of Long Binh in response to what proved to be a minor call. We drove merrily along the winding black top road that passed thru some neglected rubber tree plantations until we located the incident site. Following our directions we turned off the main road and wandered about on some two track roads to a little building in the middle of nowhere.

It was a lovely drive but proved to be a complete waste of time, for once again the reported item posed no threat to anyone. We found our way back to the highway where as luck would have it, we found a military police armored car leisurely patrolling the empty black topped road. Our unit was holding a rare party that night and we hoped to be back in time but the posted speed limit on that strip of road was I believe 35 mph. Knowing we would have to hurry to get back to the unit before all of the food was gone it was distressing to see the M.P. vehicle.

Now, our jeeps were equipped with red lights, sirens, two way radios and loud speakers on the fenders. For the most part the M.P's were pretty lenient to EOD indiscretions but we were not sure who was operating this particular armored car so I got on the P.A. system and gave them a call. The conversation continued as we drove up the highway until I joking asked them if they wanted to race to the Bear Cat turn off. Next thing I knew the road race was on, red lights and sirens echoing off the stately old rubber trees as each vehicle struggled to out run the other one. I had a fearless wheel man driving that day and he gave a good showing of our unit's fastest jeep.

The two vehicles roared along side by side for some distance until approaching the finish line where the M.P.'s had to turn off. It was decided that allowing the military police to win and save their face would be wise, so without being obvious we threw the race and yelled a congratulations over the P.A. speaker.

I should explain that when I say roaring I mean these vehicles at top speed was around 60 miles an hour. I doubt if we ever exceeded 70 mph in the race but it was still exciting in such ill handling equipment. The unofficial M.P. escort had allowed us to return to the unit on time for the party and the food that was most important to two under fed GI's. However, SFC. Smith was waiting at the unit's office door as we slid the jeep in among all the guest's vehicles parked just out front.

"Who won?" He demanded in a serious voice.

"Who won what?" I asked playing my stupid role to a tee -- it comes naturally.

"Who won the road race?"

Well you know where the conversation went from there, acquisitions and denials but as the party wore on I did my best to find out just how Smitty found out about the race. He never revealed his source and I never confessed but how he ever found out, we will never know; the word must have traveled faster than our jeep had.

I would like to say we were severely reprimanded by SFC Smith but he was much too good of a leader and gentleman to ruin the couple of rare hours of pleasure the party provided for a lot of hard working GI's.

Thanks Smitty.

GUARD DUTY WITHOUT WEAPONS

SFC Smith was a man with compassion for the underdog or the lowly; in Viet Nam this emotion was directed at low ranking enlisted men who drew the difficult, lonely, or nerve racking duty. He would take time especially at night to visit with men on bunker line duty. These men were clerks and ammo humpers who were not trained for combat and were often times not very familiar with fire arms.

Smitty always wore a wide grin that might be difficult to see in a dark bunker but somehow even strangers knew it was there. He had the ability to calm the jitters and build self-confidence in the inexperienced young soldiers.

I will give these men their just dues for serving guard duty in these bunkers. Imagine spending a long dark night with some other nervous G.I. in a hole in the ground. Oh, there were sand bags and claymore mines, if they worked and concertina wire to protect you. But V.C. sappers had learned how to crawl undetected and unscathed thru this barbed wire on steroids. Even if the V.C. didn't attack or sneak thru the wire there was plenty of nocturnal wild life prowling about to keep the dead awake.

There had been some question about the functioning or possible malfunctioning of the before-mentioned claymores on the bunker line that found Junior and me spending a day investigating the weapons operating conditions.

The claymore mine is a device filled with explosives; often times C-4 that has a layer of shrapnel attached to one side. When the explosives are detonated the shrapnel is blown in one direction like a very powerful shotgun. If used correctly the claymore is a very formidable weapon that any wise warrior will detour around.

Our bunker line was festooned with these little green plastic claymore mines that were pointed towards the enemy just as the wording on the front of the mine directed. These mines were tied in a series; the first one would be fire electrically and was initiated by a soldier in the bunker. The remainder of the mines was tied to the first by detonating cord. Det cord or primer cord as it is known, often times looks like plastic clothes line rope but the inside is filled with a very fast and powerful powdered explosive. Det cord is a fine tool and when used properly it is very reliable.

Junior and I visited the bunker line one bright clear south east Asian afternoon to investigate the report of claymores failing to detonate. We entered a bunker and explained to the two men on guard duty why we were there and what we planned to do. Once they were clear as to our intent we confiscated the little generating device used to fire the first claymore's blasting cap. I am sure these troops would not have detonated the mines while we were inspecting them but the weight of that little generator in my pocket was very reassuring.

From the bunker we could see red plastic cord running from claymore to claymore which presented a picture that everything was alright but Junior and I were always a bit more thorough in our work. Others who had gazed out of the bunker and saw the red lines assumed the mines were ready to be fired but not us; we had to get up close and personal.

We did not have to get very close to the mines before realizing that the top half of the det cord had been eaten by what appeared from the teeth marks to have

273

been rodents. Whatever had attacked the red primer cord had chewed off the top of the plastic coating, and then ate the explosives leaving the bottom of the plastic for us to see. From the bunker the remaining plastic made a person think that the det cord was in good working order but without the explosives it was just a plastic string bleaching in the intense Asian sun.

The theory of these claymore mines was to give the bunker line a massive explosive repellant if Charlie should attack in mass. The claymores were filled with explosives and a layer of steel fragmentation that was pointed to the enemy. The detonation of the claymore mines produced a very powerful shotgun effect to the front and a very destructive blast in the other directions. The mines were placed several feet in front and below the manned bunkers. If attacked they had a small hand held generator that was used to fire an electric blasting cap placed in one of the upper corners of the mine. When the first mine detonated it would in turn set off the detonation cord which would initiate the other claymores in a domino-like effect. It was a very fast domino-effect; because if everything went correctly the mines would explode at a near simultaneous rate.

We had all too quickly discovered why the claymore mines had failed to explode, but we had yet to find out why the first mine that was fired by an electric blasting cap had not functioned. When we opened up the cap-wells we found them to be full of mud deposited there by the dirty monsoon rains. We could not determine if the mud had insulated the mine from the caps initiating blast or if the normally sealed blasting caps had been soaked in rain water long enough that they became contaminated.

Whatever the reason we reported our findings to the Powers-That-Be with a suggestion that the detonating cord be inspected and replaced at shorter intervals and that the electric blasting cap wells be sealed in some manner. Whether these suggestions were taken to heart I never knew, but it seemed foolish to sct mines that would fail.

Now what has all of this to do with SFC Smith visiting the bunker line you ask? Well as it happened Junior and I were near the bunker line one dark night and decided to take Smitty's suggestion and visit the bunker where we had found the disabled claymores. We parked our jeep well away from the bunkers then approached on foot very slowly through the hot dark night.

These particular outposts where built on top of a dirt levee that prevented the V. C. from seeing our movements thus preventing their snipers from taking a shot at us. This levee had to be climbed to reach the bunker unless (as in this case) a shallow ditch had been made for easier access to the back of the bunker.

There is a set rule or protocol that most people readily obey when approaching a manned bunker at night and especially so on a dark night. The wise man crouches low as he nears the base of the levee then stops to whisper out a hailing call to the men inside. If they don't respond to your call, you try again but you never just blunder into such situations because the guards are usually nervous and they are armed with automatic weapons.

When you finally receive a whispered invitation to enter, you remain low and move quietly into the guard's nerve-racking world. These men greatly appreciate visitors not being noisy or showing lights that will give away their exact position.

On this particular night I believe Junior and I gave the guards a couple of cans of pop along with a little inspirational talk. It was obvious that both guards were very edgy but different men react differently to a like situation. Finally the question of how much action they had seen this night was asked. Both men responded that everything had been quiet and they hoped it remained that way because they did not have any weapons.

"What are you talking about?" I demanded in complete disbelief.

"Yeah that's right." One guard answered. "Could you guys stay with us for a while?" He added hopefully. "We can stay but I don't understand how you got on guard duty without any weapons." I insisted on an answer to my question.

"Oh, we have weapons, they are laying on that bench--field stripped." The guard said pointing to a plywood bench attached to the side of the bunker wall. There on the bench lay an M-16 rifle and an M-60 machine gun both of which were completely dismantled, with the parts laid out in perfect by the book order.

The guards explained that an inspection was planned for the next morning and that their First Sgt had told them to change into clean uniforms before sunrise. The First Sgt then field stripped the two weapons and laid them out with firm orders to leave them there until after the inspection.

This had to have been one of the stupidest things I had ever encountered in country. These men were our first line of defense for Long Binh Post and the idea of leaving them unarmed all night on the bunker line was tantamount to criminal act.

"If you're nervous about this put your weapons back together." I suggested still in shock at the situation.

"That's just the problem." One of the guards replied. "We don't know how to reassemble the M-60." He admitted a bit ashamed of the fact.

"Well **WE** know how to put it back together and if you want it reassembled we will be glad to do that." I offered.

"Sure we want it back together but the First Sgt will have our hides when he comes in and finds it back together." The guards insisted.

"Well you've got to decide if you want the First Sgt to have your hide or Charlie." I said with a grin.

The two guards talked it over and decided they would feel safer with machine guns that actually fired so Junior and I put the M-60 back into working order. The guards warned us that it would be hell to pay if the First Sgt found out who we were.

This was in my Don Quote days so I told him who we were and what unit we belonged to. I added that we would be happy to talk to their First Sgt anytime because I figured Junior could take this unknown First Sgt in a fair fight without problem.

Junior and I loaded a belt of ammunition into the machine gun then placed the weapon facing out of the bunker where it might do some good in case of a V.C. attack. We stayed and talked to the two young guards for a few minutes then cautiously worked our way back to the jeep. On our return to the EOD building Junior and I informed SFC Smith what had happened at the bunker line including the possibility that we might have to tangle with this unknown First Sgt. He said very little but I was sure I could detect real sympathy for the young guards.

Strangely enough I happened to be in the office the next day when the phone rang and Smitty answered with his normal official but pleasant greeting. However it was obvious that the caller was less than congenial, in fact it was the much heralded unknown First Sgt and he wanted our heads for messing up his inspection.

277

Now it usually took a lot to make Smitty hot under the collar, I should know for I tested his temper many times. But in this case he immediately got up a head of steam that came out in hot words and dire warnings. Smitty informed the Sgt on the other end of the phone line of the regulations he had broken and if anyone were in trouble it was him and not us. He then explained just how much he detested N.C.O.'s who had such little regard for their men as to endanger their lives needlessly. Finally Smitty warned the man that if anything more was said about this incident he would make the Sgt. regret the day he joined the Army and he was just the man to do it. Smitty then listed the officers that he was on first name bases with who would hear of how the men on guard duty were treated. He then explained that he and his men would be making repeated checks of the men on the bunker line in the future and that they damn well better be armed.

SFC Robert Smith was a kind hearted generous person who would and could take just about anything life handed out. But he was also the type of man you wanted to steer clear of once his Irish was up. Needless to say being the primary instigator of this row I vanished out of the side door before the telephone receiver was back in its cradle. I willingly admit that I not only disappeared, I found Junior and warned him as to what had happened. We decided to find some unsavory job that was out of sight of the office for the remainder of the day. Taking on some difficult task would make some points with Smitty if he should come looking for us or ask later in the day what we had been up to.

This may sound cheap and cowardly on our part but neither one of us wanted to tangle with Smitty when he was mad. I had a great deal of respect for SFC Smith but it wasn't his rank I feared nearly so much as the man behind the stripes.

I am glad to report that by supper time Smitty had regained his normal cool demeanor and nothing was ever said about the situation except that he still thought it a good idea to visit those guys out on the bunker line that were pulling guard duty.

This whole affair of the field stripped weapons on the bunker line is a testament to Smitty's leadership skills. Many a First Sgt would have taken the easy way out and thrown Junior and me to the wolves, but not Smitty for he was always committed to his troops and would defend them to the hilt if they were in the right. However if you were wrong he would make it abundantly clear the error of your ways. I can personally attest to Smitty's fairness because I received as many dressing downs as I did compliments from the man.

It may be difficult for anyone to believe that soldiers would be stationed in a combat area without being fully trained on the weapons they would be expected to use. The story above dealing with the bunker line or the story of the man on rear guard who was carrying an M-60 machine gun and had no idea how to load the weapon is truly shocking to me. During my limited exposure to the troops I encountered many men who had a very limited experience with the U.S. militaries commonly issued weapons. I discovered on teaching explosives classes to new men in country that the average G.I. had even less knowledge of our explosive weapons.

SAFE POLICY FOR CLAYMORES

A case in point concerns a question asked by a young soldier during one of these training classes.

The object of these classes was to introduce new men in country to ordnance, both ours and theirs that they might encounter, their dangers and what to do in case they were confronted with such hazards. We never intended these short classes to provide instructions in the use of explosives; instead the classes were for information and recognition.

Junior and I were giving a class to some new security people one hot afternoon and they were having a difficult time staying awake while I droned on about claymore mines. We had on display several inert V.C. claymores that were manufactured by hand in some local primitive shop.

As I stated before the claymore mines are a very effective weapon regardless of whether they are homemade or stamped out in some complex factory. These weapons are known as directional because when detonated the explosive charge propels pieces of metal in one direction. I suppose the term directional is what gives people the incorrect idea that it is possible to walk up behind a claymore and disarm it by removing the blasting cap. We always stressed in class that any explosion produces a 360 degree ball shaped blast wave. Just because a weapon is directional its detonation will still kill above, below, or to the sides.

"You absolutely do not want to be close to one of these items when they explode." I stated firmly hoping my words would sink into the young soldiers sleepy brains. I could see a little bit of buss among the group and thought that I might be getting to this bunch.

"How close?" One of the soldiers asked.

"It depends on if it is one of ours or one of theirs because the V.C. build their claymores in different sizes." "The more explosives the further away you want to be." I answered.

"How close can you be behind one of ours?" The same young soldier inquired.

"I believe it's a 30 meter kill zone and 60 meter wound zone." I replied, unable to recall the exact safe distance.

"Are you sure about that?" The same man demanded.

"Well let me put it this way. I personally would not want to be within 100 yards of the back of one of our claymores when it is detonated." "But why all the curiosity?" I asked.

"Well on our base when we have an alert, the Lieutenant in charge of security has us lay face down on the ground with our heads up against a sand bag with a clicker in our hands while the claymore is on the other side of the sandbag" the soldier explained nervously.

The young man's words made me shoot a look at Junior who had the strangest expression of disbelief on his face.

"You mean to tell us that you have been instructed to fire off a claymore mine that is set up on the opposite side of a sandbag from your head?" I said with a shutter.

"Well we do have our helmets on and the Lieutenant said we were completely safe." The soldier replied argumentatively.

"I take it for granted that no one has ever fired a claymore from this position?" I asked, confident that the answer would be no.

281

"But the Lieutenant said it was perfectly safe."

"Well if it is safe to fire a claymore in such a position I would demand that this Lieutenant give you a practical demonstration." I urged the young soldier.

"What do you think would happen if we did fire a claymore from behind a sandbag?" One of the other men asked.

"Well in my mind I am sure it would kill you out right, but if not you would lose your hearing and have a concussion and possible brain damage." "I would say that the least injury you would suffer would be a sand blasted body." I said in jest.

"Can we tell the Lieutenant what you said?" The group of men wanted to know.

"Of course" I agreed even going so far as to give them my name and where to contact me. It was a couple of days later that I received a phone call from the irate Lieutenant whose men had attended our class. He gave me an ear full for countermanding his orders and stated that I was an idiot who did not know what I was doing. Then came the usual command - that I put someone with respectable rank on the phone.

SFC Smith was standing nearby listening to my side of the conversation with a questioning expression on his face. I handed Smitty the phone then waited quietly for the Lieutenant to resume his verbal tirade.

Smitty listened politely to the Lieutenant who belittled Junior and I and EOD in general. Then it was Smitty's turn to explain the facts of life to this young know-it-all. He also recommended that the Lieutenant try lying down behind a sand bag and detonating a claymore mine on the other side. Smitty also made it perfectly clear that every man in our unit was, regardless of rank a qualified EOD man.

Although it was far too short I enjoyed every minute of the phone conversation between Smitty and this Lieutenant. I'll admit it was difficult to contain my desire to laugh out loud but knowing that I had once again instigated a confrontation thought it wise to merely smile.

One of our jobs was to investigate explosions whether accidental or intentional in order to determine the cause. We never heard of anyone meeting their fate from the blast of a claymore while hiding behind a sand bag so we assumed that the young Lieutenant finally got the message concerning the back blast from claymore mines.

I confess to wasting much of my miss-spent youth setting in front of a T.V. watching cartoons. Warner Bros had one character that was nothing more than a black helmet with two white shoes extending from the bottom. The humor of this little man was the music played as he walked around in the cartoon. Now as serious as this claymore incident could have been, that little cartoon character is the first thing that popped into my mind every time the subject was mention because I could visualize some poor G.I. in the same condition after firing the Lieutenant 's claymore from behind a sand bag.

INNOCULATION

This is not a bomb call story but it just came to mind so I want to get it down on paper. I had been TDY (on temporary duty) when the military in all its great wisdom declared all personnel must take a shot for some dreaded ailment whose name I can't recall. When I returned to the unit I was ordered to get the shot immediately so that everyone would have suffered equally. I agreed to go if the vaccination would prevent lead poisoning, or if it served as anti-venom against bites from the many deadly serpents in country, or hope-of-all-hopes that it might double as a mosquito repellant. I was informed the shot wouldn't have any effect on those discomforts but that I should get the shot taken within the hour and that a call would be made to the hospital to make certain I had been properly inoculated.

Junior drove me to the Medivac hospital where he elected to wait for me outside in the jeep. We avoided Medivac hospitals at all cost fearing the wounded patients bad luck might rub off. I wandered in and found a nurse who agreed to administer the shot and to record it in my file. Just at the same moment a big rangey looking grunt came in the door saying he needed the same treatment. One quick look and I knew this fellow had already been exposed to every deadly entity on this earth and that no vaccine was needed, for no germ would dare enter such a contaminated human host.

Now this guy could have served as the pattern for any book or movie description of the typical American foot soldier in Viet Nam. He was near six feet tall, 180 pounds, down from the healthy 200 he had carried back in the world. The face was lean and sunburned with hard chiseled features that did little to detract from the deep set blue eyes that seemed dazed and unconcerned. The young trooper moved slowly with a weary gate that was common in these often burned out warriors.

His uniform of the day was that of a jungle hat suspended on his back by the stampede string around his neck just above the O.D. towel these men wore like a scarf. His fatigues had what we would term today as a stone washed patina, however his were faded the hard way by too much exposure to the harsh tropical sun and mud laced monsoon rains, all while being sautéed in a sauce that is a blend of manure and human wasted from the mud of the rice paddies and gallons of human sweat. His sweat and possibly a little blood just gave that drab green costume a little color. The sweat had diluted the dark blood stains that on the shirt front formed an odd camouflage pattern.

An M-16 was slung behind his right shoulder, while two O.D. cloth ammo bandoleers made a massive "X" on his chest. A web belt around the man's waist held two plastic canteens suspended in worn out covers, plus the usual first aid kit and bayonet in a battered scabbard. His jungle boots lacked any indication that the leather had ever been black and the canvas sides and tops were in worse condition than the fatigues.

The soldier mumbled something to the nurse that he had just returned from 30 days in the field and was anxious to get a shower and some hot chow. It should be remembered that this man's uniform probably had been issued new to him 30 days before during what is known as a stand down.

The nurse, a large woman of oriental decent gave my shot then stated that it was regulation that I must wait 15 minutes after the vaccination in case of a bad reaction. I being a well trained soldier and always a gentleman responded with a polite "yes ma'am" and sat down to wait her release. Did I fail to mention that the woman was a lot larger than I am?

The grunt took his shot and headed for the door to which the nurse gave him the same directions to set down and wait for the 15 minutes to pass. The ground pounder just shot the nurse a hard but indifferent look then took another step. These men feared very little. They figured if Charlie and the hell hole of contamination they lived in hadn't killed them a little vaccination didn't stand a chance. Suddenly out of nowhere this big female nurse caught the unyielding soldier with a back-hand that lifted him off his feet and slammed him up against the wall. Like a gob of wet mud he slid peacefully down the waiting room wall before being unceremoniously deposited in a waiting folding chair.

The nurse in her most authoritative voice, one that was something similar to a bull horn blurted out a mixture of colorful phrases, instructed the private to take a seat and wait the allotted time. The man never moved a muscle while I watched the clock like a sprinter in the starting blocks watches the starter's gun. I could not wait for the magic minute when the nurse bellowed "you can go now junior." That's all it took for me to be thru the hospital door and into the waiting jeep.

I quickly related the story to Junior and we waited a few minutes to witness the lone grunt stagger out of the hospital door and disappear down the street. I always have said it doesn't pay to fight with the cook or the doctor but after that afternoon I placed nurses before either of those two poisoners. I often wondered if that poor grunt ever allowed the army to inoculate him again.

MOTORCYCLE INCIDENT

The 3rd Ord EOD served as a bed and breakfast for ordnance people moving in and out of country for such things as R&R, emergency leave, or reassignment. Some of these people were from the Republic of China, some were Australians, but most were just plain GI's looking for a bed and a ride to the airport. Everyone was welcome.

I somehow managed to do my share of transporting these guests either to Binh Hoa Air Base or Tan Son Nhut Air Base in Saigon. The former air base was located on the edge of a very old backward town, while the latter air base was located on the edge of a large busy city. Both were very scenic in their own way but Saigon, which had been labeled the Paris of the East, was definitely the more exciting of the two for GI's to visit. It being the capitol of South Viet Nam, every soldier traveling in and out of country wanted to visit the Pearl of the Orient.

Our supervising NCO's tried to tie these courtesy trips in with official business whenever possible but I didn't care what the reason, a trip off post was a trip off post. Any excuse was better than no excuse to leave the building and I became very proficient and annoying at finding reasons to be gone.

This particular drive to Saigon had been uneventful but I do remember that Junior was driving our jeep. Rain started to fall as we entered the air base's busy main gate but it proved to be a quick shower that ended just as our passenger jumped from the jeep and ran to the terminal. By the time we exited the main gate the sun had come out but the road way remained wet.

287

Neither of us was paying much attention to traffic behind the jeep as we stopped before pulling into the heavy traffic on the main street.

Just as the little green jeep came to a stop we heard a tremendous crashing sound coming from behind us. We both looked over our shoulders but seeing nothing we glanced in the jeep's little round outside mirrors but there wasn't any sign of cause of the noise.

Back in the world a person might have just driven off but this was Viet Nam and even though we were in the shadow of one of the U.S. largest Air Force bases the enemy was always present. There was always the possibility that a Vietnamese child had slipped in under our line of sight and was trying to steal our spare tire or rear gas can or even worse, drop a hand grenade inside of that five gallon gas can. These scenarios seem far-fetched back here in the world but were every day happenings in country.

Being in the passenger seat it was my place to jump out and try to determine the cause of the ominous crashing sound. I had to get completely behind the jeep before I could see the skinny rear wheel of a Honda step thru-motorcycle protruding from under the jeep. I crouched down and found not only the little cycle but a tiny young female rider crammed in under the jeeps rear axle.

I called to Junior to turn the motor off and come back to help me. He couldn't believe his eyes as we started to pull the girl and bike out of the confined space. It took some lifting and prying to free the bike but we finally managed to get the girl and her cycle back on the road with very little damage.

I was amazed that from the time the girl slipped on the wet street and became pinned under our vehicle to the point where she rode on down the street, not a single

288

word passed her lips. I am sure she was scared to death and didn't trust us but at the same time the girl was appreciative of our help and kindness. If I had slid a motorcycle under a vehicle I would have been screaming my head off. -- Different world, different people.

SAIGON

The city of Saigon itself was a huge mysterious colorful melting-pot of cultures and customs that kept one's head turning in every direction in order to take in the ever-changing sites. There were elaborate mansions with gated stone walls while nearby there were shacks made of packing crates who's only decorations were the words stenciled on the outside. The population consisted of Vietnamese, both rich and poor, along with a large contingent of Chinese, Indians and Pakistanis, many of whom were businessmen. Surprisingly enough there was a fair sized group of French nationals, remnants of their colonial days, still residing in the city.

The spires of large Catholic Churches and Buddhist Temples extended high above the tree lined boulevards. The shaven headed monks roamed the streets on foot in pairs or groups always moving but never seeming to get anywhere.

While traveling thru the city of Saigon I have experienced being shot at by South Vietnamese police, threatened by a child with a hand grenade, and had a T.V. stolen out of a moving jeep trailer in busy four lane traffic. I have been threatened by an angry mob, been broad-sided by a cyclo driver and watched a Buddhist monk burn himself alive.

This was a teaming city where anything might happen at least before curfew. These might include shootings, executions and hangings. Vendor's sat up shops on the sidewalks, spreading their wares on the hard concrete. The ill, crippled and infirm begged for money and food as they wandered aimlessly thru the hot crowded streets. Half naked children, many orphaned or

290

from poor refugee families, who had poured into the city seeking protection from the VC, ran the streets stealing or just generally raising hell. Young and old alike were on the move from the time the curfew was lifted in the morning until it was re-enforced at night, all in search of security that most never found.

The busy streets were clogged with improperly tuned buses that spewed partially burned diesel fuel. There were military vehicles of all types that usually bullied their way thru the nightmare of snarled traffic. Tiny yellow and blue taxis buzzed about in an attempt to deliver the paying passengers somewhere without delay, while at the same time the cheaper rated gas powered cyclos and pedacabs took every short cut possible to attain the same end. Riding in the front of a gas powered cyclo was often more life threatening than the war itself. These vehicles were built on motorcycle frames except that two wheels and a wide seat replaced the normal single front wheel. The passenger rode in the seat in front of the drivers who were often suicidal while enjoying the fact that you would provide an ample bumper in case of any front end collision and there were many.

Saigon had a very large fish market located on the banks of the muddy Mekong River, both of which stunk to high heaven in the intense heat of the tropical sun. I have passed over this area several times in high flying Huey's and the repulsive odor was still over powering. There was a stop light on the corner just out front of the fish market that seemed to be red all the time so Junior and I made a practice of turning on our jeeps flashing red light and sirens so that we could run the intersection while trying to hold our breath.

I suppose this was not entirely legal but many things that happen in war are not on the square.

JACK – THE DOG KILLER

Somewhere about half way thru my tour in country a new Staff Sergeant managed to slip into our little group. This was not unusual in itself since the 3rd was on the way to or from just about everywhere so it was difficult to determine if an individual was permanent party was or just passing thru.

The unit had been busy responding to calls causing me to miss out on the fact that this E-6 was assigned to the 3 Ord. This is a dead giveaway but I will call the new E-6 Jack as in Jack-the Dog Killer.

Jack was a pleasant man of slim build with quiet manners and a quick smile. These traits especially the quiet demeanor set Jack apart from the other members of the unit but once we realized that he was indeed part of our team, the members accepted him without question.

It was not unusual for the youthful members of the 3rd Ord to be rowdy and boisterous, much of which was in the form of good natured teasing, or arguing and dare I say bragging. But Jack failed to respond to our attempts to draw him into these sometimes heated conversations. Many of us began to consider the new Staff Sgt as a man of calm disposition with enough sense and self discipline to stay out of our petty exchanges.

One day Jack stated that there were a number of stray dogs running the battalion area and that several of these dogs had large sores on their bodies. He added that this seemed like an unhealthy situation and that something should be done to correct the situation. The unit members all agreed with Jack's assessment but at the same time we had come to accept Viet Nam as a world of filth, infection and disease. No one made a move to have the officials remove the ill dogs and the matter slipped our minds. That is, the matter slipped our minds until late one night when a series of gun shots drove us from our bunks. I'm not sure about anyone else but at the sound of the gunfire just outside my room, I rolled out of bed and landed with a loud thud on the hootches plywood floor.

Our hootches were built of plywood and screen wire; the bottom half of the wall was plywood while the top half was nothing but screen wire to aid in ventilation on hot humid nights. The exterior of the plywood walls were protected by a wall of sand bags. The ubiquitous green sand bag was the ultimate thing to trim buildings with in South Viet Nam and the 3rd Ord area was no different fortunately. Tex, who occupied the other room in this hootch called out to inquire what had happened. (Yes, that's what he said because Tex seldom used profanity) I replied that I didn't know but I was going to remain low enough to use the sand bag wall as cover. I headed for the screen door in the end of the building hoping to determine who fired the shots and where they originated from.

I threw open the door and rushed outside into the dark rubber tree grove expecting to find some of the local drug dealers fleeing from the scene. There wasn't a soul moving in the area so I stepped around the corner of the building where our bunker was located and where the shots had been fired. There in the shadows between the two hootches I found Jack armed with a 30 cal carbine.

"What hell are you doing?" I demanded, now sure that he had fired the shots in the direction of my bunk.

"Shooting those dogs." He replied like it was an everyday occurrence.

"Well you were shooting at my bed!" I scolded, but it was obvious my complaints were not registering with him. Jack was bent on killing the dogs and was fully prepared to fire again if the animals had been foolish enough to reappear. Deciding it was easier to go along with the canine extermination, the next question I asked dealt with how many Jack had hit.

Jack was fairly certain that one dog had been hit hard and that a second had been wounded. We fumbled around in the dark searching for any signs of dead or wounded animals but little evidence of the shooting was found. However the next day someone discovered that one of the wounded dogs had taken refuge under our main building.

That particular dog succumbed to his wounds and quickly started to smell. Of course this came as no surprise as Viet Nam was the country of rot; in fact I think they were the sole developer of rot. In country your teeth rotted, your clothes rotted, your feet rotted, wood rotted as did metal. Rot was so bad that the military had to find new materials to replace the standard cloth, leather or wood that was so prevalent in uniforms, or containers.

Being made the same old way the poor dogs had never been up-graded to more durable material so they began to deteriorate rapidly in the extreme heat of Viet Nam. When the stench became overpowering Jack was summarily volunteered to remove the odorous carcass from beneath the buildings.

Poor old Jack had to tear up the floor under the office and remove the offending remains then put the floor back in place. Most farmers in the states have better hog houses than our hootch so any minor damage done during the removal operation was of little consequence but the sweat and elbow grease expended on the hot South East Asian day was memorable.

Now just to show how much I was valued by the unit, the Powers-That-Be never mentioned to Jack that he was firing that .30 cal. carbine in the direction my bunk from less than 30 feet away. They did however object to the smell that the dead rotting dog under the office floor created around their desk. I suppose if Jack had accidentally killed me that night they would have complained about the smell of my decomposing body.

The wife and I recently attended the National EOD reunion at Huntsville, Alabama and to my surprise Jack was in attendance. It had been 38 years since last I saw Jack but he hadn't changed. Someone in the group pointed him out and asked if I recognized him in a suit and tie after so many years. I replied by walking to where he was seated, extended my hand and said I would know "Jack the Dog Killer anywhere". I was pleased to see him once again, of course I am always glad to see any EOD man who survived Viet Nam and it's after math.

The late Art Macksey's widow Barbara invited Jack, my wife and I to spend the afternoon at her lovely home. Fortunately for me I got to spend the afternoon talking to Jack one-on-one in the comfort of the Macksey home. Later that evening Jack, Barbara, my wife and I shared a table at the National E.O.D banquet.

I ashamedly admit that I had forgotten just what a kind gentleman Jack is to one and all. We past a beautiful Alabama day laughing and talking about things I had completely forgotten. I am glad for these EOD gatherings and thankful that we could attend. It is rewarding to me to see how these old comrades have weathered the years and how successful they have become. I love a mystery as well as anyone and life is one huge mystery but it is so satisfying to at last have the answer to the question of what ever happened to the men you were so close to.

A TRIBUTE TO ART MACKSEY

I can remember very well the night the 3rd Ordnance Battalion's Explosive Ordnance Disposal holding area blew up. Art Macksey and I spent the night prowling the depot's pitch black revetments filled with high explosives responding to urgent calls for help. When our holding or storage area detonated it spewed a wide variety of ordnance across a depot filled with thousands upon thousands of tons of explosive ordnance.

The C.O. was ordered to report to the battalion commanders' office where he passed the night and we were ordered into the depot in hopes of preventing a major disaster. Macksey and I departed immediately and I know that other teams followed but it was so dark after sunset that they could have been standing beside me and I wouldn't have known they were there. I don't recall a lot of radio traffic that night probably because everyone was too busy stumbling around in the dark trying to answer calls from worried depot personnel.

The demands for our services were considered urgent by those needing assistance, some of which became very insistent. Sgt. Macksey remained cool and unshaken while overbearing officers demanded that we respond immediately to their particular hazardous situation. He wisely gave priority to those items that posed the greatest threat to the huge Long Binh ammo depot. It is times like this when the real professional EOD men shine through and Art Macksey was a true bomb disposal expert.

Sgt. Macksey and I spent that long tedious night together scouring the depot for any hazardous situations that we could rectify. The first light of the morning sun

296

revealed how complete had been the destruction of our holding area by the previous night's explosion and just how close we had come to destroying the Long Binh Ammunition depot. I counted myself very fortunate to have been teamed with Art Macksey the night the EOD holding area detonated. We worked together that night and on many other incidents in the Viet Nam war and it was always reassuring to know that Macksey was at your side.

In those day's Army EOD traveled in two-man teams without escorts through a hostile country where you learned to survive by your wits while applying any knowledge you may have picked up from the people and their customs. Art was well versed in the traditions of the Vietnamese people and seemed to know instinctively which tact to take when dealing with these often unpredictable people. The two-man team theory had both its weakness and strengths in that your partner was the only thing that stood between you and a sad end. He was your only connection to our world if, while operating in the field you became ill or injured. A partner had to be loyal and dedicated to his partner to ensure that both of you returned safely while attempting to complete a mission. A partner must be cool, calm and collected to prevent any mishap while handling explosives or disarming booby traps, but one had to be especially careful in dealing with any human threats that constantly surrounded us. In either case the tiniest of mistakes could have ended in disaster. Art was a person that every team member wanted to partner with and that is saying a lot considering the size of the ego's some of us sported in those days. But not Art, he remained quiet and unassuming thru all the hype and bluster.

I always felt confident in Macksey's company and trusted his decisions without question, knowing that these delicate decisions had to be infallible and yet made on the spur of the moment without any deliberation. This was an impossible fine line that had to be walked and Macksey was one of the best at negotiating the impossible.

Sgt. Arthur Macksey was a man with a quick wit who always had a kind encouraging word when your spirits were down. He was a person who could find good in every situation and somehow managed without complaint to make the best of the worst that life handed him. Art was a great partner and to use his term, "good people".

I, like many others are proud and fortunate to have served with Art Macksey. To have teamed with such a man in a theater of war was a blessing for a young inexperienced EOD man like me. Although this is a totally inadequate sentiment, all I can say is "Thank you Sgt. Macksey and May God bless you."

JEWISH DEVOTIONALS

This is a true story that I have considered over and over for the year I have spent relating these tales, but I have until now omitted it for several reasons. I have endeavored throughout these works not to embarrass or ridicule any EOD man that served in country. However I will now make an exception to that rule by relating an incident that the late Sgt. Macksey often repeated.

About half way through my tour a young enlisted man of the Jewish faith joined out unit. I can't recall what month he arrived because as I have said before, men, especially new men, moved in and out of the 3rd Ord like osmosis. Suddenly one day you realize that a strange man was present in the bar and that someone with an old familiar face was absent. It was somehow easier not to become attached to the new men, however we never shunned anyone either.

It should be noted that this was a field where information was freely shared. No one ever said "let him learn the hard way like I did", instead men would step forward and render whatever knowledge or experience they had with the subject under discussion.

But who would have believed it I digress, so back to the story at hand, the young Jewish EOD man. Now when I first noticed this man it was my impression that he did not follow his religion very closely but as time passed he began to say more prayers and attend services more often. He began to carry a large black satchel full of kosher food while avoiding the military mess halls.

I don't mean to make light of a person's religious beliefs and the Lord knows that more than one soldier found or lost their religious convictions while in country.

You might say a tour in Nam was a moving religious experience, which path a person followed was completely unpredictable. What caused this young man to get more involved with his faith can only be guessed but from my point of view his devotionals were an aggravation.

When our holding area blew up Sgt. Macksey and I spent the entire night in the depot responding to calls. The depot seemed unusually dark that night as we felt our way from incident to incident. I have no recall of where the other team members were but I know that several of the men were performing the same type of calls that we were. It is a strange feeling to know that your team mates are performing the same type of bomb disposal operations that you are in the same situation. It is times like these that you must trust in yourself and your teammates not to make a mistake that could cost the whole ammunition depot not to mention the lives of all the EOD personnel working there.

I for one breathed a sigh of relief as the eastern sky lightened up allowing us the great advantage of being able to see the unexploded ordnance strewn about the depot. As Art and I finished our last call we slowly made our way back to the rubble of the holding area to continue in the ongoing clean up.

The day previous to the holding area's self destruction had been exhausting. The night in the depot had seemed to never end. But sleep and food are two luxuries that a soldier should never count on. Still the brilliant morning sun brought with it the gift of light but it also aided all the brass who had shown up to investigate what had caused our holding area to detonate.

The holding area was by comparison to ammo bunkers very small, maybe 60 by 100 feet that was enclosed by a dirt levy about ten feet high. A row of concertina wire stretched around the top of the dirt bank provided the only security that seemed necessary since the holding area was set deep inside the well guarded Long Binh ammunition dump. One lone frail wire gate allowed access to the small storage area.

The holding area on that day contained one conex box, a borrowed 2½ ton truck and a jeep trailer plus a few odds and ends piles of explosive ordnance. The ordnance on the truck and trailer were scheduled to be moved to our demo range for destruction. The material in the conex box, a chrome plated M-1 rifle from the palace guard in Saigon, a Russian manufactured RKG heat hand grenade, plus a wide variety of commercial ammunition were trading material and not to be destroyed. Needless to say the jeep trailer and the borrowed truck were totally destroyed by the explosive blast. I am certain no inventory of the holding area's ordnance was ever made and would have been of little consequence once the blast had scattered these hazardous items across the depot. However some of the items stored in the conex box could have been very difficult to explain if the brass were to discover them.

Several of us recognized the position the 3rd Ord and our C.O. would be in if the contraband in the conex box should come to light so without a word we began to remove or hide any questionable items. Part of this movement was performed under the guise of providing a safe area for the inspectors.

The whole team became involved in covering any tracks that the investigators might consider improper or more importantly, illegal. So you can see our efforts were more than a point of honor it was a matter of protecting our own people. I hope you get the picture, the members the 3rd Ord EOD were moving about the rubble of our holding area while investigating officers prowled back and forth like caged wild cats on top of the surrounding dirt banks above us. It was at this moment that the Jewish EOD man approached SSgt. Art Mackey to inform him that it was sunrise and time for his morning prayers. Those of us in the pit were doing our best invisible act trying not to draw the investigators attention when the young Jew asked Art for permission to perform his morning devotionals.

Macksey not wishing to draw attention to himself with a long debate or argument quickly conceded to the prayer request. We all thought the young Jew would find some private place outside the holding area for his morning devotionals. But no; instead our young religious soldier quickly unfolds his prayer blanket and other trappings right in the middle of the holding area. With his rug spread over the rubble covered ground the young Jew took up a position on hands and knees and began bowing to the east.

Needless to say the investigation came to a pause as each officer standing on top of the perimeter's tall dirt berm turned to focus their attention on the soldier chanting away on his prayer rug. I must admit to being stunned by this religious demonstration but with all the prying eyes centered on him we managed another slide-of-hand act that allowed for another piece of contraband to disappear. You might say that in a way we owed the young Jew a thank you for providing a prefect diversion. I don't remember the man being reprimanded other than a few snide remarks that I leveled at him but I do recall thinking if we ever had to fight Israel all attacks should take place at sunrise when they were already on their knees.

The night the holding area blew up was clearly a unique experience for all concerned. The fact that no one was injured and that very little damage was done is unbelievable to anyone who witnessed the detonations. A great mixture of ordnance exploded that night not to mention the items that were scattered about the depot.

If the cause of the detonation was ever determined I was never informed of it, but there was a number of theories that made the rounds. The fact that this stuff had sat in the holding area for a considerable time before several of the team members were assigned to go thru it to make certain each item was in a safe condition seems strange, and yet there was not a man of that group who would have caused the detonation, because they all knew the hazards of such an action.

I guess we must leave the question of the cause of the detonation to one of the mysteries of Viet Nam. Still I must repeat the statement I made to Tex as we stood in front of our hootch watching the colorful airborne detonations in the South East Asian twilight. "Damn that sure is a beautiful explosion."

BOTCHED JOB AT THE FRENCH FORT

The 3rd Ord had a steady turnover of First Sgts. and commanding officers while I was assigned to that unit. Truth of the matter is that so many administrators passed thru the unit that I have forgotten most of their names. In this particular instance I do remember the officers name but for obvious reasons I will not use it here.

It was another of those beautiful sunny days when I was paired up for a call with our new commanding officer who as it happened was also new to South Viet Nam. New personnel in country, even officers were teamed up with someone who had more time in country with the hope they would listen to the voice of experience. Unfortunately this was not always the case but it sounded like a good idea.

The new C.O. and I had been given the call of an unexploded artillery round in a compound in the delta. I had a rough knowledge of that area of the delta but I could not recall any camp where the instructions said we were to go. I drove because the new men in country were usually leery of the strange traffic, besides they hadn't any first-hand experience with my driving skills.

We arrived at the incident site in the late afternoon after struggling to follow directions that had seemed so plain back at the unit. Actually, for any ladies reading this we found the site only after stopping at a church and asking for directions. We were on a narrow dirt road that led to the Catholic Church by way of an old Bailey bridge over a small canal. The ends of this frail looking bridge were supported by square towers built of what appeared to be handmade adobe blocks. I found the area very intriguing for I had never seen anything quite like it in my travels around South Viet Nam. The land was as flat as a pool table with rice paddies that were being worked all around the tiny settlement. I say that the rice paddies were being worked as many of the remote farms had been abandoned to the V.C.

The church was about twenty feet wide and fifty feet long and looked like a long loaf of French bread. The exterior was constructed of mud that had been white-washed except for areas that had been recently patched. A statue of Mary sat at the rear of the churches rounded base and was the first thing one saw after crossing the Bailey bridge. The church was surrounded on three sides by badly weathered wooden buildings that formed a "U" shape enclosure. Just outside of these wooden shacks were low walls of the same adobe bricks as the bridge abutment were made of. These walls served as a divider between the shacks and a wide old mine field.

It suddenly became clear that the church and surrounding walls were very old and that this had been a French Fort during the Indo-China wars. I was intrigued by the history and the mystic of being in such a long deserted fortification; although I feared someone would want us to wade out into the tall grass of that long ago abandoned mine field to do a little clearing and that my new C.O. would want to have a go at the task. I knew that no matter what happened, I was NOT going into that mine field for any reason. I figured it had been laying there for years and years without my interference and it could damn well lay there for years and years more. Fortunately we were spared the decision making when a couple of GI's approached us saying they had a 40mm duster on the north side of the shacks that needed our assistance.

We followed the young GI's around to the back of the building where we found an armored vehicle with twin 40mm automatic guns mounted on its top. The problem as they described it was a high explosive projectile lodged in the right barrel. Now this was a fairly common occurrence that is not nearly as hazardous as it sounds. The people who design ordnance for the U.S. military are for the most part very intelligent and safety conscious. They engineer in place many safeties and procedures that prevent the injury or death of the using personnel. One of these safeties prevents the fuses in artillery projectiles from becoming armed before they have exited the muzzle of the weapon. Since these projectiles are relatively safe to handle when caught in the barrel most people use a bell rammer to drive the projectile back out of the breach. Of course there are times when no amount of battering will dislodge the rotating bands from the barrels rifled grooves.

Now some genius came up with an R.S.P. for this unfortunate predicament that sounds crazy at the onset but works great in practice. This procedure calls for elevating the barrel on the artillery piece to about a 45 degree and removing or locking the breech block open. Most people pile sand bags behind the open breech to serve as a back stop. The next step requires the EOD man to make a ball of C-4 plastic explosive of proper size that is primed with an electric blasting cap then the ball is wrapped in empty sand bags. It seems prudent to get a rough measurement of where the projectile is stuck in the barrel so that when the sand bags and C-4 are pushed down tube from the muzzle end you will know that the package is just above the nose of the fuse. Next the barrel is filled to the brim with water just before everyone clears the area in preparation for the fun.

In practice when the electric blasting cap is fired the C-4 explodes which blows the water out of the muzzle of the barrel and the projectile is forced backwards out to the open breech to be caught by the waiting sand bags. If this exercise is done properly it can be great fun to watch, if done improperly the situation deteriorates rapidly.

The situation we were handed was entirely different from the one described above in that the 40 mm round is a fixed round of ammunition much like any rifle cartridge you have seen. The larger artillery rounds are separate loading which haven't any cartridge case; instead the propellant is contained in cloth bags. The 40 mm gun we were working on had a brass case stuck in the chamber so I ran a rod down the barrel and quickly discovered that the projectile had been fired and had cleared the muzzle. In other words we had a cartridge case that had not ejected from the chamber, making this problem fall into the realm of unit armor. I explained this situation repeatedly to the new C.O. but he insisted that we try blowing the round out with C-4 the way he had heard of in school. I warned him several times that attempting this procedure would result in the destruction of the weapons action. But no matter how hard I argued the C.O. insisted that we must blow the non-existing projectile from the weapon. Well the commanding officer is the commanding officer so we set up the shot in the same manner as I had done successfully before. Since the C.O. had never witnessed this procedure performed before it was easy to convince him that we need to take cover and not watch the show.

We cleared the area, called "fire in the hole" and cranked the shot off. The resulting detonation was quite loud and so was the rattle of the shrapnel produced when the 40 mm's breech came apart from the blast of the C-4.

I never said a word as we climbed back on top of the vehicle to inspect our handy work. The gun crew who had drifted off was far from pleased when they came running at the sound of the explosion. We quietly packed up our gear, drove back across the Bailey bridge and disappeared into the beautiful Asian sunset. Back at the unit I used some creative writing skills in making out the incident report not wanting to draw attention to a botched job.

Although our work on the 40 mm went badly I greatly enjoyed visiting the old French Fort. I have stayed in a couple of the old French Villas in Saigon and Da Nang but those were probably the homes of wealthy planters or businessmen. This little outpost was where the French soldiers had lived and died. I felt a real connection with these long departed warriors as I stood looking out across the same mine field and rice paddies they had viewed so many years before. I found a strange appreciation for their little bridge and attempted fortifications, realizing that they had struggled in vain.

It was here that I first wondered if our conflict would come to the same end.

FRENCH VILLA

The French Villa I mentioned that I stayed in was located in the heart of Da Nang. This fine old two story structure now served as housing for the Army EOD unit.

As I recall it was constructed of stone with large verandas on both floors that faced towards the street. The front of the building was protected by a high metal fence courtesy of the U.S. government, which blocked the view from the first floor but the second floor veranda provided a fine place to sit in the shade and watch the war go by.

Of course the high metal fence was there to stop the V.C. from firing into the building which meant that sitting on the second floor made you a prime target for drive-by shootings. Still it was fun to sit up there and watch the Vietnamese passing by on the street below and try to decide which ones were friendly and which ones were V.C. troops entering the city.

The view from the second floor balcony also included a large lot just across the street that contained Radio Da Nang and the company of ARVN rangers who guarded the place. This ranger unit was a permanent outfit that lived in tents on the radio property and was less than cordial neighbors.

They had a boredom problem, for occasionally they would fire off a few rounds in the air, or at birds in the trees, or even at our building. The polished stone floors of the French Villa were not very forgiving when a person dove for cover from these random shootings, still it was better than diving into a muddy rice paddy.

About a block up the street laid a railroad track that as I was told upon arrival in Da Nang defined the line between us and them. It seems that Charlie owns everything on the other side of that railroad track day or night and that he controlled everything on our side of the tracks after sunset. Needless to say there wasn't a lot of sightseeing done in beautiful Da Nang; quite a contrast from the open markets of Saigon.

However I did manage to make it to the harbor a couple of times and around the city itself. I found the area very scenic with the South China Sea on one side and the high lush green hills on the other. I am shocked that it never became a tropical resort for the area certainly has all the traits needed to draw recreation minded visitors. I doubt if any of the Marines who had to hump up over those majestic green hills would be inclined to agree with my assessment.

I was TDY in Da Nang to work the cleanup of the ammo dump that had blown up making a terrible mess. EOD men of all service branches and from all over South East Asia were being rotated thru Da Nang to assist in the massive and dangerous clean up. Although others may not agree I still think that such clean ups were one of the more dangerous aspects of the EOD business. These clean ups were the most effective training aid I ever experienced because personnel were exposed to any and all explosive ordnance in every possible condition and in the most unusual positions. It really paid to be current on all ordnances and to be ready for any sudden development.

As strange as it may sound I found this hot, dirty, dangerous work very fulfilling. One might think I am referring to a sense of accomplishment of a job well done or the vast experience gained, but the greater reward came from working with some of the finest men I have ever known. I watched these men face the long hot hours day after day on a hazardous task never expecting any reward. They approached each day in good humor, completely unconcerned for their personal safety. I never heard them complain about the heat or the soot or the bad food, instead they joked and told stories or reminisced with long lost friends.

The humor was not driven by fear nor was it nervous laughter; it was truly the laughter of good men making the best of a bad situation while doing a job for which they all had volunteered.

NIGHT ON A ROOFTOP

On my first trip to Da Nang I stayed in the French Villa which was some distance from the devastated ammo dump because much of the military housing in that area had also been destroyed. I understand that there was a small Vietnamese village close to the dump that was flattened by the blast.

This villa, a large two story house was famous for being the prime objective for Charlie during the Tet Offensive of 1968. The V.C. captured the house hoping to use its second floor and roof top to fire down on the ARVN rangers across the street as a prelude to capturing Radio Da Nang. The V.C. broadcasting over Radio Da Nang would have been a major coup for the communists no matter how short lived their air time.

That was the famous Tet of 68 but this was 1969 and the Tet New Year was upon us. Those of us who were on TDY were warned several times that this villa was not the place to be on the coming holiday. I had offers to stay in other quarters but I felt it proper to remain where I was assigned.

For some strange reason the First Sgt. of the unit decided it would be wise to confiscate our ammunition. I was dumb-founded at such a move especially with a possible invasion of our building just a couple of days away. Well, I happened to mention this lack of ammo to my Marine friends out at the depot and before I knew what happened I had more loaded M-16 mags than I could carry. There were hand grenades and offers of much heavier weapons but I thought it best to sneak in small items that were less obvious.

While our ammunition was under lock and key with the First Sgt. holding the key we managed to smuggle in a modest amount of 5.56 and 45 cal. rounds with a few M-26 hand grenades just in case. One old Sgt. at the depot insisted on the grenades because he knew that in the 1968 Tet Offensive the V.C. had approached the villa by the narrow side alley. He reasoned if the V.C. followed the same attack plan we could make a good defense by dropping the grenades off of our rooftop as the enemy moved up the alley.

As the Tet holiday approached we sat on the second story balcony and watched helplessly as the traffic, especially foot traffic on the street below increased by the hour. The number of fighting age South Vietnamese men grew from a trickle to a flood. It seemed like each one was carrying a package or bundle, many were pushing bicycles loaded with bundles of 3 to 4 feet long sticks or fire wood. I questioned what was concealed within these heavy loads. That never got a straight answer other than Tet was equivalent to our Christmas and New Years so more traffic was to be expected. In my estimation this was a very naive attitude, especially in light of some of the hard fearless looks that the passer-bys on the street were rendering to the observers on the balcony.

The night before Tet the city of Da Nang was locked down even tighter than usual, curfews were strictly enforced and everyone was warned to find a place of safety. At about sunset several of us like-minded peon's moved quietly to the Villa's roof top, weapons and ammunition in hand. We were not prepared for the worst but were in agreement that we would make some semblance of a stand if the worst came.

As the sun lowered, our little group watched intently as the people began to move about the usually vacant streets, some were military units others were non-descript sulking figures. I can't recall at what time the action picked up but suddenly brilliant red and yellow

313

flares began to illuminate the night sky. Shortly the entire city and all the military bases for miles around were under an umbrella of artificial light. Artillery rounds could be heard sizzled thru the air passing over our heads, some we understood came from ships in the harbor or out to sea. Many of those artillery projectiles were dispensing flares but shortly they were replaced with high explosive rounds. Detonations large and small could be heard coming from all parts of the city and it was anyone's guess who was blowing up what.

All of this fire power was entertaining to say the least but our attention remained on defending the building we occupied. It had been made clear that if our quarters were attacked that the company of ARVN Rangers just across the street would not come to our aid even though they were the V.C.s main objective.

The action grew more intense by the hour with more and more illuminating rounds filling the sky. Our little roof top contingent kept a watch in all directions but that other end of the narrow alley seemed to draw everyone's attention the most. Then suddenly a healthy fire fight broke out at the alleys narrow opening, just a block from where we sat. Bright red tracer bullets flew across the dark opening; our side used red tracers. Those first rounds were answered by a large number of green tracer bullets of communist china manufacture, fired from the right side of the alley opening. Then all hell broke loose as streams of red and green tracers criss-crossed that narrow slot between the buildings. We cheered the friendly red tracers and held our breath at the sight of the green ones.

Although we were on a second story roof top, buildings in between us and the next street blocked our view of the combatants. It was impossible to tell who was doing the firing or how many were on each side. The worst part for us waiting up there was knowing that the outcome of this fire fight might determine our surviving the night and yet we were unable to assist those who were so bravely defending us.

The heated fighting continued for several minutes then the firing began to subside before stopping completely. We expected renewed firing between the two advisories but it never developed. We then diverted our attention to the street in front of the villa thinking that the V.C. might try an end run around the block but that also failed to develop. The main crises, at least for our building, seemed to diminish with the withdrawal of the troops from the opposite end of the alley. Our building remained unmolested but the fighting continued throughout most of the night. Our little band kept watch until the Tet Offensive of 1969 had clearly ended.

Charlie was unable to muster the type of manpower of the previous and duly famous 68 Tet Offensive. Possibly the enemies great losses the year before may have weakened their ability or resolve or maybe it became obvious that such losses were too high a price to pay for the rewards gained. Whatever the reason the whole country breathed a little easier when the sun rose the day after the 69 Tet Offensive.

I for one was glad to see the holiday pass and indeed felt grateful to those friends on the opposite end of that narrow alley, who turned back the communists who were determined to assault our building. I never knew who they were nor did they ever know that we few roof top witnesses cheered their actions and their success.

When the action had slowed I went down to the office that was situated on the first floor of the villa and reported what had taken place just outside the building. The Powers-That-Be were totally unconcerned. I stated that in my opinion they had taken this threat far too casually. They, of course, accused me of being a coward and hysterical. That may be, but consider the history of this building in the 1968 Tet Offensive and that there were no more than fifteen of us in the building that night. Additionally, the building was isolated from other friendly forces that might have come to our aid and it seemed criminal to have confiscated our ammunition at anytime let alone before an impending attack.

I had protested this ammo seizure before the holiday and had my opinion reinforced by the M.P.'s who patrolled this area as well as the Marines and other army personnel. I knew from the beginning that my words would fall on deaf ears for I had some experience with this First Sgt. when we were in the states. He had been very arrogant, domineering, and an obvious fool then and the intervening time had not improved his leadership traits. When I first arrived in Da Nang and realized who the First Sgt. of the unit was, I thanked my lucky stars that I was only there on temporary duty. He is the only man I knew who could have driven me to give up my EOD badge and go back to the ammunition field. I swore to never give up my weapon or ammo again.

I was truly glad when my first visit to Da Nang ended. I had slept in upstairs rooms with no window screens or mosquito netting and woke every morning with what looked like a terminal case of measles. The food as usual was poor and our location seemed illogical being locked away all night. The only redeeming factor was some of the other EOD men stationed there; I had known a couple of them from school and found the remainder to be exceptional men to work with.

IT'S QUITTIN' TIME

My second trip to Da Nang was completely different from the first. This time I bunked with the Marine EOD at their newly rebuilt camp located very near the ammo depot that we were cleaning up.

The new Marine barracks could not equal the opulence of the Army's down town villa but seemed more comfortable to those of us more accustom to living in a shack. The camp security left a lot to be desired for it consisted of nothing more than a couple of strands of concertina wire and a few scattered guard towers. Still there was an easy secure feeling about the camp and its defensive abilities.

I usually enjoyed spending time with the Marine EOD because they always had a positive attitude and a "can do" spirit. I was fortunate enough to work with one huge Marine Staff Sgt. at Da Nang who had witnessed some V.C. atrocities toward their own people that was causing him great anguish. We talked one afternoon while clearing a cut in a dirt bank. The temperature was unbearable and with no air moving the heat began to get the better of us. He told his story as we struggled with the impossible tangle of unexploded ordnance and burned debris that covered the cut like a blanket. The man was nearly in tears as he related the horrors he had seen in a little village on a patrol the night before. I will not relate the story for it is his to tell but it was clear the man was suffering with a memory he could not shake.

I have to give him credit for he continued to work the difficult cut without making an error or endangering us but the pain on his face was clear for all to see. We talked as we worked but no matter what consolation I offered, he could not shake those bitter images of the preceding night.

The conditions in the cut become difficult to handle as the afternoon sun bore down on us and explosive items became more hazardous to handle. The other men began to drop out until the big Marine Sgt. and I were the only two left to face the task that lay before us. We too could have stopped at any time with no questions asked but I hated to leave him alone in his grieving so I stayed, matching him item for item. It suddenly struck me that it was that old Marine Corp spirit that was driving the man to continue our suffering, for no real Marine would throw in the towel while a doggy or army man was still working. I also knew that this competition was good for him, for the heat and concentration on the work at hand took his mind off his memories.

It was at that point that I decided to do my best to match this mountain of a man step for step and item for item. We turned the topic of conversation to many other things, mostly the heat or the specific explosive devices we were finding among the piles of rubble. We worked hand in hand moving pieces of charred wood and bent metal to uncover and safe item after item.

The intense heat began to take effect manifesting itself in our staggering and stumbling but neither spoke of quitting the cut. The difficulty of trying to walk was soon and quite by accident overcome as we found it easier to crawl on hands and knees. The lack of moving air and the burning sun seemed to induce us to struggle on against all reason and common sense. The other men working in better ventilated areas of the depot had quit for the day but sick as I was becoming, I knew there was no stopping now.

The spirit of competition in a person is a wonderful thing that can propel one to great heights or it can turn inward and destroy that very person. I inwardly feared we were going to make a mistake and destroy ourselves in this madness of competitive spirit. The other men called to us to stop for they were ready to call it a day, but we refused their beckoning calls as we neared the other end of the cut bank and it became a 'do or die' situation. My head spun and my stomach knotted up and I knew the end of my day was rapidly drawing near. It was impossible to tell how the big Marine felt for the tough ones never let on or complain about mere discomfort. The struggle continued until we crawled side by side out the opposite end of the deep banked cut and a slight breeze swept over us.

I rose to my feet and with a firm voice I announced. "You may out rank me but I say it's quitting time." The big Sgt. chuckled and rose to his feet seconding the motion and declaring that we had put in a good days work. He seemed pleased with what we had accomplished and I was pleased with his obvious change of mental state. There is an old saying that time heals all wounds, a point I would like to argue with the sayings creator, but I do know that the head to head competition plus the heat, fatigue and the stress of clearing that deep cut gave the Marine Sgt. several hours of distraction from the ghosts in his brain. I considered it a miserable afternoon well spent.

LOST FINGERS

The 3rd Ord received a call from depot security explaining there had been a detonation in one of the remote areas of the ammunition depot. Junior and I immediately responded. Grabbing our tool belts, we jumped into a jeep and raced red lights and sirens blazing thru the guard's gates into the depots interior.

At the risk of the reader becoming callused at hearing how dangerous bomb disposal is, I must reiterate that any bomb call has the potential for personal injury but a reported explosion in an ammunition depot carries a much greater weight than the team's safety. You might say it is a matter of pride as an EOD man you have volunteered at your own peril to confront and contain any explosive ordnance hazard. I will admit that pride provides a great deal of the incentive to complete a mission and the thought of being the team that lost an ammunition depot the size of Long Binh is unconscionable. But aside from pride and self preservation you have to take into account the huge loss of material and hindrance the to the war effort the loss of Long Binh depot would created. Still above all, there is the potential loss of life by the hundreds of military personnel in or near the depot during such a catastrophe.

OK, this sounds very self-serving but massive depot destruction starts with one single explosion and the trick is to prevent a second detonation and the horrific chain reaction that follows. The key is to race to the point of the original explosion in time to prevent any further problems.

This may sound foolish but in an ammunition storage complex as large as Long Binh depot it was difficult to keep track of what happened in the various out of the way areas. This emergency call led our team to a facility where the government was storing captured explosive ordnance.

   We raced down a narrow dirt road and slid to a stop at what was obviously a guard post. As often happened with on-post calls there were a number of officers and other officials milling around all looking like expectant fathers.   After reporting in we were led a couple of hundred yards to an ammo cache where it was explained that a young soldier had been seriously injured by an explosion. The Powers-That-Be feared that this captured ordnance had been booby trapped by either the V. C. or possibly by the Chinese manufactures. Their fears were grounded in truth for both groups were not above such devious practice especially if they anticipated the ordnance being captured. It was also reported that this cache of captured ordnance was scheduled to be shipped back to the states for testing and evaluation. It is easy to understand the military official's case of nerves if they were to ship home a bunch of ordnance that would blow up in shipping or while being tested.

   On reaching the bunker full of captured ordnance the whole scenario became obvious to us. There, lying in the open were two 82 mm Chinese mortars and it was clear they had been tampered with. These mortars shells came sealed in individual tin cans that were shipped in wooden crates. The tin cans had been removed from the wooden crates before being ripped open. The shells nose fuse had been removed and laid out on top of a 3 foot high sand bag wall. The nose fuse on this particular mortar shell had a separated steel cap on its tip that when removed revealed a thin metal membrane that held the firing pin away from the initiating primer cap. The fuse's heavy steel removable cap and delicate metal membrane were developed in answer to a problem found

321

in the widely diverse soil of Southeast Asia. If the mortar shell had the steel cap in place when fired into soft soil such as a rice paddy it might not detonate or the shell might detonate deep in the soft soil which would result in throwing a lot of mud in the air with little effect on the target. However the steel cap when in place would allow for penetration of fortified bunkers whereas the thin metal disc would allow the shell to detonate when it encountered the least amount of resistance. This simple removable steel cap gave the mortar man a choice of different deployments for the same basic round.

The U.S. military experienced the same problem with much of its offensive ordnance which brought about the development of new fuses and ordnance. In this particular case the young soldier, without any idea what he was doing, removed the mortar fuses then unscrewed the heavy steel caps exposing the sensitive membrane beneath. What happened next is only conjecture but somehow that thin metal membrane was struck, driving the firming pin into the priming charge. Firing the primer resulted in the detonation of a healthy high explosive booster charge contained in a steel cap on the end of the fuse that is normally screwed into the mortar body.

Our team quickly reported to the officer in charge what we had found during our initial investigation. He argued that the injured soldier had stated that he did nothing to cause the explosion. He also informed us that the young man had lost a couple of fingers in the blast and that the medical people had requested that the fingers be recovered and rushed to the hospital with the hopes of them being surgically reattached. We required only a short search of the ammo pad to find the man's severed fingers, all three of them from his left hand plus a gold wedding band. We wrapped up the digits and

322

rushed them off with the certainty that the flesh was damaged far beyond their being rescued.

At this point we began an obvious and in-depth explanation of what had happened to cause the explosion and the soldier's injuries. The investigators immediately refused to accept our theory of the chain of events that lead up the blast. For some reason this group of untrained investigators were certain that these mortar rounds were not safe to handle. Of course we could not guarantee the safety of each and every round in the storage area without a visual inspection.

I explained repeatedly that the young man who was standing guard duty alone had left his weapon and deserted his post to walk some distance in order to find a souvenir. Upon reaching the pile of captured ammo the guard had opened the wooden shipping crates before removing the tin cans that held the Chinese mortar shells. He had then removed two of the fuses, and then had unscrewed the protective caps. It was at this point that the detonation occurred that caused the man's injuries. I also explained how fortunate the guard and we all were that the fuses were not screwed into the mortar shell body for the blast would have been much greater. We foolishly thought that we had heard the end of this matter but a couple of days later some of the investigating officers showed up at our building requesting that I rewrite the incident report. It seems the Powers-That-Be wanted to send this young soldier home with an honorable discharge, a Purple Heart and an Army Commendation Medal. It goes without saying that they were less than pleased when I refused to make any changes in my report and countered that I was disappointed that the man in question had not been punished for leaving his guard post, not to mention his weapon, while on a fool's errand.

Oh, I know this sounds heartless and I admit to being pretty callused in such matters but I could not see why this soldier should receive **any** recognition much less medals for being stupid. He had not been wounded in action nor faced danger other than of his own making. I simply could not reward this man when we all knew many brave men who had preformed heroic deeds without so much as a thank you. We also knew of men who had received wounds as a direct result of enemy action who were denied the Purple Heart. The argument and threats continued but we never wavered in our resolve to report truthfully what had happened at the site of that captured Chinese ammo.

I never knew the final disposition of that young soldier but I can state that nearly four decades later I feel just the same today as I did then.

AN OFF POST CALL WITH MASTER JACK

In the early days of my tour in country Master Jack called me in and offered a chance to go on an off-post call with him. As stated earlier, I had been dumped on the 3rd Ords doorstep by a practical joker, a situation that the old First Sgt did not consider funny. I was certain that he held me at least partially responsible for the trick and held a slight grudge. I felt that going on this call was an audition but at the same time considered it an honor to work with such a well known figure as Master Jack Summeral.

I of course, being new in country and lacking experience was eager to get off base to witness the sights, sounds and smells of this war. I had been kept on post near the building on an involuntary probation for a couple of weeks until the hierarchy was convinced that I was actually EOD qualified. I was thrilled to find out that this call would require Master Jack and me to catch a helicopter for the trip to some outlying fire base. This flight provided my first real aerial view of Three Corp area's flat wet terrain. I enjoyed immensely the grand view from the Huey's open side door as we fluttered and chugged high over the expanse of rice paddies below.

We landed at the fire base all too soon for my liking and the call itself proved very disappointing. The report was of a short round that had landed in the fire base compound. The term short round normally refers to an artillery projectile that for various reasons fell short of its target. If these short rounds were armed and fell without detonating in an occupied area they could threaten anyone who unwittingly encountered these items.

Our call to handle a short round proved to be nothing more deadly than an expended front section of a

4.2 inch mortar illumination round. In other words it was a short piece of 4 inch steel pipe that had functioned properly by lighting up the night sky before falling back to earth. We unceremoniously policed up the chunk of metal and threw it away. We asked for return transportation and were directed back to the little air strip. A round of twenty questions led us to a strange looking airplane that was preparing to take off. The heat was boiling off the concrete runway as we hurried to the side door of the unusual appearing plane. On approaching the air craft from the rear it was impossible to miss its extremely tall tail and the large high wings. The fuselage was long and slender but the single engine in front of the windshield seemed to stretch on forever.

The pilot who was dressed in civilian clothes was willing to take us back to Bien Hoa but it would not be a direct flight. The pilot explained over the roar of the engine that he was waiting to fly a soldier to some little air strip. We were directed to climb in and take a seat but to leave room near the door for the other passenger. I took it for granted that the late arriving passenger would be some high ranking officer, how else would you justify such a large plane being scheduled to transport one man. Not being accustom to riding in small air craft at that time I was staring nervously out of the planes side window when I noticed a soldier approaching across the sun baked runway.

The young trooper strolled casually toward the plane acting as if he had all the time in the world. He was dressed in the uniform of the day; jungle fatigues, hat and boots with an M-16 slung from the right shoulder, a backpack slung haphazardly from the left. A scan of his fatigues failed to provide any indication of rank of unit patches but his nonchalant gate cried out infantry private. I wondered what importance the military placed on this soldier to have a private plane reserved just to transport him around. In my own defense I must state that at this time I had no idea what role the private contractor Air America was to play in the Viet Nam war. There were many private contractors operating in country and all of them had civilian employees.

The young soldier casually opened the plane's side door and the pilot called out over the noise of the engine. "Rock City?"

The trooper replied to the affirmative by nodding his head and climbing inside the plane. I was still amazed that the government would go thru so much cost and effort to transport one common soldier from one point to another. In any case we taxied down the runway and climbed easily into the bright South East Asia sky.

The flight was beautiful but noneventful until we began to descend for landing. The pilot suddenly turned to the soldier and inquired if this was a secured air strip. The private who was seated between us and the pilot answered that he had no idea. "Then be ready to jump out while I'm still moving." The pilot ordered. "I ain't stopping to find out." He added obviously sure of his authority.

The pilot made a hurried dive towards a small narrow concrete runway that could be seen only thru his windshield and the spinning propeller. The landing strip was surrounded by a field of huge grey round boulders that seemed an ideal hiding place for V.C. gunners. I strained my eyes thru the right rear window certain that I would spot some V.C. with an ambush on his mind sneaking thru the rocks below.

The pilot managed a smooth bumpless landing, and then quickly slowed to a running speed before turning to the soldier and calling out. "Jump!" The

young man gathered up his gear, pushed open the side
door and jumped out. I watched as he ran out of the
path of the still moving tail fin before he came to a
complete stop. It was clear from the lost expression on
the young man's handsome face that he had no idea of
what to do next.

I was still on V.C. alert; my eye's continually
scanning the massive grey boulders for movement when
the pilot slapped the throttle open. I had expected him to
make a "U" turn and taxi to the end of the runway then
turn into the wind once more for our take off, but in less
time than it takes to tell it we had bounded into the air
again. I have never experienced a fixed wing aircraft
managing to lift off a runway in such a short distance.

The pilot made a slow turn to the right and I could
see the soldier still standing in the center of the concrete
runway just where we had left him. I did spot one lone
pajama clad old woman standing among the boulders. I
remember hoping for the sake of the young soldier that
the old woman was not a finger man for a bunch of V.C.'s
who were waiting to descend on some poor hapless
American soldier. But as so often happens in these
situations one never learns the fate of close friends let
alone passing strangers.

The civilian pilot appeared very unconcerned
about the soldier's welfare as he straightened out the
plane while trying to gain altitude. Shortly after takeoff
the pilot began to peel an orange which required both of
his hands and all of his attention. This seemed a little
too relaxed to me but I remained calm while he began to
stuff the pieces of orange peel thru a small hole in the
cockpits side window. We buzzed quietly along while
the pilot enjoyed his picnic and Master Jack dozed off. I
on the other hand, watched the pilots every movement
and at the same time watched the ground far below for

points of reference. Now I know this seems paranoid but when flying in country I always tried to scan the country side for any place I recognized or prominent feature such as the Mekong River or other waterway. Why? Well I always thought if the aircraft should be forced down and I survived, it would be handy to know which way to travel.

The flight continued on without further incident until my scouting eyes spied the long concrete runway of Bien Hoa Air Base. I felt greatly relieved knowing that we would soon be back on firm ground again in a familiar area. We began a descending turn to line up with the runway and were only a couple of hundred feet off the ground when the small single engine plane gave a great shutter. The shutter was immediately accompanied by the report of an explosion that drove us straight up some unknown distance where the aircraft stalled then began to drop straight down. Now I mean the airplane went vertically up and down without any forward movement, something fixed-winged air craft are not prone to do. In EOD School the instructors preached to their students to never set off an explosion under a low flying air craft because the blast will blow the air needed for lift out from beneath the wings causing the plane to crash.

"EOD team." Master Jack announced calmly as he looked out the side window at the ground below. The man made this revelation very matter-of-factly as the airplane dropped out of the sky like a carnival ride. The pilot remained unmoving not trying to change engine speed even though the propeller began to scream because it was being deprived of air resistance. He took no evasive maneuvers but sat calmly in his seat both hands on the steering yoke. It was obvious to me the pilot had no appreciation for the situation we were in.

We plummeted towards earth for what seemed an eternity and from where I sat staring out of the side window the blue sky was rapidly being exchanged for the green earth below. But suddenly that huge long engines high revving motor groaned as the two bladed prop began to catch hold of the hot humid air and we began to move forward. While I began to release my death grip on the airplane's spartan seat Master Jack and the pilot yawned in boredom. These two considered this little incident an everyday occurrence, but as I listened to the plane's tires impact the searing concrete runway I doubted my strength to equal the nerve of men such as these.

This may sound like a very minor everyday occurrence and I later learned to accept it as such. Little moments of such excitement were not worthy of recounting to your comrades around the bar at night for someone would surely top the tale by relating their days adventure.

I have included this yarn as an example of how jaded one can become while living in a combat zone.

STEAK SAUCE

Most possessions in our unit, from reading material to care packages from home were communal property. Men wrote home asking to be sent the usual treats like cookies or cakes but often times they requested much simpler items like steak sauce or other condiments to spice up their mundane meals. Such common everyday items were a delicacy that brought even more joy when shared with your team mates. I remember very well when our proficient unit scrounge Sgt. Lew came up with a case of frozen steaks that became the basis for a party.

I joined Lew on one of his combined EOD call & trading missions. We stopped at several different companies where Lew turned on his charm and was cordially welcomed. When Lew got rolling, the man could talk Satan himself out of his soul. It had been mentioned that the unit would need a new trader when Lew returned to the world and it was suggested that I would be a candidate. That one day of horse trading convinced me I was not that man. However, I remember stating several times that I believe in civilian life Lew would become either a rich man or a prison inmate.

In order to have a party many preparations were hastily implement, for instance rebuilding a barbeque grill, locating some picnic type tables and creating sun shade over the entire area. These minor problems were easily solved by men who are known for their gifted field expedience. However a more demanding problem arose over how to cook the prized beef steak.

There were no convenience stores just around the corner, or large super markets with well stocked shelves of Heinz 57 steak sauce so it became necessary to call in some favors from mess Sgts who were willing to donate to our cause which in turn resulted in extending the Sgts an invitation.

This was one of the few times we had access to real meat and I for one did not care to see it ruined by the application of some make-shift sauce. It is truly amazing how many secret home grown marinades can surface in one small group of men. Several strange concoctions were haphazardly developed; each one purported to be the magic elixir that would create a master piece of the donated beef.

I made it known that none of these spicy formulas appealed to my taste buds and that I wished my steak to be cooked plain. Of course that was unthinkable to the great chiefs that populated our little group. In desperation the First Sgt. declared he would brew up some of his famous beer batter. I have no taste for beer and when I learned it was normally used to fry fish I really became upset.

But over my heated protest several cans of beer were open and set out in the heat of the day until they went flat. The stale beer was then mixed with flour and salt and pepper until it became a slurry similar to wall paper paste. This odd smelling white batter was brushed all over the meat before being placed on the make shift grill. I was certain that the precious steaks would come out either tasting like fish or reeking of beer. But as it turned out I was proven wrong and the meat was an excellent treat. However, at that time I would have thought a barbequed jungle boot would have tasted good.

Fortunately most of the guests invited or not, generously contributed some food or drink preventing anyone from going hungry. No one was turned away from attending the party; no one was even questioned about their credentials for it was just the nature of the common GI's to share the bounty. The results were a great party, enjoyed by many a deserving soldier. New friends were made and old friendships were renewed that hot summer day. It is truly strange what can come from sharing a few pounds of red meat among men who were accustomed to a spartan daily fare.

HOAGIE BAIT TRUCK

As far as the world of food at Long Binh, South Viet Nam is concerned, I would judge the 3rd Ord. Battalion mess hall as one of the very worst that I ever experienced. The cooks for the most part were players in the local drug scene; while the mess Sgt's total daily calorie intake was derived from beer. But the mess halls poor quality was not completely the fault of the personnel, much of the responsibility lay with the U.S. Army. There was a period of six weeks when our mess hall was issued nothing but hot dogs. The menu consisted of boiled or fried hot dogs for lunch and dinner with the left-overs being thrown in a perpetual stew that was offered at breakfast. A trip to the mess hall was truly an adventure in dinning out.

I will give the Army credit for allowing a lunch wagon to operate in the 3rd battalion area. These stores were large metal box bodies that were mounted on two and a half ton military trucks and were know as "roach coaches" or "hoagie bait trucks" by the military. Vietnamese women with a penchant for harassing the GI's normally operated these tiny stores. Shopping in these facilities could prove very trying at times as the conversations were conducted in pigeon English or hand signs. Still they were of value to us in that our working hours did not always coincide with the hours of the mess hall. Often times it was a choice between the roach coach, C- rations, or hunger.

I have little recall of the limited selection offered by these vendors, except for their famed hoagie sandwich. These sandwiches were already prepared and separately wrapped in cellophane and consisted of a six inch bread roll holding several slices of cold meat. The key in selecting one of these sandwiches was a close inspection of the meats coloring. The cold meat, while never red, usually ranged from grey to a dark shiny green, my personal standard allowed for consuming only the cold meat in the grey to light shiny green area. I always feared that the dark slimy green meat might make me ill but since we were sick most of the time it would have been impossible to trace any food poisoning back to those roach coach sandwiches.

As my writings indicate, food was of a major concern to me both then and now. I was an exact opposite of those around me for while my thoughts centered on eating they worried over supplies of water, ammunition, explosives, or booze. I went so far as to carry a highly coveted LURP or long range patrol ration in the right leg pants pocket of my jungle fatigues.

The LURP rations were a freeze dried meal that came in a plastic bag sealed within a cloth-like O.D. pouch. These meals could easily be reconstituted by merely adding water or in a pinch could be consumed dry. A word of warning is needed here; if these freeze dried meals were eaten dry one must take care in drinking liquids afterwards, because it seems the dehydrated food will rapidly expand in the stomach as well as the shipping bag. I witnessed just such an incident in Saigon but the victim denies the whole affair. That may be but I can still recall the sound of his powerful jaws crunching that freeze dried meal, it can only be described as someone walking on broken glass.

These LURP rations are very similar to today's meal-ready-to-eat that are issued to the military and are hoarded by survivalists. In Viet Nam the freeze dried meals were a highly sought after commodity and were by far and away preferred over the notorious C-rations. I and other members of the unit made a concerted effort to acquire these LURP rations by hook or crook, usually by the later. Being a valuable commodity these rations were usually under lock and key or armed guard which necessitated other more creative forms of procurement.

I, unlike others in the unit was never adept at trading although bartering was a long established manner of commerce in the military. It is with great reluctance that I admit my strength in curing favors rested in the fine art of begging and crying. Of course this demeaning tactic usually fell on deaf ears with the hard case G.I's that we normally dealt with. However if the situation was just right even some of the toughest men would show pity on a hungry fat man.

TDY AT NAVAL BASE OF DONG TAM

On one such occasion we were TDY at the little brown water Naval Base of Dong Tam. This base can be most effectively described as the mud hole on the Mekong. The U.S. Navy operated river patrol boats know as Swift boats out of this piece of paradise. Yes, these are the same boats that Senator John Kerry made famous during his presidential bid. And at the risk of offending someone, (which in this case I don't care if you are offended.) I wondered from the first time I ever heard of John Kerry way back in the 70's how he could have survived a tour with the boat crews I knew. The swift boat men I knew lived in their own little world, they asked nothing of the military for they depended on no other than the other crew members. They in short commanded their own destinies and woe unto anyone American or Vietnamese who should foolishly interfere. Even the most insensitive unconscious boob quickly discerned that these brown water Navy men were men among men.

My first close up encounter with a boat man was just after sunset my first night at Dong Tam. I had wondered down to the dilapidated building that was jokingly known as the shower. I had just got soaped up when the sirens sounded causing everyone to race outside in search of a bomb shelter. As the mortar rounds started to detonate around the building I realized that I was not alone for just across from me stood a man casually rubbing a bar of soap all over his body.

"Ain't you going to the shelter?" He asked nonchalantly while continuing to shower.

"No." I managed to muster up my courage enough to answer.

337

"Me neither." The man stated. "To hell with Charlie, I ain't running to hide in some hole in the ground every time he wants to shell this place!"

"Yeah, me neither." I shakily agreed even though my mind raced with thoughts of grabbing my towel and heading for cover. I must admit my remaining inside the shower had nothing to do with bravery. It was just that I never did like going into those bunkers and I knew our building was too far away and was not any safer. All of that and the fact that it was dark and I had no idea of where the bunker was located, so in other words I was in a trap of my own making.

"Hey you're all right." the other man declared as he turned off his shower and began to towel off.

This had been one of those mortar attacks that are like a summer shower. They begin slowly with just a few surprising drops, and then build up to a rush only to taper off to nothing. This storm had been nothing more than a harassment attack, just a warning that Charlie was out there and he wanted us to remember that fact.

"Guess its over" the other man declared in a semi disappointed voice.

As we exited the shower the man introduced himself as a swift boat crewman and announced we were friends. I extended the same bit of bravado unwilling to confess that I was not what he thought. But the man told many of his shipmates about me and even used the incident of the mortar attack while introducing me to his friends. I was glad we were only going to be at Dong Tam for a few days because I feared that I could not live up to the standards that these brown water Navy men lived by.

NAVY MESS HALL IN DONG TAM

As the days passed we made many new friends, some of which were in the Navy's fine mess hall. A far cry from most of the Army cooks I knew, these sailors were good people who dropped by often for a chat usually with some delicacy in hand. The galley chief, a large good natured man made a habit of calling early in the morning with a pan of hot cinnamon rolls. Needless to say the chief was always a welcome visitor because we never got such treats in the Army mess halls.

One of my more memorable trips to the Dong Tam mess hall came after another EOD man and I had spent a couple of days out in the rice paddies being handed from one group to another like a couple of unwanted orphans. We stumbled into our building about lunch time covered with rice paddy muck and weary from the trip. A passing swabbie called out that they were having good eats at the mess hall but we would have to hurry if we wanted to eat. You don't have to ring the dinner bell more than once to get my attention but my team mate declared he was too tired and dirty to eat. I wanted to argue the point but since we hadn't eaten for a couple days I made a bee line for the dining hall.

Our teams were often denied entry or at least made to jump through hoops when attempting to eat in strange mess halls. But that was never the case with these brown water Navy men, they were always willing to set a place for one more person regardless of service branch. Opening the door to the little mess hall I found it packed with sailors and wondered if there would be anything left for a stray dog soldier like me. I rushed to the serving table where a young seaman standing behind the counter announced that I had my choice of fresh frozen lobster tail or steak.

Now I had just come from the 3rd Ord mess hall where we had been served hot dogs three times a day so I naturally thought this swabbie was making a joke. But I looked into big stainless steel serving pans and sure enough, one held steak and the other what appeared to be lobster tails. Now I was not accustomed to eating steak and absolutely had never tasted lobster so I just stood there mouth open in a state of shock.

"Which do you want?" The seaman demanded.

"I don't know." I replied fearing to take the lobster and then find I didn't like its taste.

"I haven't eaten in a couple days." I tried to explain while stalling for time to decide.

"Oh hell, give him both." The big good natured galley chief called out to his man at the counter.

Suddenly I found myself standing in a tiny mess hall in the middle of a Mekong mud hole preparing to enjoy a steak and lobster lunch. Man what a screw ball war.

I found a place at a table and dug in to the excellent meal. Of course my full plate drew some remarks from those seated around me because they had been restricted to one entrée or the other. I tried to explain how special I was to a bunch of men who themselves were a cut above average and who had endured their share of hungry days. Still they were good natured about some outside Army guy hustling their cooks for extra rations.

TWO SCREWBALL SWABBIES

EOD units have this magnetism that draws every odd character in the area and the 3rd Ord seemed to have more than its share of screwballs. We had the typical array of drunks, fighters, thieves, outlaws and just plain scoundrels. But two of the craziest were shipmates on a Swift boat stationed at Dong Tam. One was a petty officer the other a seaman who had also been a petty officer with twelve years in the Navy. This poor sailor had numerous tours in Viet Nam which were interrupted by short assignment in the states. It seems that every time he got back in the world some trouble would arise and back to Nam he would go. He once told me he hoped to retire as a seaman but I doubt seriously that he got his wish. This odd pair of hell raising swabbies roamed in and out of our building when ashore as if it were their home. No one ever protested the pair's visits for they were likable enough fellows besides, ejecting them might have proved painful.

Late one afternoon I could hear a fight erupting in the direction of the boat docks. The yelling moved closer and closer until it peaked my curiosity enough that I left the cooling shade of our buildings veranda and stepped out into the pleasant tropical sun. Looking into the brilliant afternoon sun I could just make out the two sailors moving slowly my way. They were yelling profanity at the top of their lungs and pausing every few feet to exchange punches. I couldn't believe my eyes and ears as I watched these two best friends in what appeared to be a bitter quarrel. It was obvious that they were heading directly for our building but their progress was impeded by the intermittent fist fight. When I could no longer resist the urge to intervene I raced down the path and stepped between the two combatants.

"What is going on?" I demanded but the squabbling and occasional wild punches continued unabated until I mediated a settlement in the form of a couple cold beers. I am now reasonably certain that free beer and a quiet place to fight was what made our building the intended destination of the two swabbies.

Once the beer cans were opened under the shade of our veranda and everyone found a place to set, the background of the sparing match began to unfold. Of course the more beer that was consumed, the more difficult it became to sort out the order of the day's events leading up to the fight but I believe this is a condensed version of what happened.

The two friends were patrolling the mighty Mekong River in their swift boat, with the petty officer at the helm while the lowly seaman was stationed in the bow with a flame thrower. The V.C. fired a self propelled grenade at the boat that blew a hole in the hull at the water line. The vessel was rapidly filling with water preventing the boat from making a hasty retreat from the heavy gun fire originating from a shore line ambush. The petty officer realizing that escape was impossible threw the helm over, cracked open the throttles and run the swift boat aground at the point where the V.C. firing was the heaviest. This desperate action placed his friend in an open position in the boats bow; he was also the closest to the enemy position. The seaman who had nowhere to hide and no choice but to run the flame thrower until a winner was determined. The argument continued with the seaman exhibiting a fresh untreated bullet wound in his arm, while the petty officer repeated that he was confident that the seaman would flame the V.C. into submission. Each new can of beer brought more charges of insanity as well as more laughter. Its funny how many disagreements have been settled one way or another over a cold beer. In fact maybe some of our world leaders would do well to exchange ideas over a brew.

Later that evening after the proper application of drinks, insults and laughs, the two swabbies stumbled out of our building best friends once more with the whole incident forgotten. They had survived a close call with team work and sheer guts. It was just another day at the office for men whose usual day was hanging your butt out of a small boat in the hopes of starting a fire fight.

A few days later the swabbies dropped by in search of a free beer when the subject of LURP rations came up. I explained how poor the 3rd Ord mess hall was compared to the one at Dong Tam and I also stated how much I liked the LURP meals and how handy they were to carry. Well the next thing I knew plans were being made for a trading run up the Mekong River. They graciously extended an invitation for me to ride along but I quickly refused after recalling past rides with more sane swift boats crews. My decision to decline the boat trip was reinforced when they could not give a return date.

The pair drank a few more beers then departed with the promise to return soon with plenty of LURP rations. I took the planned trip as drunken bravado until word got around that the pair had gone on a routine patrol but were now reported missing. I understand that other boats searched for the lost craft but nothing was found until they came slowly motoring into the dock late one evening as if nothing had happen.

The petty officer had an official story of radio malfunctions and motor trouble that with tongue-in-cheek satisfied the brass who seemed reluctant to push the subject too far. While the petty officer made his official apologies, the seaman told me they had taken the boat up the Mekong to the Bobo Canal. This was a very dangerous stream that led into Cambodia. The seaman explained they had a friend in that area that could and would trade for anything. He then handed me a couple of cases of LURP rations free of charge while explaining they had stopped farther up river to stash the rest of their trade goods so as not to cause undo questions when returning to base.

I have no proof of where these two actually went on their little trip and I never questioned what other goods they had, I was just glad I had not accompanied them to get the highly prized rations.

SWABBIE & THE STOLEN FAN

A few weeks later I was again sent to Dong Tam to assist in the pull out of the American Army troops. The GI's were to be moved up north by military transport which meant a limit would be imposed on the amount of baggage they could take along. Being unable to ship large goods the transferring soldier traded, sold and eventually gave away much of their personal belongings. The streets of the little base became parking lots for the numerous stolen vehicles that were abandoned as the GI's were shipped out. The military called these vehicles mavericks having been stolen from their issuing units and misappropriated for use by another unit. These maverick vehicles accounted for thousands upon thousands of gallons of fuel being illegally burned every month. The Army complained on and on about the stolen jeep problem but the truth of the matter is that most of the maverick jeeps were being used for military business. I wanted to take one of these abandoned jeeps back to Long Binh but it was pointed out that our unit already had one stolen jeep on its books and a second one might raise embarrassing questions. However, other more transportable, less obvious items did become the property of the 3rd Ord just to prevent them from falling into the hands of the V.C.

A day or so before we were scheduled to return to Long Binh the seaman from the swift boat asked me for a ride to the main gate. It was late afternoon and the long open road to the gate was lined with Vietnamese day-workers, most of whom were women. Nearly every one of the women was carrying some item of food or clothing that the departing GI's had given them or had simply abandoned to whoever was willing to haul it off. A bit of teamwork was required among groups of the tiny females in order to transport the larger prizes off post.

The seaman and I had not driven very far when he began to comment on the amount of booty the Vietnamese were carrying off post. I explained that the Army guys were unable to move their goods with them and because of the $ 200.00 a month spending limit it was difficult to sell for cash or bank the profits from the sales.

At that point the seaman's comments escalated to a complaint that these day laborers were carrying off property that he could not afford on his meager seaman's pay. Suddenly the seaman screamed out as if in pain calling for me to stop the jeep.

Although we were not going more than 20 miles an hour I slid the little jeep to a halt after the seaman had jumped out. He ran screaming into a group of South Vietnamese women and grabbed what we laughingly called a combat fan out of one woman's arms.

"That's my fan," the sailor yelled out. "You stole my fan." And with that the fight was on. The woman who was carrying the fan cried out that the fan was given to her by an Army Sgt, while the sailor argued it was his. The other day-workers sided with the wronged female and were threatening violence. All the noisy squabbling brought a couple of M.P.'s who were manning the gate some distance away. They had been busy checking the long line of day-worker's new found wealth to be sure none of it was U.S. property or had been reported stolen so they had not witnessed the altercation.

Naturally the M.P.'s wanted to settle the matter as quickly as possible but they still demanded to know the circumstance of the disagreement. The seaman insisted the fan was his, while the woman and her friends claimed it had been a gift from a Sgt. Then it happened since neither side had a bill of sale or knew the fans serial number the M.P.'s asked me who owned the fan. I smiled and lied in my most convincing voice that the fan did belong to the sailor but I added I didn't think the woman should be arrested for taking the fan because the sailor was always mean to the day-laborers.

The M.P.'s who had caught on to what had happened awarded the fan to the sailor and told the woman to go home or she would be reported and her work permit would be revoked. This was followed by a lot of Vietnamese profanity and a couple of death threats that meant nothing to a man of the seaman's experiences. I cussed him as we climbed back in the jeep for dragging me into such a stupid fight but it was his opinion that the woman probably didn't have electricity in the first place and that she would end up selling the fan on the street.

I started up the jeep and headed for the gate once more but he told me we could turn around and go back to the building now. It was then that I realized he had this little robbery planned from the start and that we had driven along the line of workers until he spotted a fan that looked new that was being carried by someone he thought could be easily intimidated.

I was mad at the seaman for a time but he was always a friend who, although always down and out, was willing to share anything he had. The man was always in trouble but he hadn't a clue as to why he held the lowest rank in the Navy after twelve years of active duty, several of those in country not to mention his several purple hearts and other decorations. To this day I can't remember that crazy seaman's name but crazy as he may have been, I still consider him a friend and hope that he got home. I say that with some reservation because I know he could never function in a normal society.

JEEP PROBLEM

When time came to leave beautiful Dong Tam we rolled confidently out the gate and disappeared down the lonely narrow jungle road. We hadn't traveled far although it seemed like miles when our jeep began to sputter and baulk as if it were out of gas and eventually died. This heavily forested area was appropriately enough called "Ambush Alley", as was nearly every other place in South Viet Nam that provided Charlie with easy concealment. Truthfully the road was very narrow and deserted; it was also lined the tall grass and thick vegetation that grew close enough to be touchable from the seat of a passing jeep. Where was all that Agent Orange defoliant when you needed it?

On this particular trip our team numbered three instead of the usual two members. One man became extremely nervous at out predicament; he demanded that we get the jeep running and out of the threatening area. We worked on the jeep getting it to start and run a few yards before dying once more. This jeep had a good two way radio mounted on the rear fender but our few attempts to make outside contact ended in failure. This was no real surprise to me for my experience with these radios had proven to be less than reliable. Of course this could be attributed to lack of operator training and patience with such a new fangled device.

As the third man became more disturbed with our progress we managed to learn minor tricks to extend the length or running time between each coughing and dying spell of the little motor. The struggle continued for some time without any other vehicles passing on the remote jungle route. The absence of traffic led the third man to believe we were lost and he became very indignant to the point of threatening to have us reduced in rank. This was one of the lesser of many threats I received for reduction of rank while in country. The funny thing is no one ever backed up the threat and that was probably because I didn't care about rank in the first place, but it was always interesting to listen to them recount the list of charges both real and imaginary.

I had to chuckle at the man because the only reason he thought we were lost was due to the fact that he had been dead drunk the week before when I drove him into Dong Tam on this very same road. This morning he was unusually sober so he did not recognize the route he had been over before. The little jeep's illness became very predictable in that it would run for a short distance then stop and rest for a bit then it could be restarted just to repeat the process. The third man became more disturbed each time the motor died, so much so in fact that he refused to watch the thick foliage for any signs that the V.C. were approaching. Sometime later we broke clear of the dense jungle which improved the third man's attitude a good bit even though the jeep continued to stall of its own accord.

We eventually came across a small group of mechanics and explained the symptoms our jeep had been exhibiting. They laughed, opened the hood and pointed out the small oil sensing switch located on the engine block. This switch sensed the motor's oil pressure and if it were to drop below a certain point the electricity to the fuel pump would be cut off. This was intended to be a protective device for the engine but it could prove fatal for someone driving in a combat zone. The Sgt who explained this bit of irrational thinking warned us that if this should ever happen again that we should hurriedly bypass the electrical terminal's oil sensor switch. He said they had been proven to be faulty and even if they were good and the oil pressure was low that we should bypass the switch. He figured it was better to ruin an engine than to ruin a soldier and I agreed whole heartily with the man.

It was after our mechanical misadventures in ambush alley that the other man and I agreed that we should have picked up one of those abandon jeeps in Dong Tam. We both would have gladly set the complaining third man free in the maverick jeep while we nursed the ailing vehicle home.

I have never named this third man for he has been dead for many years now. He was one of my least favorite partners because we shared other similar incidents; but I am told in the end he gave a good accounting of himself and that is what matters in the EOD field.

TDY DA NANG

As I look back on my days in country there is a reassuring theme that the 'Powers-That-Be' conspired to send me on TDY assignment or at least somewhere afield. Now I'm sure that other men drew more TDY than I, but I have many memories of off-post calls. If this is true then there must have been some nefarious plan by the upper echelon to absence me from the building. However I haven't any idea why such a plan would have been initiated but it worked in my favor. I loved traveling throughout the countryside where we had a chance to get to know the people. For the most part I found the Vietnamese people to be friendly and hospitable even though they wanted to kill us. It was one of those love-hate relationships I guess. It's like the people who invite you to their church on Sunday then try to skin you in a business deal on Monday. Business is business everywhere in the world except the Vietnamese people's business was killing us if possible.

As much as I find fault with TDY at Dong Tam, I found trips to Da Nang just the opposite. Truthfully our living conditions were on par for both bases. The living quarters were meager at best while the food being Navy in Dong Tam and Marine in Da Nang was excellent. Since both were supplied by the Navy their mess halls had real meat, real milk, and (God bless the Navy) real ice cream. None of these staples had passed through the 3rd Ord mess hall doors in months.

Dong Tam was a small half forgotten base that lay on the flood plain of the Mekong River that was blessed with a topography that was as flat as a pool table. Da Nang on the other hand was a large harbor city situated on the beautiful South China Sea. A row of tall green mountains served as a contrasting back drop to all the civilian and military structures in the sprawling city.

I remember making an oath while standing on the perfect white sandy beach at Da Nang and gazing into the hypnotizing clear blue water of the harbor, that when the war ended I would return to this very spot and build a magnificent resort hotel. The Army EOD man with me stated that he wanted to be a partner in such a sure thing. He thought as I did that such an enterprise would become world famous and that we would become filthy rich. Well so much for day dreams but war ravaged or not it was a beautiful place and I am glad to have had the opportunity to have seen it.

On my first trip to Da Nang I was billeted with the Army EOD down town in a large house. The second time I stayed with the Marine EOD outside of town near the large ammo dump. The ammunition dump had exploded destroying the entire facility, a small village and the Marine camp in the process. The Marine camp, while not entirely completed had just been rebuilt in time for my second visit. The camps security consisted of a few strands of concertina wire, a couple of guard towers and several hundred armed and well motivated Marines. Staying on this Marine base had a whole different feeling than life in the Army camps. The descriptive words, remote, primitive or scary all come to mind.

I was fortunate enough during my short enlistment to spent time with all four branches of the military. It is difficult to rate one service against another because each individual unit has an assigned mission that affects the living standards of the personnel on that installation. I spent nearly a year on a small reserve air force base in the midwest where the duty was easy, the food great and the security minimal. The Naval Ordnance School at Indian Head had a little tighter security but the duty and the food were on par with the air force. The Army had poor food, poor barracks and a lot of extra duty time.

Although I knew several Marines at Indian Head plus our class spent a week at Quantico, my TDY with the Corp at Da Nang was a real learning experience. It seems they have rules and areas that pertain only to those below the rank of E-6; in fact they set out big signs that state "Only God and E-6 and above in this area". I had a deep burning daydream that a dud rocket or mortar round would land in that area so that I could just for spite refuse to work on it. Of course it never happened but it certainly would have been a lot of fun to tangle with those NCO's.

I'LL JUST HELP MYSELF

One of my first confrontations with the Marines came of course on the evening of my first day in camp. I had returned from the destroyed depot in time for the evening meal. The Marine team I was staying with was delayed so I was told to go ahead to the mess hall and they would meet me there later. Now, I should have known that a lone dog face walking thru a Jarhead camp unescorted would be asking for trouble but hunger, as usual had overcome my common sense. I patiently endured a couple of rude comments and accidental bumping of shoulders as I strolled quietly thru the rows of olive drab tents.

Even though my little army uniform managed to attract a good deal of attention from my host I managed to find the highly desired mess hall. Fortunately it sat just this side of the dead line where 'only God and E-6' could enter or I would have had to starve to death. The building was obviously new, the old one having been damaged when the ammunition depot was destroyed some months earlier. Cautiously entering the shiny new facility I was surprised to find an absence of the usual long line leading to the serving window. In fact there were only a half dozen men in the whole dining room and they were already seated. I thought the empty building a great stroke of luck and hurried to the food servers fearing I would shortly be overrun by a flood of starving Marines.

I picked up one of those stylish compartmentalized tray and utensils and stepped in front of the young marine who was serving the food. The steam table held large stainless steel pans filled to the brim with fried beef steak and real vegetables while at the far end of the line was ice cream; I mean real ice cream, not the imitation

354

stuff the Army offered, but vanilla and chocolate real ice cream, in large paper containers that were covered with frost. How long had it been since I had seen real ice cream or frost for that matter I wondered aloud. I was wearing a huge smile when I extended the ugly brown tray towards the slick sleeved Marine cook standing on the opposite side of the serving line. The young man stood arms folded across his chest while giving me his meanest scowl.

"Just what the hell do you want doggy?" he snarled.

"Fixing to eat supper," I replied in my most polite voice, still wearing my winning smile.

"Not in here you ain't," came his vindictive forcefully reply.

I did my best to explain that I was on TDY here for a couple weeks and this was the mess hall I had been instructed to eat in. The rebuff to my courteous explanation was met with a long stream of barracks language and the promise that he would never serve any Army soldier.

I said "fine with me" as I grabbed up the serving tongs from the meat tray. This brought on screams of protest and dire death threats from the young man but that did not prevent my piling several steaks in the middle compartment of the tray. Now that I had converted the dining hall to self-serve, I quickly bypassed all the fresh vegetables and moved directly to the cartons of real ice cream. I quickly filled the remaining compartments of the tray with ice cream then made my way to a private table.

The heat in this unairconditioned mess hall was so intent that my precious hard packed real ice cream was already turning soft. I was becoming upset that the real chocolate ice cream in the small right tray compartment

355

was melting and running over into the real vanilla ice cream in the left tray compartment. All this melting ice cream made consuming the pile of steaks in the large center tray compartment all the more urgent.

Somewhere in the distant background of my famished subconscious was detecting a great deal of yelling and cussing, but my conscious mind was completely absorbed with eating at least one of the steaks before the real ice cream became blended into a brown soup. When I finally looked up from my plate I found my little table was completely surrounded by several irate Marines. The leader of the lynch-mob was a really big gunny Sgt who spouted one profane death threat after another. I politely smiled at the Sgt and his merry men and continued to eat the big beautiful beef steak. But I guess having a quiet steak supper was not in the cards as the commotion became so intense that I had to muster up my most courteous personality to ask for some peace and quiet during my dinner. These Marines were very rude and became even more vocal as their numbers grew until some ten or twelve men were involved.

I simply continued to eat the steak and take an occasional spoonful of real ice cream to prevent it from invading the steak compartment. I love steak and ice cream but not mixed in the same bite of food.

Although it took a few minutes, I soon realized that two of the men surrounding my table were Marine EOD men who were trying to make sense of all the commotion. It was interesting to listen to the EOD men argue with their mess Sgt while at the same time trying to explain to me why I could not take food especially several steaks at one time. It seems they only had so many steaks to begin with and that I wasn't in the original head count. They continued to explain that if I ate all those steaks that someone would have to go hungry. I listened politely to their arguments, while still eating then asked if they wanted the ice cream back also. They allowed, as how the ice cream was nearly melted that I could keep it but the steaks had to be returned. I had remained pleasant and polite from the minute I walked in the front door but now I stood up and faced the big gunny Sgt and made my demands clear to him and his crowd. I would return the steaks only if he agreed that whenever I came in this mess hall for the extent of my stay that I would be served just like any other member of the U.S. military. I didn't want or need any snide remarks from a slick sleeved cook but I did want him to do his job. I said this knowing the Marines place a lot of value in rank. I being an E-5, it was not proper for a Marine private to cuss me as the server had done.

Of course there was some resistance to my demands, but in the end the mess Sgt agreed to my terms. The next morning at breakfast everyone was very military and of proper bearing as I moved thru the serving line. I know there was no love lost and I even wondered if they might poison me but I decided the results were worth the risk. I ate every one of the mess halls fine meals in a state of complete relaxation. I always wonder why the gunny Sgt and his men did not get physical and simply take the steak laden tray away from me. I had learned from some of the best that making firm demands and running a bluff, blessed with a little luck, can at times achieve your ultimate goal.

DA NANG LATRINE

One hot sultry evening a couple of days after the mess hall incident we had just returned from a miserable hot day of cleaning up the ammo depot when a trip to the latrine became an urgent matter. I must explain at this point that bowel problems were a constant factor in South Viet Nam. The combination of bad water, poor food, anti-malaria pills and a world that was always in the final stages of decay made diarrhea a national past time. Everyone from the meek to the mighty suffered with this ailment at one time or another.

In any case it was just dusk as I raced to the large wooden out house located some distance from our building. This necessary structure was constructed of a wooden bottom and sides made of wire that allowed for ventilation and provided a pretty fair view of the area while seated on the four-holer. Only the Marines would build an outhouse with its back to a small hill facing across a valley towards some bright green hills.

I had just chosen a seat in the empty facility and was admiring the beautiful Asian sunset when suddenly a huge explosion ripped thru the air causing the building to move all about me. To say I was startled would be an understatement for I thought at first the mess hall crew was seeking revenge on me or we were under a rocket attack or a satchel charge had detonated in the nearby perimeter wire. My head spun from side to side looking for the source of the detonation while at the same time trying to pull up my pants for a rapid departure. I made great haste to flee the outhouse because the last thing I wanted to have happen was to meet my fate in an outhouse in South Viet Nam. As I headed for the door I spotted a large bright white cloud suddenly forming in the clear blue-black evening sky over the far range of green hills. One of the first things a new man in country

358

must learn is the different sounds that incoming or outgoing artillery make. The artillery shells being fired out produce a deep thud while incoming shells are more of a sharp report. In this case the 175's muzzle blast was so close I couldn't tell the difference. A second explosion shook the wood-frame building and it was only then that I realized the source of the blasts was coming from the top of the short hill just behind the outhouse. Unbeknown to the Marine EOD team, a large 175 mm artillery piece had set up shop just behind the company latrines. The muzzle blast from such a weapon is terrific and could prove deadly if a person were to get too close to the weapon when firing.

I hurried back to our building and informed the other shocked EOD men of my experience. They had a good laugh but had no idea that the 175 mm had been placed on the hill behind the outhouse. Everyone agreed that it was probably fortunate for me that I was already seated when the first round was fired.

In the interest of inter-service rivalry I want to state that the 175mm gun crew who fired those rounds was not simply attempting to terrify a poor Army soldier, the gun crew was firing for registry which is a common practice. This registry often takes place at dusk after an artillery piece is set and the forward observer is in place. The forward observer calls in a co-ordinance to the gun crew who then fire a white phosphorus round that is easily seen at that given position. The forward observer then makes adjustments so that the artillery shells can be placed on target in the area. Once the gun crew has these co-ordinances registered or written down the forward observer can redirect the artillery fire no matter how dark or stormy the night might get.

A WILD GUESS

One of the stranger duties, or maybe I should say services that the 3rd Ord provided for Long Binh Post involved the investigation of every explosion within the base boundary. This may sound simple but Long Binh was a very large post and accidental detonations were common, as were fraggings. Fraggings were incidents where one GI tried to blow up another GI. The weapon of choice was normally a hand grenade of some type but every now and then some irate soldier would get inventive, which made such calls much more interesting. Most of the before mentioned calls were merely time consuming but the Army took the investigation of impacted V.C. rounds much more seriously. When the call came in for a team to investigate incoming fire we were urged to arrive at the scene as soon as possible.

The standard crater call consisted of rushing to the sight of the impact as if it would magically vanish. A small crowd mostly made up of officers would be gathered around a shallow hole in the ground impatiently waiting our arrival. This clustering of personnel around and impact site was an act of stupidly in its self. The V.C. commonly fired rockets or mortars into our facilities in a haphazard fashion that prevented them from striking exactly the same place twice. That being said repeated rounds did strike the same place twice especially when fired by our own artillery while using the wrong co-ordinance. Although it never happened, the possibility of these weapons containing chemical warheads was at least feasible. In fact, in late 1969 Army intelligence warned that a Russian officer with a full chemical outfit had been killed south of Saigon.

If these little sightseeing parties had stumbled into a crater where a projectile filled with nerve gas or mustard gas had detonated they would have been displaying signs of the exposure long before we arrived. In chemical storage areas cages of birds and small animals are strategically placed along roads and buildings as an early warning device with the theory being that they are more susceptible to toxic agents than humans. Junior and I made a habit of looking ahead on approaching a crater to determine the condition of those gathered around the area. In essences the group of sightseer's became our 'little animal' early warning system.

On arriving at the crater the officer in charge would demand to know what piece of ordinance had made the hole in the ground and the exact place it was fired from. The type of weapon was usually very easy to determine by examining the fragmentation lying about, in addition we could often render a good guess as to the country of manufacture. The firing position was another matter altogether.

We knew the maximum ranges of the different munitions and the direction they came from by looking at the crater itself. The inquiring minds standing around wanted us to provide a back azimuth so that it would be possible to pinpoint the firing position. This information always seemed quite foolish to me because the rockets at least were normally launched remotely or by time delay at night. We on the other hand were seldom called to investigate until daylight, hours after the weapon had detonated and the perpetrator was miles away.

If we were in a hurry the report was short and simple. "107 mm rocket came from out there somewhere," we would say pointing out in the middle of nowhere. However if we had plenty of time and the officer in charge was stern and demanding, a small play was put on just for his benefit. We started by making a thorough examination of the weapons remains, then we stepped off the size of the crater. The investigation process took on a very serious nature as we made several long calculations to determine the trajectory and flight path of the weapon. Our next step involved a whispered consultation between the team members before rendering a very serious straight faced finding to the officer. "107 mm rocket came from out there." The truth of the matter is that both of the findings were the results of a wild guess.

I was always surprised at how often the officer on the scene commended us for our professional work, sometimes they would even call back to the unit to report how pleased they were at being bilked. I am sure now that at times my teammates and I carried these little scams to extremes but as long as no one got hurt or in trouble and we made ourselves look important then there was no harm done.

DEATH IN THE FAMILY

This is a story that I have been reluctant to tell but I felt it important if the reader is going to understand the life in the old EOD. The tale doesn't have a happy ending or even an ending for that matter. There isn't any humor or lesson to be learned, just an event that helps shape who we become. The story is about an exceptional EOD man from another unit; a unit that the 3rd Ord EOD socialized with a great deal.

The man, I guess I will call him Jerry although he was best known by his last name, visited our unit on many occasion because he was a friend of all the men but was especially close to SFC Smith. Jerry, a warm good natured individual who always seem to liven up any gathering no matter the situation, was always welcome in our unit. But Jerry was best known in the field as an accomplished EOD man and this was proclaimed by men who often sported big heads and swollen egos.

Jerry was one of the good people, the type of man you always wanted to work with and learn from. He was the guy you always considered invincible, a man who could not make a mistake; the type of man who you looked to for reassurance; the type of man whose repeated successes in the field instilled confidence in younger less experienced EOD men like me.

It was on one of those heady evenings that Junior and I returned from the field full of pride and self importance because we had managed to survive through sheer dumb luck a particularly touchy bomb call that we were informed of Jerry's mishap. Someone met us at the buildings back door with the somber word that Jerry had been severely injured while working on a mine in the middle of the road.

The description of his injuries was horrific to say the least and I will not report them here other than to say he was not expected to live. We were both surprised to hear that at the last word Jerry was still alive but on the other hand he was known as a strong man who would fight to survive to the bitter end.

I must confess the news of Jerry's mishap stunned me beyond belief. I somehow had never considered the possibility of such an incident occurring to Jerry. There were others in the field who if injured would not have come as a surprise but for Jerry to fall prey to a booby trap was unthinkable.

Junior and I both knew of the close friendship between Jerry and SFC Smith so we walked softly and unspoken out of respect for the two men as we passed Smitty's desk upon entering the building.

I have said many times that Smitty had an unnatural sense or gift if you will to decipher his surroundings to the lowest common denominator. This was one of those times and it may be that he picked up on the fact that I was neither bragging nor complaining about something as I passed his desk.

"Hold it." Smitty ordered, rising from his chair on the opposite side of the desk.

"What is the matter with you two?" he demanded.

"We just heard about Jerry," we managed to stutter out.

"There won't be any of that around here." "We don't mourn in EOD," Smitty snapped out in a firm voice. "We honor those we lose." He paused for a moment giving us a hard look before continuing to explain. "Jerry was a good EOD man but he made a mistake." "He would be the first to tell you not to mourn his loss but instead go in the bar and have a drink to his memory or if you want to say a prayer for his soul, but don't mourn."

"Now remember that Jerry, like all the rest of us volunteered for this field and he loved what he was doing." Once again Smitty paused, this time to appraise our response before deciding if he needed to say more.

"Alright if that's settled, you better get down to the mess hall before it closes." Smitty said dismissing us while trying to work up a weak smile before settling back down in his desk chair.

"Yes sergeant," we replied in the stoutest voices we could muster before hurrying out the office door.

Junior and I hurried toward the mess hall glad to take the opportunity to be away from the building. Of course Jerry and Smitty were the topic of our conversation for we both realized just how difficult it was for Smitty to give us that lecture during his own moment of grief. We both gave him credit for handling the situation so well plus a bit of praise for setting us straight on such matters.

They are both gone now, Jerry died in the hospital a few days later. Smitty completed his tour in country and passed away only a couple of years ago surrounded by his loving family and friends.

Jerry and Smitty were both good men, who enjoyed life and loved family and country. Both served at the same time in nearly the same place ignoring the dangers and accepting the challenges of a profession that is hazardous enough in peace time without the added risks of operating in a war zone.

Both men, similar in so many ways have now met their fate. One's young life was forfeited in the middle of a hot, dirty little road in a far away land to a vengeful enemy. The others life ebbed away on a cold day in a small Midwestern town due to a combination of a hard life and old age.

Sometimes when I am all alone working in some dank dirty basement I can't help but defy Smitty's edict not to mourn those of our little brotherhood who have gone before. I know that all too soon all of this group will expire and I grieve in advance knowing that men of this caliber will no longer be allowed to follow in their footsteps.

BROTHERHOOD OF VIET NAM EOD

I'm sure that at times some of our EOD men, me included, became a bit conceded. There are those who would argue that we became insufferable and that may be true. These swelled heads became quickly deflated after an accident, injury, or death in the field. We were all aware of the inevitability of such tragic occurrences; however it is human nature to reason that the bad luck will strike the other guy.

Like many jobs in this world a feeling of invincibility is essential to perform the duties of an EOD man. With all this said I passed my time in country resigned to a powerful feeling that I would not survive the experience. I am now certain that after recounting the many mistakes I made that fate must have been on a holiday or that the grim reaper had more fruitatious opportunities at the moment. However the truth of the matter most likely lays in the fact that my father, a W.W.II veteran raised me with the idea that one day I would also have to serve my country. I believe his training as well as the fine instructors I had at Indian Head put me on a good footing for my time in country. All of that was preparation that would have to be put into practice in an alien world far removed from my own.

I would have to give a great deal of credit for my returning from Viet Nam to the outstanding men that I call my brothers. It was these good men who endured my hot temper and hard headed ways, even to the point of defending my misguided ways.

Terms of endearment or affection such as brotherhood are a little used part of my vocabulary. I am not a person who seeks to belong to churches, civic groups or organizations even to the extreme of not socializing with what is considered the norm with other couples. So it should be clear when I use the word brotherhood it is done so with great reverence.

While I respect all bomb disposal personnel, the definition in my heart of this brotherhood encompasses all EOD men of whatever rank or military branch that served in Viet Nam during the war years. This may ring of elitism and snobbery but the EOD veterans that served in the Viet Nam war shared a unique experience that not only left an indelible mark on our lives, it became the mold that formed the characters we would be for the remainder of our lives.

I fully appreciate and honor all bomb disposal people who have come before and after those Viet Nam years but at the same time I did not share the pressure of their existence just as they were not witness to the pressure before, during, and after our tours in country.

The point of all this lecturing is just this: These tales are the stories of my everyday life while serving in a typical EOD unit in South Viet Nam. I have for the sake of propriety neglected to relate some stories that the non-veteran might not understand. There are also some untold events that might embarrass part or all of those participants who endeavored to do their level best and yet came out looking bad. I also thought it wise not to put in print any actions that could result in the need for anyone to plead the 5th amendment.

These tales as I said happened to me, but being of a common type adventure was probably experienced by many other in country veterans. Knowing this commonality to be the case I make no reservations or restrictions on the verbal use of these stories by other members of the brotherhood of Viet Nam Veteran EOD personnel. This does not however give license or permission for any non-Viet Nam Veteran EOD personnel to use, reprint, retell, or copy in any manner for their use, or profit, or education of this material in whole or any part.

This all sounds foolish but I do not want to find these stories in one of those stupid anti-war movies, novels or documentaries. I am now and always have been a patriot, who loves this country above all else and would be crushed to learn that my simple stories would be used in any way that would detract from the glory that is the United States of America or blemish the gallant military who defends it daily.

The Viet Nam EOD veteran who, for whatever reason, does not wish to share with others their own experiences are encouraged to use my stories. You may change or embellish at your discretion any part of said tale especially if the narration will gain you a free drink, good meal, warm smile from an attractive female or all of the above. If however, you are like me and must stoop to spinning these yarns to impress some dense pimply faced teenage group of kids in the next booth at a fast food restaurant, try to remember that you were once a **highly trained, fearless EOD man who wore a Seiko watch, owned a demo knife and enjoyed living an exciting life of daring do! ! !**

I will end these tales with a short story and a quote that I always remember as befitting the time and place. We had some Australian EOD friends who frequented our bar whenever they were in the area. One of these was a Sgt Smith, which I believe was an alias. He was a man's man as were most Aussie soldiers and a real character who managed to keep any gathering lively.

Sgt Smith stopped by for one last beer and to say good bye the day he was to rotate back home. We all bid him a sincere but happy farewell because we were always glad to see a good man live to return home. I recall very clearly as Sgt. Smith exited the rear door of our bar he hesitated mid way thru the opening to call back. "I'll see you blokes in the next war."

It was one of those last word goodbyes that you couldn't and didn't want to top because we were kindred spirits with these hearty people. I felt good knowing that Sgt. Smith still cherished the comradery of being under arms with us even after all he had experienced in the Viet Nam War.

I hope that no one takes offense at the telling of these stories because they were never meant to harm but rather to inform and possibly amuse the reader. I know that many of my brother EOD men have far more interesting accounts of their adventures in bomb disposal and I heartily encourage them to make a recording of these events. I fear that bomb disposal and the world in general has changed so much since our days in Viet Nam that without our input, people will never know the true facts of our participation in that war.

I also hope that you will overlook the many errors in spelling, grammar and composition that are so evident in these writings. This effort was never intended to be a polished piece of prose and as stated before my lack of education would prevent anything of that quality. I have spent an hour or two every day for approximately a year to produce these poor works of literature, some days were more difficult to work and recall and some recollections were difficult to write about. I humbly ask that you be kind in your criticism and judge these stories kindly in light of the many years that have past and the fading memory that accompanies the passing years.

THE END